AF662093

Higher English Grammar and Composition

M.P. Sinha
A.K. Awasthi
S. Kumar
H. Kaur

ATLANTIC
PUBLISHERS & DISTRIBUTORS (P) LTD

Published by
ATLANTIC
PUBLISHERS & DISTRIBUTORS (P) LTD
7/22, Ansari Road, Darya Ganj, New Delhi-110002
Phones : +91-11-40775252, 23273880, 23275880, 23280451
Fax : +91-11-23285873
Web : www.atlanticbooks.com
E-mail : orders@atlanticbooks.com

Branch Office
5, Nallathambi Street, Wallajah Road, Chennai-600002
Phones : +91-44-64611085, 32413319
E-mail : chennai@atlanticbooks.com

Copyright © Authors, 2018

All rights reserved. No part of this publication may be reproduced, stored in a retrieval system, transmitted or utilized in any form or by any means, electronic, mechanical, photocopying, recording or otherwise, without the prior permission of the copyright owner. Application for such permission should be addressed to the publisher.

Disclaimer

The authors have taken every effort to the maximum of their skills, expertise and knowledge to provide correct material in the book and they have fully tried to follow the copyright law. However, if any work is found to be similar, it is unintentional and the same should not be used as defamatory or to file legal suit against the authors/publisher. The publisher shall have no liability to any person or entity with respect to any loss or damage caused, or alleged to have been caused directly or indirectly, by the information contained in this book.

If the readers find any mistakes, we shall be grateful to them for pointing out those to us so that they can be corrected in the next edition.

All disputes are subject to the jurisdiction of Delhi court only.

Printed in India at Nice Printing Press, A-33/3A, Site-IV,
Industrial Area, Sahibabad, Ghaziabad, U.P.

Preface

Why another book on grammar and composition, when there are Nesfield's *English Grammar* and Wren & Martin's *High School English Grammar and Composition* available in the market? The older generation will say that grammar books written by Indian authors are a pale shadow of these two classic works. Nesfield, Wren and Martin are the final words.

We cannot challenge the merit of these two grammar books. Yet the fact is that J.C. Nesfield and P.C. Wren are outdated. Their grammar was written more than a century ago. English language has changed considerably and so has its grammar. John Seely writes in *Oxford A-Z of Grammar and Punctuation* (2000).

> The grammatical terms used in this book are those in current use in modern grammar. Some of them may be unfamiliar to readers accustomed to more traditional terminology. For example, if you are used to talking about "parts of speech" it may be jarring to see them referred to as "word classes". However, these changes in the terminology of grammar are intended to make the way language is described much more accurate and consistent. (p. XIII)

New terms like "pre-determiner", "determiner", "classifier", "disjunct", "countable noun", "uncountable noun", "complement clause", "relative clause" and such others have been coined to describe the structure of language. Structural linguistics began with Ferdinand De Sassure who made a distinction between "langue" and "parole". Langue is the system of language and parole the actual speech act. The system of a language is limited but the speech acts are infinite. Linguistics, therefore, can study langue, the system that makes combination and permutation of words. Grammar is, as such, a description of a language. It does not prescribe rules but describes them scientifically. The new terms have been coined to describe the system of language accurately.

Since this book is meant primarily for students, school and college teachers, we have presented modern grammar in the simplest way possible. We have explained every new term in the text itself, for example "classifier" (a noun which functions as an adjective in a noun phrase).

Besides, there are chapters on synonyms, antonyms, homographs and homonyms. We hope *Higher English Grammar and Composition* will serve the needs of both teachers and students.

We owe our indebtedness to C.C. Fries' *The Structure of English*, R. Quirk and others' *A Grammar of Contemporary English*, N. Chomsky's *Syntactic Structures*, and John Seely's *Oxford A-Z of Grammar and Punctuation*.

M.P. Sinha
A.K. Awasthi
S. Kumar
H. Kaur

Contents

Introduction

Robert Lowth's *A Short Introduction to English Grammar* (1762) dominated the eighteenth and nineteenth centuries in general. It was primarily meant for students, teachers and general public. It prescribed rules for correct usage and guided people how to use words and frame sentences. Any deviation from the rules was not permitted. This grammar was replaced by J.C. Nesfield's grammar. As English language had considerably changed towards the end of the nineteenth century, Nesfield updated Lowth's grammar and framed new rules. Wren and Martin wrote *High School Grammar and Composition* for Indian students, following J.C. Nesfield. Nesfield's and Wren's grammars were prescriptive grammars like Lowth's, full of "do's" and "don'ts". However, we cannot blame them for writing prescriptive grammar books: their contribution to English language learning and teaching is invaluable.

The first descriptive grammar was written by Otto Jespersen of Denmark. It is a massive book in seven volumes published during 1909-1949, and it is one of the most comprehensive books on English grammar. Besides, it is based on modern linguistics. After Jesperson's book came two other great books on English grammar: *The Structure of English* by CC Fries appeared in 1950, and the second, *A Grammar of Contemporary English* by Quirk, Svartvik, Rosenbaum, and Leech in 1980.

The revised and enlarged edition *A Comprehensive Grammar of Contemporary English* appeared in 1985. All these new grammar books deviated from Lowth's traditional grammar. The structural linguists and grammarians criticized Lowth, Nesfield, and other traditional grammarians on the following grounds:

1. Negligence of the Spoken Form: The traditional grammarians focused their attention on the written form only and neglected the spoken form. They did not know that speech is primary and writing is a method of preserving it for record or future use. Naturally they studied grammar under the following heads:

(a) Orthography
(b) Etymology
(c) Syntax
(d) Punctuation
(c) Rhetoric and Prosody

Besides, their English grammar was based on Latin grammar. They were confused in explaining clearly the use of "a" and "an". In speech, "hours", "heir", "S.D.O.", "M.Sc.", and many other words like these begin with a vowel sound, but "one", "university", "European", "utopian" and such other words begin with a consonant sound. Therefore, the first group of words takes "an" and of the other group "a". Besides, the traditional grammarians declared the most common expressions in the spoken form either wrong or substandard.

2. Prescriptive Fallacy: The general attitude of traditional grammarians was rather haughty. They assumed that they were the masters of language and it was imperative for learners and common people to follow their prescribed rules. They forgot that language is ever-changing and that there is a difference between correctness and appropriateness. A sentence is grammatically correct when it is saturated on the system of language. Appropriateness is related to the use of word/words in context. Look at this sentence:

I saw him not.

It is not a normal sentence. By the standards prescribed by Nesfield and Wren, it is incorrect. But it may be appropriate in a poem or drama. H.J.C. Grierson wrote about Tennyson's famous poem *Maud*: "A great poem *Maud* is not." He made use of inversion for the sake of emphasis. Now we use the terms "acceptable" and "unacceptable". If a construction is commonly used by native speakers or is acceptable to them, it is grammatically correct.

Look at these sentences:

(a) It's me.

(b) She's more intelligent than me.

According to the traditional grammar, there should be "I" not "me". Now-a-days, very few people use "I" in sentences like these. So is the case with "due to" and "owing to". Nesfield and Wren say that the use of "due to" in "I could not go to school due to rain" is wrong and it should be "owing to". Now, nobody observes this distinction.

3. Logical Fallacy: The third flaw in the traditional grammar is the belief that its rules are based on logic. But, the fact is that the basis of language rules is convention. We cannot explain why the plural of "fox" is "foxes" but of "ox" is "oxen". Similarly, the commonly used expression "He's friends with me" is ungrammatical but it is acceptable in the English speaking world. Likewise, the old grammarians did not allow the use of "more" or "most" before "perfect". But scholars even in the time of Nesfield, Wren and Martin, and other grammarians used "most perfect", "of the very best quality" and "roundest of all". Logic says that the meaning of "perfect" is faultless and no improvement can be made upon it, but people use "more/most" and "very" for the sake of emphasis.

Modern grammar says that convention is the basis of grammatical rules; we cannot go by logic always.

4. Historical Fallacy: The next drawback of traditional grammar is illustration of grammatical rules through the writings of past writers. No doubt, the quoted authors were great men of letters but their language became archaic in the latter half of the nineteenth century. Nesfield's and Wren's grammars are outdated as English language has changed considerably. Nesfield's grammar is the grammar of the nineteenth century and we are living in the twenty-first century.

5. Unscientific Classifications and Definitions: The traditional grammarians, being unaware of developments in linguistics, had little idea of the true nature of language. Staunch nationalism restricted them from looking around and studying other European languages disinterestedly. They relied solely on Latin grammar and moulded their English grammar accordingly.

There are six cases in Latin as in Hindi, but there are three cases only insofar as English is concerned—nominative, accusative and possessive. The traditional grammarians wrote a number of pages in classifying 'moods' and laboured fruitlessly in explaining the so-called "four moods". Now-a-days, nobody bothers about "mood".

They mixed different criteria in defining word classes (part of speech) and bundled them together confusedly. For example, the definition of noun is that it is "the name of a person, place or thing". The criterion of this definition is semantic. An adjective is defined as "a word which qualifies a noun or another adjective." The criterion is functional. In short, the definitions of word classes follow different criteria.

Modern English grammar has its base in descriptive linguistics and describes the structure/system of English language under the following headings:

(a) Sound System
(b) Word System
(c) Syntax
(d) Punctuation

The second part of the book focuses on the use of English, which is basically the practical application of grammatical rules. Grammar cannot be taught in isolation. Pupils must learn language in real-life situations and apply the rules of grammar in producing acceptable sentences. As language is a means of communication, the sole aim of the speaker/writer is to convey her/his ideas and emotions to the listener/reader fully and clearly. Besides, the speaker/writer should be able to understand the message of the listener/reader. In other words, both the addresser and addressee should be competent speakers and listeners at the same time.

As the basic elements of language are word/lexis, grammar/structure and meaning, the learner should possess a good vocabulary, practise the art of sentence construction and produce meaningful sentences acceptable in her/his speech community. For this, the second part lays emphasis on vocabulary and use of language in real-life context. Comprehension, précis, and essay-writing are the best means of mastering the target language. Now the first chapter begins with the structure of English language.

Chapter One

The Structure of English

Outcome of the Chapter

(a) The sound system (phonology)
(b) The word system (morphology)
(c) The sentence pattern (syntax)

Every language has its own structure. Structure means the organized whole of the basic components of an object. Let us take a human skeleton. It is a structure organized in human form made of bones. The entire structure is built under a system. Let us take the body of a living human being again. The living body has flesh and blood that covers the bones. The first structure is dead and the second living because of flesh and blood. The living human body functions under a system and that system is specific to all human beings. Likewise every language has its own structure and functions under a system which is its GRAMMAR. We shall study the structure of English under the following heads:

(a) The sound system (phonology)
(b) The word system (morphology)
(c) The sentence pattern (syntax)

(a) The sound system or phonology: Language is primarily speech. The writing system is a method of recording speech acts. A native speaker learns first how to speak language; he learns the alphabet later on. There are altogether forty-eight sounds in English, forty-four sounds called phonemes and four variations, allophones of p, t, l and k. Out of these forty-four phonemes, twenty are vowels and the rest are consonants. The vowels are divided into pure vowels numbering twelve and diphthongs, numbering eight.

The great mistake of the traditional grammar was that it ignored the fact that language is primarily speech and gave value to the written form only. As a result of this, traditional grammarians spoke of five vowels and twenty-one consonants.

(b) The word system or morphology: We said that English language recongnises forty-four sounds or phonemes. These phonemes form words. The word 'set' is formed by combining the phonemes s, e and t. Earlier "word" was supposed to be the next higher unit in grammar. Now we know that "morpheme" is the next higher unit. If we analyse the word "goodness", we find that it is made of "good" and "ness". It can be pertinently asked if "good" is a word, what "ness" is. The answer is that it is a morpheme.

Morphemes are of two kinds, free and bound. A free morpheme can stand by itself. "Road," "class", "room" and "air" are free morphemes and they can be words by themselves. "Ness', "trans", "-ed" and "un-" must be attached to a free morpheme or a word. They cannot stand by themselves. Therefore, they are bound morphemes.

The concept of morpheme has solved a number of problems. Let us take words like "output", "blackbird" and "overtake". These words, if divided meaningfully, will have different meanings from those they have as wholes. In fact, they are made of two morphemes, which have their own meanings. Similarly, "s" and "-es" are plural morphemes and "-d" and "-ed" are past morphemes.

Words according to their structure are divided into three classes, **simple, complex** and **compound.**

(a) Simple words are made of one morpheme only; for example: air, chair, cart, hundred, force, tray and zoo.

(b) Complex words are made of one free morpheme and one or more bound morphemes. Airy, chairs, carts, forceful, nationalize and inexperienced are complex words.

(c) Compound words are made of two or more free morphemes. They may have one or more bound morphemes also.

Classroom → class + room, both are free morphemes

Football → foot + ball, both are free morphemes

Computer programmers → compute + er + programme + er + s

happy – go – lucky = happy + go + luck + y

The phrase is a group of words systematically positioned. For example:

On the hill

A small boy

A wonderfully designed dress

In all these phrases, words are grouped together under the system of English language. The headword, noun comes at the end and if we change its place, it will not be acceptable to a native speaker of English.

(c) **Sentence pattern or syntax:** Words and phrases are organized to form sentences in a special way. Any change in the order will lead to change of meaning.

"A cat chased a rat" is different in meaning from "A rat chased a cat".

The sentence is the highest unit of language for grammatical analysis. It usually consists of a subject and a verbal or a noun phrase and a verb phrase. The nucleus of a sentence is its verb. Therefore, the verb alone can make a sentence. For example:

Go. Run. Help!

The difference between a phrase and a sentence is that the verb in a sentence carries tense but a phrase does not. For example, "*A horse is running*" is a **Sentence** but "*a running horse*" is a **Phrase.**

The length of a sentence is not determined. It can be as short as "Birds fly" and as long as the last sentence of James Joyce's *Ulysses*, which sprawls over fifty pages.

To summarise, what has been said in the previous pages, there is a hierarchy in the grammatical system of English. The phoneme is at the bottom of the structure and at the top is the sentence. It can be diagrammed thus:

Sentence
↑
Clause
↑
Phrase
↑
Word
↑
Morpheme
↑
Phoneme

Let us analyse the hierarchy of structure in the following sentence:

He said that he had seen a snake.

There are two clauses in the sentence:

(a) He said (b) that he had seen a snake

The clause (b) contains the phrase a snake

The phrase a snake consists of two words "a" and "snake"

The words "said", "had" and "seen" are made of two morphemes each : say+ed; have+ed and see+en

The morphemes "say", "have" and "sea" are free morphemes and "-ed" and "-en" are bound morphemes.

There are two phonemes in the word he → h and e.

The relationship between clause and sentence is that of between morpheme and word. A free morpheme can be a word, and an independent clause can function as a sentence. Since the sentence is a larger unit, it can have two or more clauses.

God is great.—One clause

I know that he is ill.—Two clauses

Structurally, sentence is classified into simple, complex and compound.

A simple sentence is made of only one clause. The complex type has an independent clause and one or more subordinate clauses.

She is brave.—Simple sentence

We know that she is brave.—Complex sentence

The compound sentence contains two or more independent clauses. In addition, it may have one or more subordinate clauses. Let us study this sentence:

> *"The Concise Oxford Dictionary is designed to be as straightforward and self-explanatory as possible* ***and*** *the use of special dictionary symbols and conventions has been kept to a minimum".*

This is a compound sentence. The two independent clauses are joined by the conjunction "and". The following sentence consists of two independent clauses and one subordinate clause.

> *"The core meaning is not necessarily the oldest meaning* ***nor*** *it is always the most frequent meaning, because figurative and extended senses are sometimes the most frequent."*

The two independent clauses are joined by "nor" and the subordinate clause begins with the subordinator "because"

Every grammatical unit—phoneme, morpheme, word, phrase, clause and sentence has its form and function in the system of language. Form and function should not be confused. The same word can function as noun or verb in a sentence. Therefore, modern grammarians have given formal and functional classification separately to words and sentences.

Form, Function and Meaning

There are three main aspects of every component of language. They are form, function and meaning.

Form: It is the physical appearance of an object. Let us take the word "bit". The form is b+i+t. We see the letters in print or hear the word and recognize it. The letters in print and the total sound of the letters pronounced give us the idea of word "bit".

Function: Function is the role played by a word in a sentence. Let us take the word "water". Water is both a noun and a verb. It functions as noun in:

I drink water.

It functions as verb in:

I water the plants.

Meaning: Meaning is the idea, information or feeling/emotion expressed by a word in a sentence or utterance. Meaning follows structure. Modern English Grammar classifies words according to their form and function. The classification of words into word-classes (formerly called Parts of speech) is formal classification. The classification of words into subject, verbal, complement, object, adjunct, disjunct and conjunct is functional classification. We shall study these two kinds of classification in Chapters 3, 4 and 5.

As the terms noun, pronoun, article, adjective, verb, adverb, preposition, conjunction and interjection are parts of formal classification. Similarly, noun phrase, verb phrase, verbal group, prepositional phrase and adverbial phrase are formal classification.

The terms subject, verbal, object, complement, adjunct disjunct and conjunct are named according to their function.

The following sentences can be classified according to form and function both.

1.	*Love*	*is*	*blind*	*Love*	*is*	*blind*
	noun	*verb*	*adjective*	*subject*	*verbal*	*complement*

2.	He	loves	her	blindly	He	loves	her	blindly
	pronoun	verb	pronoun	adverb	subject	verbal	object	adjunct

Functional analysis and labelling is important in explaining the ambiguity of sentences. An ambiguous sentence has two structures usually.

"The wizard made the prince a frog".

This sentence has two meanings. The first is that the wizard made a frog for the prince and the second the wizard changed the prince into a frog. The formal analysis and labelling will not help us in explaining the two structures. We have to take the help of functional labelling also:

1. *First meaning* : $\frac{\textit{The wizard}}{\textit{subject}}\ \frac{\textit{made}}{\textit{verbal}}\ \frac{\textit{the prince}}{\textit{indirect object}}\ \frac{\textit{a frog}}{\textit{direct object}}$

2. *Second meaning* : $\frac{\textit{The wizard}}{\textit{subject}}\ \frac{\textit{made}}{\textit{verbal}}\ \frac{\textit{the prince}}{\textit{object}}\ \frac{\textit{a frog}}{\textit{complement to the object}}$

Some sentences or utterances have more than one meaning. Such sentences are called ambiguous. Ambiguity is of two types: (a) Contextual and (b) Linguistic. An utterance can have one meaning in one context and a different meaning in another context. Since grammar is not concerned with context as it is undefinable, we will confine ourselves to the linguistic ambiguity. Linguistic ambiguity is of two types: lexical and structural. When a word with double entendre is used in a sentence or utterance, it is ambiguous. Shakespeare has used words of double entendre profusely in his comedies. This device of playing upon words is called "pun".

Let us take the following sentences:

(i) He was found by the bank.

(ii) The lamb is too hot to eat.

"Bank" has two meanings: The bank of a river and the place where money transaction takes place.

Lamb may mean either "a live lamb" or "mutton". Hot may mean "passionate" or hot "burning hot".

These are the examples of lexical ambiguity. Similarly, Robert Frost's famous lines are a good example of lexical ambiguity:

And miles to go before I sleep,
And miles to go before I sleep.

Structural ambiguity arises out of the positioning or ordering of words. Let us take two famous examples.

(i) Those men's hostels.

(ii) We decided on the boat.

In the first sentence, "men's hostels" can be read as possessive + noun (hostels of those men) and a compound noun (those hostels of men) also. Similarly, the sentence can be dissected (i) we decided on + the boat meaning "we took decision about the boat" and (ii) we decided + on the boat meaning "we took decision when we were on the boat".

Honestly speaking, these are bad/odd structures. To avoid ambiguity the structure could be: "Those hostels of men" and "Hostel/s of those men". In fact, most of the time structural ambiguity occurs on account of weakness of framing sentences or conceptual frigidity and sometimes deliberate.

Mark that these two sentences are without an ambiguous word. Ambiguity arises here because of their peculiar structure.

IC Analysis, Phrase Structure Grammar and Transformational Generative Grammar apply modern technique in analyzing the structure and formation of words, sentences and their meanings.

EXERCISES

1. Point out the clauses in the following sentences:
   (a) It is difficult to guess how he will react to our advice.
   (b) The two friends went to the nearby river which was one mile wide.
   (c) I wanted to help him but he refused bluntly.
   (d) This is the boy who won three gold medals in the sports event.
   (e) It is important to know the people in our neighbourhood as they are the only people who can help us in our need.
2. Find out the phrases in the sentences in Q.N. 1.
3. Break the following words into their morphemes:
   globalization, preponderantly, immunity, dehumanizing, adaptability, possibility, sequential
4. The following phrases/sentences have more than one meaning, write their meanings:
   (a) Old men and women.
   (b) Shooting of hunters.
   (c) Flying planes can be dangerous.
   (d) He left her sad.
   (e) The policemen were asked to stop drinking after midnight.

Chapter Two

The Sound System of English

Outcome of the Chapter

(a) Phonetic symbols
(b) Syllable
(c) Stress and intonation

There is no exact correspondence between written symbols (called letters) and the sounds they represent. For example, the letter "c" represents three sounds: /k/ in "cat", /s/ in "certain" and /ch/ in "chat". The reason is historical. English or Celtic was spoken in England before Julius Caesar conquered the country. Perhaps, the English people had their script or writing system. It may be a reason for their difference and imposed the Roman script for his own convenience. Unfortunately, the 26 letters could not accommodate all the sounds of English Language. At present, there are 44 sounds, called phonemes, of which 24 are consonants and 20 vowels. Apart from 24 consonants, there are four allophones. These allophones occur in stressed positions. The allophone of /p/ is like Hindi "ph" (फ), of /t/ like Hindi "th" (ठ), of /k/ like Hindi "kh" (ख) and of /l/ is dark /l/. As the 26 letter of the alphabet cannot accommodate the 48 sounds, there is always confusion for the Indian learner.

The second peculiarity of English system is its three-tier relation which is symbol/letter, the name of the symbol/letter, the sound it represents. Because of this complex and irregular relationship Indian students find it an uphill task to memorize the spellings of words and their pronunciation.

Standard dictionaries print the pronunciation of words in International Phonetic Alphabet within slant lines for the convenience of foreign learners. The traditional grammarians ignored the fact that the language speech is primary and writing is a method to record it. Naturally, they spoke of five vowels, nineteen consonants and two semi-vowels.

Here is the list of phonetic symbols used in most dictionaries. The consonants and vowels which are available in Indian languages are also given in *Devnagri* script.

Consonants

1. /p/ (प) : ***p**ain* /pein/, **ca*p*** /kæp/, **ha*pp*en** /hæpᵊn/
2. /b/ (ब) : ***b*an** /bæn/, ***b*ad** /bæd/, **ru*bb*er** /rʌbəʳ/
3. /t/ : ***t*ime** /taim/, **lo*t*** /lɒt/, **ma*t*** /mæt/
4. /d/ : ***d*rink** /driŋk/, **par*d*on** /pɑ:dᵊn/, **no*d*** /nɒd/
5. /k/ (क) : ***c*at** /kæt/, **ma*k*e** /meik/, **sha*k*e** /ʃeik/
6. /g/ (ग) : **get** /get/, **begin** /bigin/, **log**/lɒg/
7. /tʃ/ (च): ***ch*in** / tʃin/, **suggestion** /sədʒestʃᵊn/, **mu*ch***/mʌtʃ/
8. /dʒ/ (ज): ***j*ust** / dʒʌst/, **ra*g*e** /reidʒ/, **lo*dg*e** /lɒdʒ/
9. /f/ (फ) : ***f*ine** /fain/, **coug*h*** /kɒf/, ***ph*easant** /fezᵊnt/
10. /v/ : ***v*ine** /vain/, **ha*v*e** /hæv/, **ra*v*e** /reiv/
11. /θ/ : ***th*in** /θin/, ***th*rough** /θrʊ:/, **ba*th*** /bɑ:θ/
12. /ð/ : ***th*is** /ðis/, ***th*ough** /ðəʊ/, **wi*th*out** /wiðaʊt/
13. /s/ (स) : **sit** /sit/, **mi*ss*** /mis/, **last** /lɑ:st/
14. /z/ (ज़) : **i*s*** /iz/, ***z*oo** /zʊ:/, **rai*s*e** /reiz/
15. /ʃ/ (श): ***sh*ip** /ʃip/, ***sh*oot** /ʃʊ:t/, **sugar** /ʃʊgəʳ/
16. /ʒ/ : **mea*s*ure** /meʒəʳ/, **gara*g*e** /gærɑ:ʒ/, **vi*s*ion** /viʒᵊn/
17. /h/ (ह): ***h*at** /hæt/, ***h*eight** /hait/, ***h*abit** /hæbit/
18. /m/ (म): **ra*m*** /ræm/, ***m*ight** /mait/, **sa*m*e** /seim/
19. /n/ (न): ***n*et** /net/, **ca*n*** /cæn/, **begi*n*** /bigin/
20. /ŋ/ (ङ): **ri*ng*** /riŋ/, **si*ng*** /siŋ/, **ha*ng*** /hæŋ/
21. /l/ (ल): **let** /let/, **till** /til/, **clay** /klei/
22. /r/ (र): ***r*ay**, **c*r*y** /krai/, ***r*ide** /raid/

23. /j/ (य): *y*et /jet/, *y*ou /jʊ:/, *y*east /ji:st/
24. /w/ : *w*et /wet/, *w*eary /wiəri/, *w*ine /wain/

Vowels

Pure Vowels

- No closure or narrowing at any point
- There are 12 pure vowels:
  1. /i/ (इ): **s*i*t** /sit/, **l*i*p** /lip/ , **polit*i*cs** /pɒlətiks/
  2. /i:/ (ई): **k*ee*p** /ki:p/, **l*ea*ve** /li:v/, **t*ea*** /ti:/, **k*ey*** /ki:/
  3. /e/ (ए): **b*e*d** /bed/, ***a*ny** /eni/, **l*eo*pard**/lepəd/
  4. /æ/ (ऐ): **b*a*d** /bæd /, **att*a*ck** /ətæk/, **m*a*p** /mæp/
  5. /ʌ/ (अ): **bl*oo*d** /blʌd/, **en*ou*gh** /inʌf/, ***o*ven** /ʌvən /
  6. /a:/ (आ): **c*a*rd** /ka:d/, **l*a*rge** /la:dʒ/, **c*a*r** /ka:/
  7. /ɜ:/ ( ): **g*ir*l** /gɜ:l/, **b*ur*n** /bɜ:n/, **w*or*se** /wɜ:s/
  8. /ə/ (अ॒): ***a*ccount** /əkaʊnt/, doctor /dɒktər/, enter /entər/
  9. /ɒ/ (ऑ): **h*o*t** /hɒt/, ***h*onest** /ɒnist/, **f*o*llow** /fɒləʊ /
  10. / ɔ:/ ( ): ***a*ll** /ɔ:l/, **h*o*rse** /hɔ:s/ , **s*aw*** /sɔ:/
  11. /ʊ/ (उ): **b*oo*k** /bʊk/, **p*u*t** /pʊt/, **f*u*ll** /fʊl/
  12. /u:/ (ऊ): **l*oo*m** /lu:m/, **t*u*be** /tju:b/, **appr*o*ve** /əpru:v/

Diphthongs

1. /aɪ/ (आइ): **eye** /aɪ/, **die** /daɪ/, **pilot** /paɪlət/
2. /eɪ/ (एइ): **male** /meɪl/, **grate** /greɪt/, **shape** /ʃeɪp/
3. /ɪə/ (इअ॒): **career** /kərɪər /, **here** /hɪər /, **peer** /pɪər/
4. /ʊə/ (उअ॒): **tour** /tʊər/, **lure** /lʊər/
5. /aʊ/ (आउ): **owl** /aʊl/, **doubt** /daʊt/, **cow** /kaʊ/
6. /əʊ/ (अ॒उ): **own** /əʊn/, **boat** /bəʊt/, **mould** /məʊld/
7. /ɔɪ/ ( ): **toil** /tɔɪl/, **noise** /nɔɪz /, **boy** /bɔɪ/
8. /eə/ (एअ॒): **air** /eər/, **tear** /teər/, **care** /keər/

Allophones

An allophone is a member of phoneme family. The phoneme is the smallest meaningful unit in the sound system of a language. All the forty-four vowels and consonants of English are phonemes. Replacement of one phoneme by another brings about change of meaning. For example:

Bad, dad, had, lad, mad, pad and sad

A phoneme exists in contrast to another. Two allophones are complementary to each. It means if one allophone occurs in a particular environment, the second will never occur in that position. The allophone of /p/ is /pʰ/. /pʰ/ occurs in stressed positions and /p/ in the rest. Similarly, /kʰ/ occurs in stressed positions and /k/ elsewhere and so is the case with /tʰ/ and /t/; clear /l/ occurs before a vowel and dark /l/ before a consonant. The other important features of English sound system are word-stress and intonation. How each sound is pronounced can be best learnt from the news readers and discussion made on television channels.

Syllable

The next higher unit is the syllable in the sound system of English language. We cannot speak with consonants only. As consonants are produced by the blockage of air in the oral passage, it is impossible to speak after the articulation of four consonants in succession. The air in the mouth or oral passage must be released. Vowels release the pulmonic air. Once the air in the oral passage is released the syllable is formed. Naturally, the number of syllables in a word are counted by the number of vowels. Look at these words:

cry, tie, heap, bound, dream, deep, strange, people

Each word is monosyllabic. Do not go by the number of letters. Write them in phonemic script and you will find that each word has only one syllable. Now read the following words:

argue, crying, bitter, reader, throughout, through

You will find that each word consists of two syllables.

Stress

Stress is a very important feature of English sound system. It is an extra-muscular effort in the production of a syllable or word. English-speaking people do not give equal value to all words or syllables. The content words (nouns, adjectives, verbs and adverbs) are given more value as they contain meaning and so they are, stressed. If a content word contains more than one syllable, it receives stress on one of them. Look at these words. The stressed syllables are given a vertical mark on them

ar'rival, trai'nee, a'bout, 'feeling, sup'port, al'low.

Intonation

Intonation is the variation in the pitch and quality of speech sounds. We never speak on a fixed scale of sound. We raise the pitch of our voices and lower it, too. We use four tones generally. They are falling tone, rising tone, fall-rise tone and rise-fall tone. Read J.D.O' Connor's *Better English Pronunciation* and listen to news, group discussions and speeches telecast on your television set or you can take the help of Internet.

EXERCISES

1. Count the vowels and consonants in English.
2. What is a diphthong?
3. How many allophones are there in English?
4. What is the difference between a phoneme and an allophone?
5. How will you explain the difference between a vowel and a consonant?
6. What is stress? Which words are stressed in English?
7. What is a syllable?
8. How many kinds of tone are used in English?
9. Count the number of vowels in each of the following words: condition, rely, daily, economy, national, photography, habitual, fantasy, sprightly.
10. Mark the stressed syllable in each of the following words: horrible, predictable, umbrella, signify, hatred, certain, effort, afford, troublesome, afternoon, appear, wonderful, message, random, cheaply, beginning.
11. When do we use a falling tone while talking to people?
12. When is rising tone used in conversational English?

Chapter Three

The Formal Classification of Words

Outcome of the Chapter

(a) Noun
(b) Pronoun
(c) Article
(d) Adjective
(e) Verb
(f) Adverb
(g) Conjunction
(h) Preposition

It is already discussed in the first chapter that form is the physical appearance of an object. A 'Bucket' is a word with its own form. It consists of sounds b A K I T when it is spoken and six letters when written. Formal classification groups words in classes according to their form. Grammarians have divided words into two major groups. They are (a) content words and (b) structure words. Content words are called open-ended words as their number is ever increasing. Structure words are close-ended, because number is fixed.

1. Content words include
   (a) Noun
   (b) Adjective
   (c) Verb
   (d) Adverb
2. Structure words include
   (e) Pronoun
   (f) Article

(g) Preposition

(h) Conjunction

These eight classes of words are known as "parts of speech". We will discuss there in next sections.

NOUN

A noun is a word that can be made plural by adding "- s" or "- es" or some other plural marker. It takes the possessive form if we add apostrophe (') or apostrophe and "s" ('s).

(a) **Plural forms: cat → cats, dog → dogs, mango → mangoes**

(b) **Possessive forms: man → man's, men → men's, people → people's, boys → boy's**

Classification of Noun

Nouns are classified into (a) **countable** and (b) **uncountable nouns. Countable nouns are usually counted in number.** For example, one man, two chairs, fifty trees, a hundred rupees note.

The countable noun is of two types:

(i) Proper Noun

(ii) Class Noun

The proper noun refers to only one object. John, Patna, Sunday and India are proper nouns as they refer to only one object.

The class noun refers to the whole class. Cat, tiger, house, pine and hill are class nouns as they refer to a class or genre.

The collective noun is a part of the class noun. It refers to the whole class of an object which is a group. For example, cabinet, government, fleet, jury, police and corporation.

These nouns are used as singular in collective sense and plural in distributive sense. For example:

The fleet was moving slowly.	The fleet were scattered in the storm.
The jury has given its decision.	The jury were divided in their opinion.

The other difference between the proper noun and the class noun is that the former is not made plural nor does it take an article, in general. The uncountable noun is not counted in number, it is measured in quantity. An article is also not used before an uncountable noun normally. We use **"many" before a class noun and "much" before an uncountable noun.**

Many boys, many trees

Much water, much milk

The uncountable noun is of two types:

(i) Abstract noun

(ii) Material noun

The abstract noun does not have the plural form usually and it ends with such suffixes as "- ity", "- try", "- ship", "- ion" and "- tion". For example:

> ability, gravity, goodness, helplessness, complexion, formation, gradation, hardship, fellowship, industry, chemistry, gratification, satisfaction, succession.

However, nouns made after adding the suffix "- tion" may have plural forms, for example, limitation – limitations; derivation – derivations; plantation – plantations.

The abstract noun refers to an idea, not a concrete object. The material noun on the other hand refers to a concrete object, which is measured in quantity. It does not have a plural form nor does it take an article in general. Words like "water", "gold", "rice", "wheat", "mustard" and "ice" are material nouns.

Forms of the Noun

There are four forms of the noun, which are determined by number, person, gender and case.

(A) Number: There are two forms of the noun according to number: singular and plural. A singular noun refers to one object and the plural noun to more than one.

Rules for making a noun plural:

(i) The common rule is to add "- s" or "- es" at the end of a singular noun to make it plural

Cat - cats
Horse - horses
House - houses
Pen - pens
but
Child - children

If a noun ends with "o", "sh", "z", " tch", "ch" or "x", the plural marker "- es" is added

Mango - mangoes
Tomato - tomatoes
Potato - potatoes
Kiss - kisses
Ass - asses
Wish - wishes
Church - churches
Witch - witches
Fox - foxes
Tax - taxes
but
Ox - oxen

The following nouns take "- s", though they end in "o": dynamo, kilo, kimono, memo, piano, photo, radio, rhino.

(ii) The plural marker "- ves" is added to the nouns ending in "f" and "fe"

Calf - calves
Half - halves
Knife - knives
Leaf - leaves
Life - lives
Sheaf - sheaves
Shelf - shelves
Thief - thieves
Wife - wives
Wolf - wolves

But the following nouns ending in "f" and "fe" take "s" only

Chief	-	chiefs
Cliff	-	cliffs
Handkerchief	-	handkerchiefs
Safe	-	safes

The following nouns take both "- s" and "- ves"

Hoof	-	hoofs, hooves
Scarf	-	scarfs, scarves
Staff	-	staffs, staves
Wharf	-	wharfs, wharves

(iii) Nouns ending in consonant "y" are made plural by dropping the "y" and adding "ies"

Baby	-	babies	lady	-	ladies
Country	-	countries	liberty	-	liberties
Fly	-	flies	smithy	-	smithies

If a vowel precedes "y", the regular plural marker "- s" is added

Boy	-	boys	Key	-	keys
Day	-	days	Guy	-	guys
Donkey	-	donkeys	Ray	-	rays

(iv) A few nouns are made plural by vowel change.

Foot	-	feet	Goose	-	geese
Louse	-	lice	Man	-	men
Mouse	-	mice	Tooth	-	teeth
Woman	-	women			

(v) Some words of Greek and Latin origin still retain the original plural from, especially in technical writing

Axis	-	axes
Crisis	-	crises
Erratum	-	errata
Memorandum	-	memoranda
Oasis	-	oases
Parenthesis	-	parentheses
Phenomenon	-	phenomena

Radius	-	radii
Terminus	-	termini
Thesis	-	theses
Matrix	-	matrices

The rest of the Greek and Latin words take the English plural makers also.

Aquarium	-	aquaria or aquariums
Appendix	-	appendices or appendixes
Datum, data	-	data, datas
Cactus	-	cacti or cactuses
Formula	-	formulae or formulas
Fungus	-	fungi or funguses
Gymnasium	-	gymnasia or gymnasiums
Lacuna	-	lacunae or lacunas

(vi) Compound nouns are made plural by adding "- s" to the last element

Breakdown	-	breakdowns
Boy friend	-	boy friends
Break-in	-	break-ins
Education minister	-	education ministers
Travel agent	-	travel agents
Paper work	-	paper works
University teacher	-	university teachers
Week day	-	week days

If "man" or "woman" is the first element, both are made plural

Man servant	-	men servants
Woman novelist	-	women novelists
Woman doctor	-	women doctors
Man hour	-	man hours (exception)

(vii) Some nouns denoting pairs are always used as plural: forceps, pincers, scissors, trousers and tongs. When we want to mean only one, we say "a pair of trousers" or "a pair of scissors."

(viii) Some adjectives become noun when "s" is added to them, but their meaning is changed.

good – goods, blue – blues (the blues = feeling of melancholy) green – greens (meaning vegetables), second – seconds (meaning goods of inferior quality), white – whites (meaning white clothes), new – news.

(ix) Some nouns when added "- s" denote a different meaning. air – airs; cloth – clothes, date – dates (the years of a person's birth and death; the beginning or end of a period or event); "Dos" is always plural. It is also written "do's"; it means a party or other social event. "Do's and dont's" means rules of behavior.

Future – futures (meaning: contracts for assets)

Surround – surrounds (meaning: surroundings)

(x) Compound nouns with prepositional phrases are made plural by adding the plural makers to the first element.

Commander-in-chief	-	commanders-in-chief
Officer-in-command	-	officers-in-command
Sister-in-law	-	sisters-in-law

(xi) Acronyms and abbreviations are made plural by adding "- s"

M.P.	-	M.P.s	VIP	-	VIPs
UFO	-	UFOs	RADAR (radar)	-	RADARS
Id	-	Ids	M.L.A.	-	M.L.A.s

(xii) Some nouns have the same form whether used as singular or plural

Animals: deer, sheep

Fish: cod, mackerel, salmon, trout

The word "fish" has the same form whether singular or plural but has the form "fishes" in expressions like "a variety of fishes".

(xiii) **Some nouns, especially garments, tools and instruments of two parts have always plural forms and use.** For example, Binoculars, breeches, clothes, forceps, glasses, pants, pincers, pliers, scales, scissors, shears, spectacles.

(xiv) **Some nouns are plural in form and are used as plural.** For example, Airs, arms (weapons), damages (compensation), details, earnings goods, greens (vegetables), grounds, outskirts, pains, particulars, premises, quarters, riches, savings, spirits, stairs (but staircase), surroundings, valuables.

(xv) **Some words are plural in form but are singular in meaning and are used as singular nouns:** Aesthetics, economics, ethics, linguistics, mathematics, physics, politics, billiards, bowls, darts, draughts, innings, meshes, mumps, news, prickly heats, rickets, shingles and summons.

(xvi) **The collective nouns can be used as both singular and plural. The use depends on the meaning of the context:** audience, cabinet, crew, fleet, government, jury, team.

(xvii) **"People" and "police", though singular in form are always used as plural.** The word "people" has the plural form in expressions like "peoples of different countries."

(B) Person: There is no special form of a noun so far as "person" is concerned. Only pronouns have three forms of persons, namely first person, second person and third person.

(C) Gender: There are three genders in English: (a) masculine, (b) feminine and (c) neuter. Yet, the gender of a noun cannot be known by its form. This is because adjectives, verbs, adverbs and prepositions do not carry gender. The gender of a noun is known by its pronoun. However, a few nouns have masculine and feminine forms.

1. Human relations:

Masculine	**Feminine**	**Masculine**	**Feminine**
Father	mother	Uncle	aunt
Husband	wife	Son	daughter
Brother	sister	Nephew	niece
Bridegroom	bride	Man	woman
Widower	widow	Boy	girl
Lad	lass	Gentleman*	lady*

* Now, "gentlemen" and "ladies" are used in special cases only.

2. Designation:

Masculine	**Feminine**	**Masculine**	**Feminine**
King	queen	Duke	duchess
Earl, count	countess	Lord	lady
Prince	princess		

3. Profession:

Masculine	**Feminine**	**Masculine**	**Feminine**
Actor	actress**	heir	heiress**
Hero	heroine	host	hostess**

The word hostess is used in the compound noun "air hostess" only. The tendency is to use gender free language.

4. Animals and birds:

Masculine	**Feminine**	**Masculine**	**Feminine**
Bull, ox	cow	Cock	hen
Dog	bitch	Ram	ewe
Lion	lioness	Stag	doe
Gander	goose	Stallion	mare
Tiger	tigress		

(D) Possessive Forms: Pronouns have their specific possessive forms but nouns do not. There are two ways to indicate possession. The first is to add apostrophe and "s" or apostrophe only. The second method is to link the two nouns with the preposition "of". The first method changes the form. For example:

1. Raja Ravi Verma's paintings or The paintings of Raja Verma.
2. Prashant's diary or The diary of Prashant.

Since the use of the preposition "of" does not change the form, we shall consider the use of apostrophe with "s".

(a) Apostrophe is placed at the end of a singular noun, especially classical names, when it ends with a hissing sound like "s", "z" or "sh" .
Sophocles' plays, Aeschylus' *Prometheus Bound*.

** Double starred words are no more in use.

(b) Apostrophe is placed at the end of a plural noun ending with "- s" or "- es". Boys' hostel, citizens' demand, three days' work.

(c) Apostrophe and "- s" are placed at the end of other nouns other than those described in (a) and (b). Jane's pencil, people's verdict, men's hostel, my teacher's house.

(d) The possessive marker apostrophe or apostrophe with "s" is added, to the last element of a compound noun. My sister-in-law's office, the commander-in-chief's order.

(e) The possessive marker is not attached to an inanimate noun except in these cases:

  (i) Time expressions: today's newspaper, a month's vacation, five hour's delay.

  (ii) With "sake": art for art's sake, for heaven's sake, for goodness' sake.

  (iii) Ships and boats: the ship's mast, the boot's owner.

  (iv) Poems, novels and plays: the poem's theme, the novel's technique, the play's ending.

  (v) When the second noun is dropped as the chemist's (shop), dentist's (clinic), Midland's (shop), James's (house).

We usually write.

(i) We brought the medicine at the chemist's.

(ii) He has gone to the dentist's.

(iii) We are going to Midland's.

(iv) We met him at James's.

EXERCISES

(a) **Write the plural forms of the following nouns:**

mouse, appendix, fungus, minister of state, radio, thesis, ox, goose, chef, beau, phenomenon, hippo, hippopotamus, rhino, rhinoceros, M.L.A., M.P., commander-in-chief, knife, wife, cliff, chief, belief, impurity, variety, height, hero, mongoose, church, latch, water, tax, axe, half, education officer, woman doctor, man servant, man hour.

(b) **Write the possessive forms of the following nouns:**
Men, children, heaven, brother-in-law, hero, church, judge, Socrates, Venus, boys, people, crowd, James, England, India, lady doctor, health minister painter, Bradley, Becky.

(c) **Write the possessive form of the following nouns:**
adding a noun after each of them: Men, children, heaven, brother-in-law, hero, church, judge, Socrates, venus, boys, people, crowd, James, England, India, Lady doctor, health minister, painter, Bradley, Becky.

PRONOUN

Pronouns are structure words and their number is fixed. Functionally, a pronoun comes for a noun or noun phrase which has been mentioned earlier.

(a) John is a good student. He is my neighbour.

(b) I saw a small girl in front of my house. She was carrying a big doll.

The pronoun "he" comes for the noun John (masculine) and "she" for the noun phrase a small girl (feminine) in front of my house.

Pronoun is classified as:

(a) **Personal pronoun:** I, me, my, mine, we, us, our, ours, you, your, yours, he, his, him, his, she, her, hers, it, its, they, them, theirs

(b) **Reflexive pronoun:** myself, yourself, ourselves, yourselves, himself, herself

(c) **Relative pronoun:** who, whose, whom, that

(d) **Demonstrative pronoun:** this, these, that, those

(e) **Interrogative pronoun:** who, which, whom, what

Pronoun has four forms: person, number, gender and case.

(a) Person: There are three persons: first person, second person and third person. The speaker is the first person, the listener is the second person and the person spoken about is the third person.

First person: I, we

Second person: You

Third person: He, she it, they and these

(b) **Number:** There are two numbers: singular and plural. Since the number of pronoun is fixed, the singular and plural forms are fixed and the plural maker "- s" or "- es" is not added except in the case of reflexive pronoun.

Singular	Plural	Singular	Plural
I	we	Me	us
We	our	My, Mine	our, ours
He, she, it	they	His, her, hers, its	their, theirs

The second person pronoun has the same form whether singular or plural except in the case of its reflexive form.

Singular	Plural
Yourself	yourselves
Myself	ourselves
Himself	themselves
Herself	themselves

(c) **Gender:** There are three genders: masculine, feminine and neuter. The first and second person pronouns are gender free. The third person pronoun has gender forms.

Masculine	Feminine	Neuter
He	she	it
his	her, hers	its
him	her	it

But they have the same plural forms: they, their, theirs, them and themselves.

(d) **Case:** There are three cases: nominative, accusative or objective and genitive or possessive. The following is the pronoun paradigm:

	Nominative	Objective	Possessive
First person singular	I	me	my, mine
First person plural	We	us	our, ours
second person	you	you	your, yours
Third person singular			
masculine	He	him	his, his
feminine	she	her	her, hers

neuter	It	it	its
Third person plural	they	them	their, theirs

Possessives are of two kinds: possessive determiner and possessive pronoun. My, our, your, his, her, its and their are possessive determiners and always come before a noun. Mine, ours, yours, his, hers and theirs function as pronouns and can be subject and complement to a verb. For example, My book is old but yours is new. This car is hers.

The possessive forms my - mine, our - ours, your - yours, her - hers and their - theirs have the same meaning but are used differently. My, our, your, her and their are placed before the noun of possession but mine, ours, yours, his, hers and theirs after it.

1. This is my book. — This book is mine.
2. This is our house. — This house is ours.
3. Now it is your turn. — Now the turn is yours.

However, the pronoun "yours" is used in expressions like yours truly, yours sincerely or yours faithfully before the noun.

Reflexive pronoun is formed by adding "- self", to the possessive form of the first and second persons, myself, ourselves, yourself and yourselves, but to the objective form of the third person, himself, herself, itself and themselves, it is used for emphasis on the doer.

I did it myself.

Do it yourself.

She washed clothes herself.

This, that, these and those are demonstrative pronouns. They can function as subject, object or complement to a verb.

(a) This is my book.

(b) I want this, not that.

(c) What is this?

But when they come before a noun they become determiners.

(a) She led me to that room.

(b) I don't like those grimly painted dolls.

Interrogative and relative pronouns are the wh - words: who, whom, whose, which and what. "That" is a relative pronoun, not an interrogative pronoun. In fact, the terms interrogative and relative are functional. The same pronoun can function as both interrogative and relative pronouns.

(i) **Interrogative function:**

Who wrote this book?

Whose pen is this?

Whom do you want?

Which pen will you buy?

(ii) **Relative function:**

This is the man who rescued me yesterday.

Did you find out the book which you were searching in the morning?

Please call the candidates whose names are in the list.

This is one of the best books that are available in the market.

EXERCISES

1. Fill in the blanks with the appropriate form of the pronoun given in brackets at the end of each sentence:

(a) Do you know .... he is? (who)

(b) I can't say .... book is this? (who)

(c) Those .... live in glass houses should not throw stones at others. (who)

(d) He completed the work all by .... (he)

(e) Clean the table .... (you)

(f) I do not know .... he will select. (who)

(g) He .... is down knees fear no fall. (that)

(h) This is .... painting. (he/she)

(i) He threw .... ball into the river but retained .... (he, I)

(j) This is your idea, not .... (I)

(k) It is difficult to follow .... plan. (he/she)

(l) The boy .... you called for interview has arrived. (who)

(m) John asked .... if .... would go with .... (I, I, he)

(n) The naughty boy played a trick on .... (she)

(o) .... could not decide what .... should do when .... friend arrived. (she, she, she)

2. Fill in the blanks with the appropriate form of pronoun.

(a) This handwriting is .... (your, yours, your's)

(b) Her house is nearby...................... (our, ours, our's)

(c) This small dog has got one of .... legs broken. (it, it's, its)

(d) I asked Sita if the book belonged to her. She replied that it was not. (hers, her, her's)

(e) Amit is my .... son. (brother's-in-law, brother-in-law's)

ARTICLES

Articles are structure words. They are three in number A, An, and The; **A** and **An** are indefinite articles and **The** is the definite article. *A* and *An* are in complementary distribution. It means that the places where **A** occurs, **An** does not. **A** occurs before the words that begin with a consonant (sound) and **An** before the words which begin with a vowel (sound).

The best method to know whether a word begins with a consonant (sound) or vowel (sound) is to transcribe it into phonemic script or write it in *Devnagari.*

Let us take a few examples:

cat /kæt/ - the word begins with /k/ - a consonant

honest /ɒnɪst/ the word begins with /ɒ/ - a vowel

M.A. /em ei/ the word begins with /e/ - a vowel

Europe / jʊərəp/ the word begins with /j/ - a consonant

One /wʌn/ word begins with /w/ - a consonant

The Uses of A/An

(a) **Before a singular class noun which is referred to for the first time and which is not known to the reader/listener beforehand:**

I saw a bird.

They caught a big fish.

She gave him a rupee.

He left this place an hour ago.

She is an M.A. from a reputed university.

(b) **Before a singular class noun to refer to the whole class:**

An owl can see in darkness.

A Jersey cow gives milk up to 35 litres every day.

An intelligent man can see through things.

A small child needs great care.

A camel can live without water for many days.

(c) **Before a proper noun which is insignificant:**

A Mr. Kamal came to see you, sir.

(d) **Before a proper noun in figurative use:**

He wanted to be an Einstein.

My friend considers himself to be a Premchand.

She is a Hitler.

(e) **In certain expressions of quantity and number:**

He ate a lot of laddus.

I waited an hour for him.

She spent a couple of days in Nainital.

They bought a number of handkerchiefs.

Uses of The

(a) **Before a class noun which is already known to the listener/reader. (Previous reference)**

I saw a snake. The snake was a cobra.

The definite article "the" is used before "snake' in the second sentence because it has occurred in the first sentence. It may be the same noun, which is referred to twice in the same sentence. For example: I remember the time when my first child was born. References are of two types: (a) anaphoric and (b) cataphoric. Anaphoric reference comes before the noun and cataphoric after the noun.

The book you gave me is missing.

Here the definite article "the" is used before "book" as it is referred to in the sentence "you gave me". In fact, the sentence is made of.

(a) You gave me a book.

(b) The book is missing.

(b) Before a class noun to refer to the whole class. In such a case the article a/an can also be used.

The crow is black. (A crow is black)

The elephant has a trunk.

The African lion is very ferocious.

These sentences can be written with a/an and the meaning shall remain unchanged.

(c) Before a proper noun in figurative sense:

Kalidas is the Shakespeare of India.

(d) Before surnames when more than one person is referred to:

The Bradleys are coming.

The Smiths live next to my brother's house.

(e) Before the nouns that are only one. (Unique reference):

The Sun, the Moon, the Sky, the Prime Minister, the Milky way, the earth

The Sun rises in the east.

The Earth moves round the sun.

The Prime Minister is arriving today.

(f) Before material noun in specific sense. In other words, the definite article "the" is used before a material noun when it is specified and excluded from the rest.

The water of the Ganga.

The gold of the Kolar mines.

The rice of Dehradun.

(g) **Before names of rivers, lakes, seas, oceans, groups of islands, mountain ranges, newspapers, ships and some classical books.**

The Thames, the Nile, the Volga

The Chilka, the Salt Lake

The Arabian Sea, the Caspian, the Red Sea

The Maldives, the Andaman and Nicobar Islands

The Himalayas, the Vindhyas, the Andes, the Alps

The Times, the Hindustan Times

The Patna, the Titan

The Bible, the Ramayana, the Mahabharata, the Gita

(h) **Before a noun which is followed by the preposition "of".**

The front of my house

The pages of my diary

The rotten part of this apple

But when a noun is in apposition, the definite article is not used.

(i) Arundhati Roy, author of *The God of Small Things*, has become a political activist.

(ii) Mr. A. Nigam, owner of this house, is my friend.

(i) **Before an adjective in superlative degree:**

(i) She is the brightest girl in the class.

(ii) This is one of the most interesting books I have read.

(j) **With comparative degree when there is increase or decrease in activity:**

(i) The more he received the more he wanted.

(ii) The sooner you start the better for you.

Zero Article

(a) **No article is used before the following class nouns when they are parts of daily routine.**

Home, church, temple, hospital, masjid, prison, work, sea, town, market, railway station, bus, train, bed, court, school, college, university, office, father and mother.

He is going home.

I go to church every Sunday.

She was admitted to hospital yesterday.

Father is out of station.

Mother is in the kitchen.

He was confined to bed for three days.

(b) **No article is used before material and abstract nouns unless they are specified.**

He bought five bars of gold.

The small child needs care.

Virtue is its own reward.

(c) **Plural class nouns, unless they are specified, do not take an article.**

Boys will be boys.

Ants are industrious.

Old men should be helped.

There is income tax relief for senior citizens.

EXERCISES

A. Fill in the blanks with a/an in the given sentences:

(a) I saw .... white tiger in the zoo.

(b) Let us have our lunch in .... hotel.

(c) She gave me .... one hundred rupee note.

(d) He met .... European in Rameshwaram.

(e) He is .... M.S. from Princeton University.

(f) There is .... university in Jhansi.

(g) I know that Shankar is .... honest man.

(h) This gift is .... honour to me.

(i) They broke .... stone with .... large hammer.

(j) It was .... unanimous decision.

B. Fill in the blanks with 'a, an or the' in the given sentences:

(a) .... seeds you sowed last week have sprung up:

(b) .... bird was flying leisurely in the sky.

(c) It is such .... difficult task that only .... few are capable of doing it.

(d) Look at .... sky; there are .... sun and .... moon shining together.

(e) He had .... lot of money but now is .... spend thrift.

(f) You can't deny .... fact that this revolver is yours.

(g) Are you going to see .... world cup cricket match in West Indies?

(h) Will you send .... mechanic to repair my car?

(i) They have left me in .... unenviable position.

(j) .... prime minister asked his ministers to arrive at .... unanimous decision.

C. Fill in the blanks with appropriate articles in the given passages:

(a) Little over .... year ago Rama Rao went out of work when .... gramophone company, of which he was .... Malgudi agent, went out of existence. He had put into that agency .... little money he had inherited, as security.

(b) There is .... enemy beneath our feet .... enemy more deadly for his complete impartiality. He recognizes no national Boundaries. Everyone in .... world is threatened by him. .... enemy is .... Earth itself. When .... earthquake comes, ... whole world trembles .... power of .... quake is greater that anything man himself can produce.

(c) One of .... most impressive sights I have ever witnessed was .... birth of .... porpoise in .... tank at .... oceanarium. A biologist friend had invited me for .... big moment, and as we watched .... blue and .... grey, bottom of .... pool, ... baby appeared.

(d) Democracy, ... word which has come down to us from ancient Greece, means literally "............... supreme power or authority of .... people" and it embodies .... political conception expressed by Abraham Lincoln. But democracy is .... old word, ... sense in which we use it today is new.

(e) It is most unlikely that .... governments of .... worlds will formally agree on an international auxiliary language but mean while, whether we like it or not, there are signs that English will gradually become accepted as .... second language by .... majority of .... people all over .... world.

D. Explain the following terms in the context of use of articles:

(a) Exophoric

(b) Situational

(c) Linguistic

(d) Anaphoric

(e) Cataphoric

ADJECTIVE

Adjective is a word that comes before or after a noun or pronoun. It is possible that three or four adjectives may come before or after a noun or pronoun.

A small boy is sitting on the table.

A beautiful small bird is singing on the tree.

He has bought a beautiful red and black Chinese doll.

I saw him sad, serene and thoughtful.

Adjectives are classified according to form, type and sentence position.

A. Form. There are three forms of adjective: Positive, Comparative and Superlative. The positive is the normal form, the comparative is used when two nouns are compared and the superlative is used when the number exceeds two.

The common rule is to add "- er" and "- est" to the positive forms to make them comparative and superlative respectively when they are monosyllabic (one syllable) or disyllabic (two syllables). For longer words "more" and "most" are placed before them.

1. Monosyllabic and disyllabic adjectives

Positive	**Comparative**	**Superlative**
fit	fitter	fittest
early	earlier	earliest
hard	harder	hardest
swift	swifter	swiftest
busy	busier	busiest
heavy	heavier	heaviest

2. Longer adjectives

Positive	**Comparative**	**Superlative**
Trustworthy	more trustworthy	most trustworthy
Intelligent	more intelligent	most intelligent
Respectful	more respectful	most respectful

A few adjectives have irregular comparative and superlative forms:

Positive	**Comparative**	**Superlative**
bad	worse	worst
far	farther	farthest (distance)
good	better	best
little	less	least
many, much	more	most
old	older, elder	oldest, eldest

An adjective may be preceded by an intensifier. An intensifier is a word which gives extra weight to an adjective or adverb. The most frequent intensifiers are: very, extremely, too, awfully, terribly and painfully.

John is very happy.

I am extremely sorry.

This is awfully bad.

It is too expensive.

He is terribly slow.

B. Type. There are two types of adjective: classifying and qualitative.

1. Classifying adjectives.

   Classifying adjectives help to divide persons, things or ideas into groups or classes. Read the following sentences:

   (a) Bihar, UP, Uttarakhand, Madhya Pradesh and Rajasthan are *Hindi* area.

   (b) Sports meet is an *annual* event in our college.

   (c) Our committee consists of *four* male and *three* female members.

   All the adjectives used in the sentences are classifying adjectives. Classifying adjectives are called "classifiers".

   Classifying adjectives cannot usually be graded, that is, intensifiers cannot be placed before classifying adjectives. In other words, we cannot place, very, extremely, too, awfully, painfully and other intensifiers before classifying adjectives like Indian, British or bi-annual.

2. Qualitative adjectives.

   Qualitative adjectives describe the quality of a person, thing or idea. Let us take the following sentences:

   (a) She is a <u>bright</u> student.

   (b) This is a <u>sharp</u> knife.

   (c) I admire your <u>brilliant</u> idea.

   We can place the intensifier 'very' before the underlined adjectives in the sentences given above.

C. Sentence position adjectives. Adjectives can be placed before or after a noun. Some adjectives can be placed before a noun only, some can be placed after a noun only and the rest before or after a noun. The adjectives that come before a noun only are called attributive, those that come after a noun only are predicative and the rest at both places. Thus, there are three types of adjective according to their position. They are:

(a) Attributive
(b) Predicative
(c) Attributive-predicative

(a) Examples of attributive adjectives
   (i) It was a wrong decision.
   (ii) This is a beautiful scene.
   (iii) She achieved the perfect ten.

   Here, wrong, beautiful and perfect cannot be placed or positioned after their nouns.

(b) Examples of predicative adjectives
   (i) I saw a woman in the temple. She was <u>alone</u>.
   (ii) The place was absolutely <u>calm</u>.
   (iii) We went to the river. The landscape was <u>serene</u>.

   We cannot place the underlined adjectives before the nouns they qualify, that is, "alone woman" "the calm place" and "the serene landscape. If we do so, it will sound un-English.

(c) Examples of attributive-predictive
   (i) Her voice is sweet. She has a sweet voice
   (ii) We looked at the leaves. They were lush and green.

   We looked at the lush green leaves.

   Most of the adjectives are attributive-predicative

   The following diagram will help you know the classification of adjectives. It is taken from John Seely's *Oxford A-Z of Grammar & Punctuation* (p. 5)

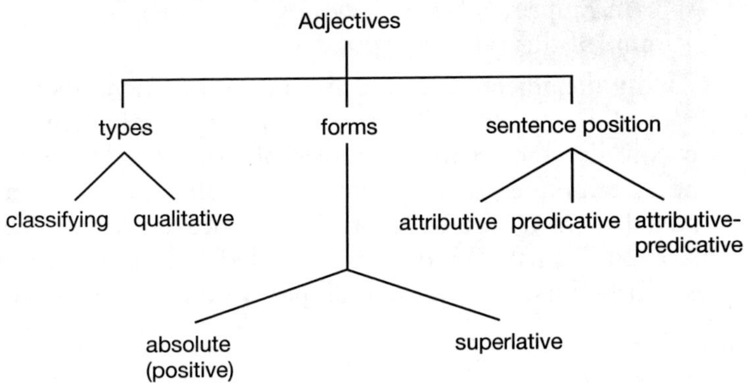

The Traditional Classification of Adjectives

Traditional grammarians classified adjectives into (a) Adjectives of Quality (b) Adjectives of Quantity and (c) Numeral Adjectives.

(a) Adjective of quality qualifiers the attributes of a noun. For example, a red flower, a small boy, a sharp knife

(b) Adjective of quantity qualifies the amount/measure of the noun it qualifies. For example, much water, very beautiful, deep well.

(c) Numerical adjective shows the number of a noun. It is of two kinds: cardinal and ordinal. The cardinal adjectives are one, two, three and all other numbers. The ordinal adjectives show the order of numbers. For example, first, second, third and so on. "Last" and "foremost" are ordinal adjectives.

As grammarians found the traditional classification inadequate, they revised it in the grammar of our time. We will read more about cardinals and ordinals in Adjective Phrase section.

EXERCISES

1. **Mark the adjectives in the given passage.** The Cambridge teachers were much influenced by Freud, and felt that just as human action is a product of hidden motives, so the richer type of poetry contains underlying meanings. The early practitioners of analysis were adept at discovering subtle implications, of which the poet was probably unaware. William Empson's *Seven Types of Ambiguity* is a supreme example of this type of approach.
2. **Classify the adjectives in the given passage.** Richards learnt from Moore to scrutinize apparently simple statements, and to consider their various shades of meaning. He applied these techniques to imaginative literature, and gradually moved towards the conception of critical analysis. When in 1926 English Tripos was extended Practical Criticism established itself as an essential part of the examination.

ADVERB

An adverb is a word that is placed before or after a verb or an adjective. Most of the adverbs end in "- ly". Generally, an adverb is formed by adding "- ly" to an adjective or a noun.

Adjective	Adverb	Noun	Adverb
Bad	Badly	day	daily
Careful	carefully	hour	hourly
Loud	loudly	man	manly
Complete	completely	time	timely
Beautiful	beautifully	week	weekly
		year	yearly

But comely, homely and lovely are adjectives, though they end in "ly".

The following adverbs are not derived from adjectives.

Always, ever, fast, however, never, nevertheless, nonetheless, sweet, whatever, whatsoever and well. 'Fast', 'hard', 'sweet' are adjectives as well as adverbs but they are not derived from adjectives. Fast+ly, sweet+ly are not in use. The word hard+ly is in use but the meaning in changed; it is different from 'hard'.

The function of adverb is to modify a verb, an adjective, another adverb or a sentence.

(a) Modification of verb
- (i) He walks slowly.
- (ii) She acted wisely.
- (iii) You spoke well.

(b) Modification of adjective
- (i) I am very sorry.
- (ii) This is awfully bad.
- (iii) He was mercilessly beaten.

(c) Modification of a sentence
- (i) Generally, they are punctual.
- (ii) He welcomed us all cheerfully.
- (iii) They went to him, hesitatingly.

(d) Modification of another adverb
- (i) She was going very slowly.
- (ii) He returned quite soon.
- (iii) She acted superbly well.

Like adjectives, adverbs have three forms: Positive, Comparative and Superlative. Almost all adverbs are made comparative and superlative by placing "more" and "most" before them. But the adverbs which have the same form as adjectives follow the pattern of adjectives.

Positive	**Comparative**	**Superlative**
Fast	faster	fastest
Hard	harder	hardest
Well	better	best
Badly	worse	worst
Much	more	most

EXERCISES

1. Point out the intensifiers, adjectives and adverbs in the given sentences. The first sentence is done for your guidance.
   (a) It was awfully bad.
   (b) He looked about curiously at our friends.
   (c) He looked at me very blankly and tiredly and said, "Thank you very much."
   (d) The light shone palely down the stairs.
   (e) Moved chiefly by his pride, he finally agreed to fly.
   (f) Moye and I naturally responded to the idea.
   (g) He made careful notes and drawings, went home for tea and slept soundly for an hour.
   (h) Operation flood requires genetically superior cattle which in turn have to be provided with fodder, now in extremely short supply all over the country.
   (i) The forces that generate condition conducive to crime and riots are stronger in urban communities than in rural areas.
   (j) As disputable as such action may seem to be, it results in fewer recorded violations of the law compared to the big cities.
   (k) Urban areas with mass population, greater wealth, more commercial establishments and more products of our

technology also provide more frequent opportunities for theft.

Solution of the sentence (a): awfully: intensifier
bad: adjective

2. Adverb and Intensifier

The relationship between adverb and intensifier is like that of class noun and collective noun. Collective noun is class noun but it differs from other class nouns as it denotes a group and can be used as both singular and plural according to the context. In the same way, intensifiers are basically adverbs but they stand apart from the rest of adverbs. Intensifiers heighten the quality of an adjective, another adverb or verb. They never come alone. Read the following sentences.

i. The situation is really bad.
ii. The patient's condition is slightly better.
iii. She performed extremely well in the examination.
iv. This sherbet is too sweet.

The underlined words are intensifiers and adverbs too.

Now read the following sentences. The underlined words are adverbs but not intensifiers.

i. He approached me hesitantly.
ii. She looked cheerful apparently.
iii. You can go now.

The following adverbs are intensifiers:

awfully, extremely, too, very, terribly, painfully and horribly.

3. Adjunct, Disjunct and Conjunct

These three terms are functional labellings. The term "adverb" is formal labelling and "adverbial" functional labelling.

(a) Adjunct is basically preposition phrase. Read the following sentences:

i. We found the ball in a bush.
ii. They followed us for an hour.

The underlined words are **preposition phrases** by formal labelling and adjuncts by functional labelling.

(b) Disjunct modifies the entire sentence and occurs at the beginning or end of a sentence, look at these sentences.

i. Unfortunately, the dense fog delayed our train by six hours.

ii. We escaped the accident, luckily.

Here "unfortunately" and "luckily" are disjuncts.

(c) Conjunct connects two or more clauses and sentences to maintain a logical sequence. Let us take a sentence, first, where there are two clauses.

In spite of my advice she did not read seriously; consequently she obtained very poor marks in the examination.

The word "consequently" is a conjunct.

The following sentences contain three conjuncts:

We would like to submit the following for your consideration.

Firstly, the new time table of working hours is not practicable in the winter season; Secondly, the period of lunch break is very short. It should be half an hour. Finally, the working hours were of eight hours but now it is 8½ hours, which is against existing rules.

Here "firstly", "secondly" and finally" function as conjuncts. Earlier 'firstly' was considered incorrect and 'first' was common expression but now 'firstly' is frequent word.

EXERCISES

1. Use the following intensifiers in sentences of your own:
   very, extremely, awfully, absolutely, decidedly
2. Use the following words as adjective and adverb:
   fast, hard, sweet
3. Regroup the following words into adjectives and adverbs.
   Homely, solely, hard, hardly, comely, terribly, too, fondly, lovely, vain, idle.

VERB

The verb is a word or phrase indicating an action, an event or a state, e.g. take, organise, line. Mostly, it carries the tense along its use. Functionally, the verb is the nucleus of a sentence and is governed by the number and person of its subject. It is a word which is made singular by adding "- s" or "- es", in the present tense and has "- ing" and "- en" forms. There are five forms of Verb:

Present form	-	be (am/is/are), do, go
Past form	-	was/were, did, went
"- ing" form	-	being, doing, going
"- en" form	-	been, done, gone
Infinitive form	-	to be, to do, to go

The verb assumes other forms during the process of synthesizing; these were classed under 'participle' and 'gerund' in traditional grammatical rules. These are:

Present Participle

Example: By using verb + ing form in action verb only but which is not used as stative verb, i.e. not used as emotion (love, hate, want, need), sense (see, hear, smell, seem), possession (have, own, want, belong), and thought (know, believe, remember); it also functions as an adjective to the following noun. It is used with the verb that gives sense of continued action. The 'ing' form of verb (v + ing) is present participle and normally used in continuous progressive tenses.

He took hasty steps. He reached the station on time.

Taking hasty steps he reached the station on time.

He ran a race. He touched the winning mark.

Running a race he touched the winning mark.

I observed my students. They were working hard.

I observed my students *working* hard.

The soldiers were retreating. The enemy chased them.

The enemy chased the *retreating* soldiers.

Past Participle

Example: By using 'en' form of the main verb; in other words the third form of the main verb called Past Participle. It functions as an adjective and denotes completed action.

He had a shirt. It was torn.

He had a *torn* shirt.

A window broke. It is hanging on the wall.

A *broken* window is hanging on the wall.

The team was finalized. It was sent to BMC for approval.

The *finalized* team was sent to BMC for approval.

Perfect Participle

By using have + ing + en form of the main verb. When one action being complete follows another in continuation it is used with verb denoting completed action.

I saw a tiger in the jungle. I ran helter-skelter.

Having seen a tiger in the jungle I ran helter-skelter.

I finished my lunch. I went to school.

Having finished my lunch I went to school.

GERUND

Gerund looks like a verb/present participle but it functions as a noun. Some uses of the gerund are given here:

As a subject of the sentence:

Smoking is a bad habit.

Flying makes me nervous.

As the complement of the verb 'to be':

My intention is *making* sure you understand English grammar.

One of my duties is *attending* meetings.

As object of a verb:

I enjoy *watching* TV late at night.

After preposition:

She is good at *painting*.

I can't sneeze without *opening* my mouth.

After phrasal verb:

Can you think of *giving* up *smoking*?

He kept on *asking* for money.

Some phrasal verbs ending with 'to' generally take a gerund; these are not part of infinitive like *to take to, to look forward to,* etc.

I look forward to *hearing* from you soon.

When will you get around to *studying* English?

Some other expressions:

Mohan is giving me *driving* lessons.

It's no use *trying* to displease your brother.

There is *swimming* pool in our backyard.

Verb is classified into: (a) auxiliary verb, (b) Auxiliary modal and (c) main verb.

(a) Auxiliary verbs are three in number: be, do and have.

(i) They function as main verbs when they are alone in a sentence.

He does his work.

There are five tigers in this zoo.

My school is at a distance of two kilometers.

I have a pen.

(ii) They carry tense when they are alone in a sentence or are with the main verbs.

We are playing football.

They have finished their work.

Did you see him yesterday?

But they do not carry tense when they are with auxiliary modals.

They will be playing football.

He may have gone home.

She can be helpful.

(iii) Auxiliaries are used for short answers:

Is he all right?

Yes, he is.

(b) **Auxiliary modals,** usually called **modals,** are thirteen in number.

They are:

can, could, may, might, shall, should, will, would, must, ought to, dare; need and used to.

The difference between auxiliaries and modals is that the latter are unaffected by the person and number of their subjects.

I	can
She	could
You	may, might
We	need not
They	ought to
He	used to

(c) Main verbs are content words, they carry meaning. Auxiliaries and modals are structure words and make the structure of a sentence. Auxiliaries and modals are close-ended because their number is fixed. Main verbs are open-ended as their number is always increasing.

Main verbs are classified into transitive and intransitive verbs. The transitive verbs take an object but the intransitive do not. The auxiliaries "do" and "have" are transitive when they function as main verbs. The verb *be* is intransitive. It functions as main verb in Subject + Verb + Complement (he + is + my friend) constructions.

Transitive verbs are of two kinds, Mono-transitive and Di-transitive. The former takes only one object and the latter two.

1. Mono-transitive verb:

   I write a letter

   She knits a sweater

   You have cleaned the room.

   She is doing her home work.

2. Di-transitive verb:

   She bought me a pen.

He gave me five hundred rupees.

The wizard made her a doll.

We shall read more about verbs under the heading Tense system.

EXERCISES

A. Point out the auxiliaries, auxiliary modals and main verbs in the following sentences:

(a) He may be hiding in the bush.

(b) He could do the work easily.

(c) We are planning to organize a party in her honour.

(d) It was difficult for her to check her emotions.

(e) Can you solve this problem?

(f) They have spoiled the whole show.

(g) Why has he come here at this hour?

B. Point out the main verbs and state whether they are monotransitive or ditransitive in the following sentences:

(a) She bought me an umbrella.

(b) The chairman awarded him a gold cup.

(c) We taught him a lesson.

(d) People love to do easy things.

(e) We could not identify the dead body.

C. State whether the verbs in the following sentences are transitive or intransitive:

(a) He looks pale.

(b) She ran a mile.

(c) The judge has heard the arguments.

(d) At last, we were able to know his reality.

(e) Can you lift one hundred kilograms?

(f) She prevented him from coming here.

(g) They thanked me for my services.

(h) I would like to have a cup of tea.

(i) You ate nothing during the breakfast.

(j) It rained heavily in the morning.

CONJUNCTION

Conjunction is a word that joins two words, two phrases or two clauses. Look at these sentences:

John *and* Jane are friends.

He is *not only* intelligent *but also* considerate.

We found him *by* the river.

I do not know *what* he is going to do.

She swam in the pond for an hour *and so* did I.

The italicized words are conjunctions.

Conjunctions are of two kinds: coordinating and subordinating.

The American structuralists have called them co-ordinator and subordinator. The co-ordinator joins two independent units and the subordinator joins the dependent unit(s) with the independent unit.

The co-ordinating conjunctions or co-ordinators are: *and but, yet, get, either...or, neither...nor, or, therefore, not only... but also, otherwise, else, so, still, till, however, nevertheless, nonetheless, however* and *besides*. The co-ordinator or co-ordinating conjunction joins two independent units to form a sentence. Read the following sentences:

(i) He went straight to the tree *and* then turned back.

(ii) I wanted to disclose the secret *but* something stopped me.

(iii) He is quick *but* accurate.

(iv) She was ill, *yet* she attended the meeting.

(v) *Either* he *or* she will do it.

The italicized words are conjunction.

The subordinator or subordinators are:

If, whether, when, while, why, how, what, through, although, as, that, unless, and the interrogative pronouns.

Look at the following sentences:

(i) I do not know; *when* he will come.

(ii) *While* he was going home, he met his old friend.

(iii) I know *that* he will come.

(iv) He cannot pass the examination *unless* he works hard.

(v) We saw the moon *in* the east.

The subordinators if, while, that, and unless join two clauses. They occur at the beginning of the subordinate clauses or dependent units. The preposition *in* is a subordinating conjunction or subordinator in the fifth sentence and it joins the dependent unit "the east" with the independent unit "We saw the moon."

EXERCISES

1. Point out the subordinating and co-ordinating conjunctions in the following sentences:

(a) I can't say when he will come.

(b) If you put out a candle, you will have a foul smell.

(c) He was crying for help but they did not go to him.

(d) He went to the window and threw the bag down.

(e) The doctor examined the patient and prescribed him some medicine.

(f) He behaves as if he were a king.

(g) She does not know where to go.

(h) It all depends on how the weather behaves.

(i) I saw a few boys who were carrying a big log to the river.

(j) Ram did not know how to drive a car, therefore, he thought it proper to go by bus.

PREPOSITION

Prepositions function as conjunction words and they form a separate group. They usually precede a noun or pronoun. They indicate direction, attachment, detachment, continuity, position and relation.

(a) **Direction:** She ran to me.
They went down the road.

(b) **Attachment:** This man is attached to her.
The picture is hanging by the wall.
You must stick to your principles.

(c) **Detachment:** The boy fell from the tree.
He cut off all his relations.
T.S. Eliot made a break with the tradition of the Victorian poetry.

(d) **Continuity:** Go on.
It has been raining since morning.
He has been a teacher in this school for ten years.
He ran on and on.

(e) **Position:** He is sitting in my room.
There is a frog on the table.
She is at her table.

(f) **Relation:** This building belongs to Madhav.
A leg of this table is defective.

The following are most frequently used prepositions:

about, above, after, against, among, at, away, byre, behind, below, beneath, beside, between, by, down, for, from, in, into, of, off, on, out, over, since, through, to, up, upon, with, within and without.

Out of these about, above, below, down, over, round, since, and through are adverbs also; the other adverb "away" sometimes functions as particle (preposition which is a part of the phrasal verb).

Since the same preposition can have different meanings when used in sentences, Indian students should read a lot to master their use. Some important prepositions and their general meanings are given here.

(a) *About* indicates time, place and whereabouts:

(i) My house is about three kilometres from here.

(ii) I have no idea about him.

(iii) It is about three hours ago that he left this place.

(iv) It was about 4.30 in the morning when I saw the tiger near my window.

(b) *Above* indicates position and direction (upward):

(i) The moon shone above in the sky.

(ii) The bird blew high above.

(iii) There is nothing above God.

(c) *After* means behind in place or time:

(i) Please come after me.

(ii) The world scenario changed after the Second World War.

(iii) Why is he after me?

(iv) You must come after 9 o'clock.

(d) *Against* is used to mean opposition and also face-to-face position:

(i) She is very much against me.

(ii) I have nothing to say against him.

(iii) The players of the two football teams stood against each other before the play started.

(e) *At* shows time, place and nearness:

(i) He arrived at 10 p.m.

(ii) At what time shall we meet?

(iii) He lives at Bithoor.

(vi) She is at her desk.

(f) *Away* shows distance and separation:

(i) Ravi decided to go away.

(ii) I cannot go away from my principles.

(iii) Come away now. Its 12 o'clock.

(iv) When I picked up the mug, the handle came away in my hand.

(g) *Below* means down, under or beneath. It is opposite to *above*:

(i) Nishant's home is above mine but Prashant's is below.

(ii) It is below my dignity to go there uninvited.

(iii) Look below, there is a scorpion.

(h) *Beside* means by the side. It also indicates nearness:

(i) I would like to sit *beside* you.

(ii) There is nothing *beside* you and me.

(i) *By* indicates nearness. It is used with the logical subject in passive voice and with the vehicles we travel by:

(i) She was sitting *by* her friend.

(ii) There is a tree *by* the wall.

(iii) This picture was painted *by* Niket.

(iv) We came *by* train.

(v) They go to office *by* bus.

(j) *Down* is used to show direction when the subject is in motion. It has the meaning of low position and is opposite of *up* in meaning:

(i) He ran *down* the street.

(ii) Please don't look *down* upon the poor.

(iii) We came *down* from the tree.

(iv) Sit *down*.

(v) The road is not plain. It goes *up* and *down*.

(k) *For* indicates favour, purpose, reason and the length of a period:

(i) Who is going to speak *for* the motion?

(ii) I won't do anything *for* Narendra.

(iii) Shanta came to me *for* money.

(iv) We struggled *for* our survival.

(v) You cannot give any reasons *for* your failure.

(vi) It has been raining *for* two days.

(l) *From* indicates separation, origin and *with* to in continuity of a period or time:

(i) The monkey fell *from* the tree.

(ii) A fruit dropped *from* the basket.

(iii) He comes *from* a village.

(iv) Where do you come *from*?

(v) He worked *from* 10. a.m. to 6 p.m.

(vi) We swam in the river *from* 6 p.m. to 7 p.m.

(m) *In* shows position and time:

(i) There are five fans *in* the hall.

(ii) We sat *in* the room and discussed the problem for an hour.

(iii) We arrived *in* time.

(iv) I will be back *in* an hour.

(n) *Into* indicates motion:

(i) He ran *into* my room. We cannot use "in" at the place of "into".

(ii) The diver ascended the board and made a perfect jump *into* the swimming pool.

(iii) The wood-cutter's axe fell *into* the pond.

(o) *Of* is used to mean relation:

(i) Five pages *of* this book are damaged.

(ii) I have no idea *of* his plan.

(p) *On* shows continuity and position over something but with contact:

(i) We went *on* and *on*.

(ii) The small boy went *on* crying.

(iii) They kept *on* watching the stars.

(iv) There is a cat *on* the table.

(q) *Over* is used to mean that there is no contact:

(i) A bird flew *over* the tower.

(ii) Planes are flying *over* town.

(r) *On to* indicates motion:

The cat jumped *on to* my table.

(s) *Off* shows separation or end of an action:

(i) She cut *off* all her relations with her husband.

(ii) The strike was called *off*.

(iii) The light suddenly went *off*.

(t) *Out* is opposite of *in*:

(i) He came *out* successful in the competition.

(ii) I will go *out* tomorrow.

(iii) The doctor is not *in*; she is *out*.

(u) *Over* with verbs like fly means *above* but with verbs like run and spill means making contact. We have already seen the difference between *on* and *over*. Here are examples of contact:

(i) A car ran *over* the dog.

(ii) The news has spread all *over* the world.

(iii) The retired officer handed *over* the charge to the new incumbent.

(v) *Since* is used to show continuity:

(i) It has been raining *since* morning.

(ii) They have been working *since* Monday. In most of the cases *since* is used as adverb.

(w) *Through* is different from "by". It means the middle and indicates direction:

(i) A bullet passed *through* the window.

(ii) I can see *through* your design.

(x) *To* is one of the most frequent prepositions. It indicates direction, attachment and continuity:

(i) We went *to* the zoo.

(ii) The girl ran *to* her mother.

(iii) She is attached *to* me.

(iv) The board is fixed *to* the wall.

(v) She visited the place from Monday *to* Saturday.

(vi) We work from ten *to* five.

(y) *Toward/towards* shows direction:

(i) He ran *towards* me.

(ii) His attitude *towards* me is rather inimical.

(z) *Up* shows position and direction:

(i) Look at the birds high *up* in the sky.

(ii) He climbed *up* the tree.

(AA) *With* indicates attachment, association, the instrument used to perform something:

(i) Please pack this notebook *with* my books.

(ii) She will not part *with* her husband.

(iii) He lives *with* his friend.

(iv) She is going *with* us.

(v) He cut the plant *with* an axe.

(vi) We see *with* our eyes.

(AB) *Upon* shows up position with or without motion but the object touches the other. According to *Concise Oxford English Dictionary,* it is a more formal use of 'on'.

(AC) *Within* and *without* are in contrast like *in* and *out*. If we draw an imaginary circle the object inside the circle will be indicated by *within* and outside by *without*.

(i) He will be back *within* a week.

(ii) Please manage the budget *within* five thousand rupees.

But in modern times, the preposition "without" has come to mean "not accompanied by" or "unless".

(i) It is difficult to run a school without good teachers.

(ii) She cannot live without her husband.

These are the general meaning of prepositions but in different contexts they have other meanings than described above.

Some Prepositions Differentiated

1. At and in

At refers to a place, *in* to a-position within.

(a) He is *at* Ashok Nagar *in* Kanpur.

2. At and on

At refers to nearness; *on* to close contact.

(a) He is *at* his table.

(b) There is a cat *on* his table.

But it shows nearness in expressions like

(a) My house is *on* the main road.

(b) The castle is *on* the river.

3. In and into

In shows things at rest and *into* motion

(i) They are sitting *in* the hall.

(ii) They went *into* the hall.

(iii) There are frogs *in* the well.

(iv) The frogs jumped *into* the well.

4. By and with

By is used with an agent, but *with* agrees with an instrument.

(i) This table was bought *by* Sita.

(ii) Sita is writing *with* a ball pen.

5. For, from

For is used to indicate a period of time.

(i) Mr. Shrivastava has been a teacher *for* fifteen years.

(ii) He has been working on this project *for* six months.

From is used to mean separation.

(i) The boy fell *from* the tree.

(ii) He has come *from* a long distance.

It also indicates continuity from one point of time to another, when used with to.

(i) I will be available in my office from 9 a.m. to 2 p.m.

(ii) We worked from 7 p.m. to 10 p.m.

6. On and onto

On indicates things at rest and *onto* in motion.

(i) There is a dog *on* the bench.
(ii) The dinner is set *on* the dining table.
(iii) The cat jumped *on to* the roof of the house.
(iv) I boarded the wrong coach of the train but went *on to* the right coach through the vestibule.

7. On and over

On indicates contact but *over* above the object.

(i) There is a monkey *on* the tower.
(ii) A bird flew *over* the tower.

8. Out and away

Away indicates distance but *out* does not mean so. It means 'away from inside but not far'. It is mostly used with 'of'.

(i) He is *out* of home. It means he is not far *away* and may return after some time.
(ii) He is *away* from home. It shows distance and may not return soon.

Some verbs have fixed prepositions. These prepositions are also called appropriate prepositions. They are given below.

1. Abound in
2. Abstain from
3. accede to
4. accuse of
5. acquit of
6. adapt to
7. add to
8. adhere to
9. admit to
10. agree with
11. aim at
12. argue with
13. amount to
14. apologize for
15. approve of
16. attach to
17. attend to
18. become of
19. believe in
20. benefit by/from
21. boast of
22. borrow from
23. care for
24. complain against

25. convince of
26. cry for
27. delight in
28. derive from
29. differ from
30. dream of
31. excel in
32. escape from
33. attach to
34. exclude from
35. faint with
36. fail from
37. feel for
38. fill with
39. gaze at
40. guard against
41. heal with
42. hide from
43. hit at
44. impose on
45. indulge in
46. insist on
47. intend to
48. interfere with
49. introduce to
50. involve in
51. laugh at
52. lean against
53. listen to
54. long for
55. look at
56. part with
57. pray to
58. prepare for
59. protect from
60. punish for
61. recover from
62. result in
63. send for
64. separate from
65. smell of
66. subtract from
67. supply with
68. suspect of
69. stare at
70. surrender to
71. submit to
72. succeed in
73. sympathise with
74. think of
75. tower above
76. usher in
77. veer round
78. wear out
79. wait for
80. weed out
81. wish for
82. wonder at
84. yearn for
84. yield to

Some nouns take fixed or appropriate prepositions

1. access to
2. acquaintance with
3. admission to
4. affection for
5. alternative to
6. admission to
7. apology for
8. appetite for
9. approach to
10. attitude to
11. cruelty to delight in
12. dependence on
13. escape from
14. exception to
15. expenditure/expenses on
16. experience of
17. fear of
18. flair for
19. freedom from
20. gratitude for
21. liking for
22. limit to
23. neglect of
24. obedience to
25. offence against
26. passion for
27. proof of
28. relationship with
29. release from
30. relief from
31. reputation for
32. result of
33. sense of
34. slave to
35. victim of
36. view of
37. want of

Some adjectives have fixed/appropriate prepositions

1. addicted to
2. allied to
3. ambitious of
4. angry with
5. ashamed of
6. armed with
7. attend to
8. attached to
9. aware of
10. averse to
11. bent on
12. bored with
13. bound to
14. busy with
15. capable of
16. concerned with
17. conscious of
18. cruel to
19. deficient in
20. delighted with

21. dependent on
22. dressed in
23. engrossed in/with
24. equal to
25. equivalent to
26. excessive of
27. faint with
28. familiar with
29. faithful to
30. far from
31. favourable to
32. fond of
33. free from
34. full of
35. good at
36. grateful to
37. innocent of
38. intent on
39. interested in
40. involved in
41. lack of
42. jealous of
43. just of
44. keen on
45. knowledge of
46. known to
47. liking of
48. loyal to
49. married to
50. obedient to
51. opposite of
52. painful to/for
53. partial of
54. passion for
55. pleased with
56. polite with
57. popular of
58. profitable to
59. related to
60. sensitive to
61. satisfied with
62. sincere to
63. sick of
64. tired of/with
65. timed/with/of
66. weak in
67. trained in

The following Latin adjectives ending in *i* and *or* take the preposition *to*:

1. junior
2. senior
3. inferior
4. superior
5. interior
6. exterior
7. prior

EXERCISES

1. Fill in the blanks choosing the right prepositions given at the end:
   (a) We travelled .... Delhi .... Chennai .... Tamil Nadu Express.
   (b) We walked .... foot .... four kilometers.
   (c) He waited .... the instruction.
   (d) When the gun shot, the competitors dived .... the pool.
   (e) A plane flew .... the town.
   (f) This ring is made .... gold.
   (g) He was sitting .... his desk and writing .... a pen.
   (h) Our office is closed .... Saturdays and Sundays.
   (i) The book is lying .... the table .... the next room.
   (j) The fan .... us is not functioning.

   (above, at, after, from, by, to, on, about, into, for, of over, on, with, in, on)

2. Fill in the blanks in the following passages with prepositions:
   (a) .... 1897, ... the age .... forty Ross made one .... the greatest medical discoveries. He proved that malaria was transmitted .... mosquitoes.
   (b) .... the beginning .... October, thirty new students collected .... St. Swithins Hospital Medical School, London, ... a lecture .... welcome and introduction .... the Dean. Carrying a new and shiny loose-leaf folder .... my arm, I walked .... the stone steps .... the first time and entered .... the dingy, small entrance hall.

(c) The ghost that got .... our house .... the night .... November 17, 1915, raised such a hullabaloo .... misunderstandings that I am sorry, I didn't just let it keep .... walking, and go .... bed. Its advent caused my mother to throw a shoe .... a window .... the house next door and ended .... with my grandfather shooting a patrolman.

The police were .... hand .... a commendably short time. A ford sedan full .... them, two .... motorcycles, and a patrol wagon .... about eight men .... it, and a few reporters. They began banging .... our front door.

(d) But there was one happy moment .... Ravi's childhood that was, ... some reason, trapped .... my mind, beautifully iridescent, like the bubbles .... a glass paper weight. We had gone .... a restaurant .... Ambegaon, and Ravi said something cheeky .... a loud voice, ... which everyone there had looked .... him and smiled. Each time I met Ravi, I thought .... that child, beaming .... pride .... being the centre .... attention and looking .... the man he had become, I felt a thickening .... my throat as if I was .... to burst .... tears. Its not that life is cruel, but that .... the very process.

Chapter Four

The Formal Classification of Phrases

Outcome of the Chapter

(a) Noun phrase
(b) Verb phrase
(c) Adjective phrase
(d) Prepositional phrase
(e) Adverbial phrase

As described earlier, *form* and *function* are two different things. When we say that a word is a noun, we label the term noun according to its form. A noun can be the subject or object of a verb. The terms subject and object are labelled according to function. Now we shall discuss the larger units than words and label them according to their form.

1. Formal or categorial labelling: A sentence can be divided into clauses, if it is a complex or compound sentence. A clause consists of phrases which are named after their head words (the most significant words).

The sentence "The small boy ate two cakes without water" can be divided into

(a) The small boy: **Noun phrase or NP** and
(b) ate two cakes without water: **Verb phrase or VP.**

The VP "ate two cakes without water" can be further divided into

(a) ate: **Verbal Group.**
(b) Two cakes without water: **NP.**

The NP is divided into

(a) two cakes: **NP.**

(b) without water: **Prepositional Phrase or PP.**

(c) Phrases are named after the key words in them.

In all there are five kinds of phrase.

(a) Noun phrase (the head word is a noun).

(b) Verb phrase (the head word is a verb).

(c) Adjective phrase (the head word is an adjective).

(d) Prepositional phrase (the phrase begins with a preposition).

(e) Adverb phrase (the head word is an adverb).

Noun Phrase: There is a quality in English, which is called recursiveness. It means that an element can occur again and again in a sentence. We saw in the division of the first sentence that the noun phrase occurred three times.

The structure of the noun phrase: A NP consists of a number of elements which have their fixed place in the phrase. It is called classifying-adjective by British grammarians. They are Pre-determiner, Determiner, Ordinal, Quantifier, Adjective phrase, classifier and Noun.

We shall start from the classifier which is closest to the head word.

1. A classifier is a noun that functions as adjective in the noun phrase.

   Sunday morning

   Education officer

   Flower pot

   Here Sunday, education and flower are classifiers.

2. Adjective phrase comes just before the classifier. We shall discuss adjective phrase after noun phrase.

3. Quantifier is a word which refers to quantity or number.

   Five boys

   All girls

Much milk

Many chairs

Here five, all, much and many are quantifiers.

4. Ordinals are structure words and they are derived from numbers.

   For example; first, second, fifth, hundredth

5. Determiners precede ordinals. There are three kinds of determiner.
   (i) Articles: a, an, the.
   (ii) Demonstratives: this, these, that, those.
   (iii) Possessives: my, our, your, John's, Jane's.

These three cannot come together. We can place only one of these three in the slot of the determiner.

A pen
My pen } a/my/this pen
This pen

6. Pre-determiner comes before a determiner. Half of, some of, a few of are pre-determiners. "All" becomes pre-determiner when it precedes a determiner.

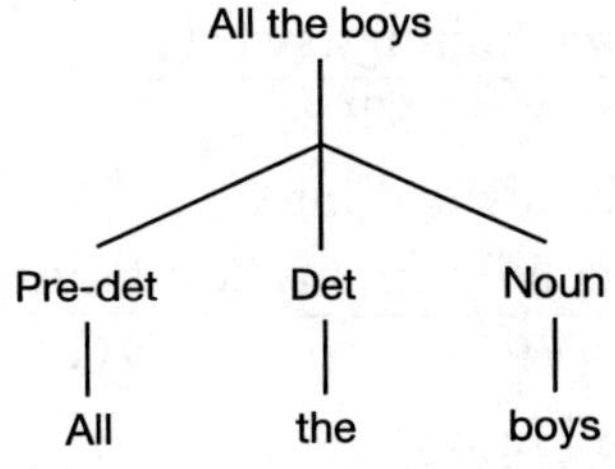

Adjective phrase: The head word of the adjective phrase is an adjective. In some cases, it may be preceded by an intensifier. An intensifier is a word that gives intensity to the adjective. The important intensifiers are already described.

It should be:

Look at this NP

A	very nicely	drawn map
determiner	adjective phrase	noun

The adjective phrase consists of two intensifiers "very" and "nicely" and one adjective "drawn".

Let us note that the intensifier is attached to the adjective, not to the noun in the phrase "a very nicely drawn map."

Sometimes two or three adjectives may come before a noun in a noun phrase.

A beautiful small girl.

A pretty red Indian doll.

The rule is that subjective adjective comes first and is followed by an objective adjective. The adjective derived from noun comes last. In the first noun phrase "small" is adjective and in the second "red" is adjective and *Indian* is derived from the noun India.

The Verb Phrase: The nucleus of the verb phrase is the verbal group. There may be noun phrase, adjective phrase, prepositional phrase or adverb phrase within a verb phrase. Let us take the following sentences:

1.

John	ran
NP	VP

The VP consists of the verbal group only

2.

A small girl	was kniting a sweater
NP	VP

The VP is further divided into

3.

Jane	looked sulkily at him	was kniting	and	a sweater
NP	VP	VG		NP

The VP is divided into

looked	sulkily	at him
VG	Adv. Phr.	PP

The structure of the VG is tense and the main verb. Auxiliaries and modals are helping verbs and –ing and –en are their aspects. Let us examine the following sentence:

1. $\dfrac{\text{He}}{\text{NP}}\ \dfrac{\text{ran}}{\text{VP}}$

The VP "ran" is verbal group. This verbal group consists of past tense and the verb *run.*

2. She has run.

Here "has run" consists of present tense + have + verb in past participle.

3. She has been running.

Here, "has been running" consists of present tense + have + been + run + ing

4. She may have done it.

The verbal group "may have done" consists of present tense + may + have + verb in the past participle.

Grammatically speaking, the structure of the verbal group is Tense + modal + perfective + progressive + main verb.

The form of perfective is have - en and of progressive be - ing. There is one rule called *affix movement*. It makes the affixes - en and - ing move onto the next verb. Here are two illustrations.

1. She may be going.

   She + present tense + may + be - ing + go

By affix movement rule Present Tense is attached to the modal "may" and the suffix - ing to the verb *go*.

2. It has been raining since morning.

It + present tense + have - en + be - ing + rain + since + morning. By affix movement rule present tense is attached to have, - en to "be" and - ing to "rain".

Prepositional Phrase: The prepositional phrase consists of a preposition and a noun phrase. Look at the following phrases.

in a room

on the roof

for example

down the line.

There is a preposition in each of these phrases. Since it supports the noun phrase in the structure of a sentence, it is called prepositional phrase.

The adverb phrase: The head word of the adverb phrase is an adverb. It can be preceded by an intensifier.

He works very slowly.

She ran terribly fast.

Here the adverb consists of an intensifier and an adverb. In most cases, there is an adverb only.

The students left the class gradually.

It rained heavily.

EXERCISES

1. What is the difference between a word and a phrase?
2. What is the basic criterion of naming a phrase?
3. Which is the most important component of a verb phrase?
4. Describe the different components of a noun phrase.
5. What is the difference between a pre-determiner and a determiner? Enumerate the determiners.
6. Describe the structure of the verbal group with examples.
7. What is a classifier? Illustrate the use of classifiers in noun phrases.
8. Give five examples of five verb phrases and make their structural analysis. One example is given for your guidance.

   It has been raining since morning.

   NP : It

   VP : has been raining

   PP : since morning

$$\text{VP} \rightarrow \text{Verbal group} \rightarrow \frac{\text{have + present tense}}{\text{has}} - \frac{\text{be + en}}{\text{been}} - \frac{\text{rain + ing}}{\text{raining}}$$

9. Differentiate an adverb phrase from a prepositional phrase.

Chapter Five

Functional Classification

Outcome of the Chapter

(a) Subject
(b) Verbal
(c) Object
(d) Complement
(e) Adjunct
(f) Disjunct
(g) Conjunct

Words and phrases function in a sentence. They are labelled according to their function. The following are the main labels:

1. Subject
2. Object
3. Verbal
4. Complement
5. Adjunct
6. Disjunct
7. Conjunct

The nucleus of a sentence is verb. A verb can alone be a sentence. Some imperative sentences have the verb only.

Go, come, march, proceed.

However, a full sentence has a subject and a verb. Let us examine these two sentences:

i. The small boy lifted a heavy bag.
ii. She is intelligent.

The first sentence has:

1. The small boy: **subject**
2. Lifted a heavy bag: **verbal + object**

The second sentence has a subject, a verbal and a complement.

She : subject
is : verbal
intelligent : complement

Adjunct is not an integral part of a sentence, that is, if we remove the adjunct from a sentence, the sentence remains meaningful.

She ran down the hill.

She : subject
ran : verbal
down the hill : adjunct

Subject - Subject is the doer. It governs the verbal. The subject is of two kinds: (a) grammatical and (b) logical.

The grammatical subject governs the verbal.

She is washing clothes.

Clothes are being washed by her.

In the first sentence, "she" is the grammatical subject; it governs the verbal "is washing". Similarly, "clothes" is the grammatical subject as it governs the verbal "are being washed".

The logical subject is the doer. Coming to the previous sentence, the grammatical subject "she" is logical subject also. But "clothes" is not logical subject in the second sentence. The logical subject is "her" because it is the doer, not "clothes".

2. Object is the word or phrase which is affected by the action of the verbal.

I want to see him.

He ate an apple.

In passive sentences, the object is placed in the nominative case and the logical subject in the objective or accusative case.

Objects are of two kinds: direct object and indirect object. The direct object is affected first.

He bought me an umbrella.

She gave me five hundred rupees.

In both the sentences, "me" is indirect object as it is affected later; 'an umbrella" and "five hundred rupees" are direct objects.

3. Verbal: Verbal is the verb group of categorial labelling. The verbal is of two kinds: transitive and intransitive. The transitive verb is divided into mono transitive, and di-transitive. The former takes one object and the latter two objects.

They chased a thief. Mono-transitive

They bought her a car. Di-transitive

4. Complement: A complement completes the meaning of the subject or object in a sentence. It is an integral part of a sentence and if it is removed, the sentence will be incomplete.

He is nice.

She is gentle.

Complements are of two kinds: complement to the subject and complement to the object.

He is nice.

She is gentle.

Here "nice" and "gentle" are complements to the subjects "he" and "she" respectively.

I found him *dull.*

Here *dull* is complement to the object "him".

5. Adjunct is an extra part of a sentence.

They were dancing *in the hall.*

She is swimming *in the pool.*

Look at the tree *on the top of the hill.*

The underlined phrases are adjuncts.

All adjuncts are prepositional phrases.

6. Conjunct: It is a term coined by British grammarians. It is a type of adverbial used to show the connection between a sentence and an earlier sentence. "Firstly", "Secondly", "thirdly", "finally" are common conjuncts. Other conjuncts are "namely", "as follows", "for example", "as a result", "consequently", "accordingly", "naturally", "additionally" and "decidedly".

7. Disjunct: A disjunct modifies the entire sentence. It often occurs either in the beginning or end of a sentence.

Admittedly, he proved a great help to us.

He hit her, unintentionally.

She acted in that critical hour, wisely.

Disjunct is also called "Sentence Adverb".

EXERCISES

A. Divide the following sentences into phrase units. The first sentence is done for you.

(a) The green revolution / has solved / India's food problem/ to a large extent.

The green revolution /	has solved /	India's food problem/	to a large extent.
NP	VG	NP	PP

(b)

We	shall meet	in the hall	tomorrow.
subject	verbal	adjunct	adjunct

(c)

It	is	difficult	for me	to help him.
subject	verbal	complement	adjunct	adjunct

(d) We saw a small boy with his mother.

(e) The black cat has drunk our milk.

(f) A gentle breeze blew early in the morning.

(g) The athlete fainted in the field.

(h) He told us an unbelievable story.

(i) *The Arabian Nights* is one of the most interesting story books in the world.

(j) The wall collapsed in the torrential rain.

(k) The boy who won the first prize did not turn up to receive the medal.

(l) The recent flood destroyed all the crops.

(m) He fell exhausted after walking seven miles.

B. Analyse the structure of the following sentences assigning functional labels. The first two are done for you.

(a) We shall meet in the hall tomorrow.
(b) It is difficult for me to help him.
(c) He met me after a long time.
(d) The little mouse in the tub laboured hard to come out.
(e) The man who lives next door is related to the local MLA.
(f) We could not decide on the matter.
(g) A few burglars were arrested by the police.
(h) The headmaster of the school punished the erring boys.
(i) Markets are flooded with mangoes in this season.
(j) The sun rose as usual.
(k) We did not know his whereabouts.
(l) The stars twinkled in the sky.

C. Underline complements and adjuncts in the following sentences and name them:
(a) He is a gentleman.
(b) He is going home tomorrow.
(c) The prisoner was released yesterday.
(d) Some boys were fishing in the pond.
(e) She made him happy.
(f) He looks sad.
(g) It appears defective.
(h) The sun rose, making the sky crimson red.
(i) At last we found him in a hotel.
(j) He was in a state.

D. Underline the direct and indirect objects in the following sentences and name them:
(a) She bought me an umbrella.
(b) They gave him a beautiful pen.
(c) Please write me a letter.
(d) We threw him a rope.

(e) They sacrificed their today for our tomorrow.

(f) The old man told us a wonderful story.

E. (a) What is conjunct? Write a small passage to illustrate the use of conjuncts.

(b) Write five sentences, using disjuncts.

(c) Write five sentences, using adjuncts.

(d) What is the difference between a prepositional phrase and an adjunct?

(e) Make distinction between an object and a complement with examples.

Chapter Six

Tense

Outcome of the Chapter

(a) Difference between time and tense
(b) Usage of tense
(c) Auxiliary modals

Tense is a subsystem of grammar to indicate the time of an action or event. Let us look at these sentences:

She is knitting a sweater.

They came back home.

I will go home tomorrow.

The first sentence indicates, present time, the second past time and the third future time. We should not confuse tense with time. Time is for practical purposes and is universal. Tense is a part of grammar and specific to language. Each language has its own tense system. In English language, tense is attached to the verb. If there is the main verb only in a sentence, tense is attached to it, in other cases to the auxiliary. If we look at the sentences given as examples we find that tense is attached to the auxiliary "be" (is) in the first sentence, to the main verb "come" (came) in the second sentence, and the modal "will" in the third sentence.

Time and Tense

Time is universal. We measure time by the Earth's diurnal course and divide the period into day and night. We measure the length of a day by the Sun's position in the sky in relation to the Earth. Suppose, the midday sun is the present or now, the time before is the past and what is coming or will come is future. The division of time in past, present and future is universal. Action or an event is the point which decides our notion of time.

Tense is grammatical, a way to convey an event/action, that occurred in the past, is occurring at present or will occur in the future. Since the verb denotes the idea of action, it carries tense.

There are two tenses in English: Present Tense and Past Tense. It is erroneously assumed that there is a future tense also. In fact, it does not exist. The *Oxford English Dictionary* defines grammatical tense as "any one of the different forms or modifications (or word groups) in the conjugation of a verb which indicate the different times (*past*, *present*, or *future*) at which the action or state denoted by it is viewed as happening or existing."

As we know that Tense refers to the location of an event or action in time, either the present or the past. It is marked by an inflection of the verb or modification in verb:

Rahul *plays* the football. (present tense)

Rahul *played* the football. (past tense)

To represent other times—the future, for instance—can be made in a number of ways, by using the modal auxiliary *will*, or the semi-auxiliary *be going to*:

Rahul *will* the football.

Rahul *will be playing* the football.

Since the expression of future time does not involve any inflection of the verb, we do not refer to a "future tense". Strictly speaking, there are only two tenses in English: present and past. English has ample of ways to represent the future actions, in terms of base verbal morphology there are only two tenses in English: present and past because they require a change in the finite form of the verb. Constructions such as the present progressive or past perfect are analysed in terms of aspect, although the present and past tenses express aspect too.

For example, regular verbs have four forms. In the case of *play* they are *play, plays, playing, played.* In third person singular, the present tense is *plays* and the past tense is play*ed.*

There are five forms of the verb.

Present: be (is, am, are), go, will, can;

Past: was/were, went, would, could;

Infinitive: to be, to go (see appendix 'B' for participle, gerund, etc. which also do not carry tense)

- ing form: being, going;

- en form: been, gone;

The last three forms do not carry tense. For example:

I have to go	Present
I had to go	Past
He is going	Present
He was going	Past
She has gone	Present
They had gone	Past

We see that the infinitive, - ing and - en forms remain the same in all cases, whether the sentence is in the past or present tense.

There are four forms of the present and past tenses.

1. Simple present	1. Simple past
2. Present progressive	2. Past progressive
3. Present perfect	3. Past perfect
4. Present perfect continuous	4. Past perfect continuous

MEANING AND USES OF TENSE

Present Tense

1. Simple Present: The form is that the main verb carries present tense.

Simple present is used in the following cases:

(a) **To state timeless truth:**

The sun rises in the east.

Ice is cold.

Sugar is sweet.

These statements are true in all times: past, present and future.

(b) **Routine work:**

I go to school by bus.

The office opens at 10 a.m.

I polish my shoes every day.

Shatabdi Express leaves Kanpur at 5 p.m. for Delhi.

(c) **Present time activity:**

He is in the kitchen.

There are two doors in the room.

He has a sword in his hand.

He writes a letter.

How do you do?

(d) **Performative use:**

I name thee husband and wife.

I declare the meeting closed.

(e) **Commentaries:**

The bowler takes the ball. He runs fast.

He delivers the ball. It is a bouncer.

(f) **Future time activity (fixed plan):**

Our exams begin tomorrow.

The Prime Minister arrives today.

Advertisers use simple present often: Come to Nainital any time. We are ready to offer you a lot of enjoyment. Our hotel is opposite the lake. We offer nice bed tea at 7 a.m., sumptuous breakfast at 9 o'clock. We provide taxi to see Nainital and the adjacent areas.

(g) **Declaration and stage directions:**

Now, the meeting is over.

Team a is the winner.

There are three chairs on the stage.

Tanmay enters the stage from left.

He makes a round and then sits in the middle chair.

2. Present Progressive: The form of the verb "be" or a modal is in present tense and the main verb in the - ing form:

It is raining.

We are playing.

They will be reading.

The present progressive indicates an action that began sometime in recent past and is in progress at present. The time of past is not known.

Present progressive is not used normally with the stative verbs of emotion, thought, possession and sense like forget, believe, feel, see, smell, hear, sense, doubt, dislike, understand, suspect, loathe, own, belong, know, like, need, want, seen, mean, remember, prefer, hate, love. But be, taste, see, have, think are stative as well as dynamic, i.e. when they mean usual action, they can be used in continuous tense.

(a) Present time activity:

She is writing a letter.

We are watching a programme on T.V.

He is washing his car.

(b) Future time activity (immediate plans):

I am going to Delhi next week.

They are going to run a risk in that enterprise.

The exams are starting from tomorrow.

(c) Continual activity:

He is reading Shakespeare

She is writing a novel.

Janardan is working on a project.

Here the work is in progress but there are breaks in the middle as it is a prolonged one. Contrast these two sentences.

I am writing a letter.

I am writing a novel.

(d) Frequently repeated action which is annoying or unreasonable:

He is always taking leave.

My maid servant is breaking cups and plates frequently.

3. Present Perfect: The form is have + verb with the - en form

I have done the job.

She has come, just now.

The train has arrived.

Uses of Present Perfect

(a) Recent Past:

I have received your message.

He has washed the car.

He has gone to England and will be back next month.

(b) Resultative Past:

I have cut my finger. (It needs bandaging, hurry up!)

The train has arrived.

I have seen a strange animal moving there.

(c) An activity that is still continuing:

I have been a teacher in this university for ten years.

I have stopped smoking.

(d) Experience:

I have been to England. I have been a good cricketer. There is a difference between

He has gone to England.

He has been to England.

The meaning of the first sentence is that "he" is still in England and of the second that "he" has returned from England (or he is no longer in England) and the country is a part of his experience.

4. Present perfect continuous:

The form is have + been + verb with - ing

It has been raining since morning.

We have been working for eight hours.

This tense is used for an action which began in the past and is still continuing.

5. Present perfect and present perfect continuous contrasted:

Present perfect is used generally for a completed action but present perfect continuous shows that the action is still going on.

I have written this letter.

I have been writing this letter.

(Normally, time is mentioned in perfect continuous and there is sense of progression)

She has read the novel.

She has been reading a novel.

Past Tense

1. Simple Past: The form is verb in past tense:

She woke early. (Up follows this verb in certain cases especially in imperative sentences).

I slept well.

He was absent.

Simple past is used in the following cases:

(a) Actions completed in the past without time reference:

I met him by chance.

She did it herself.

They forgot to remind me.

(b) Actions completed in the past with time reference:

He wrote his first novel in 1985.

They worked here for four years.

I cut my finger ten minutes ago.

(c) Habitual activity in the past:

I smoked five cigarettes every day.

They begged door to door during the famine.

(Compare: modal 'used to': I used to smoke five cigarettes daily.)

(d) Polite use:

Did you call me, sir?

I wanted to ask you a question.

There is a difference in meaning between:

(i) I cut my finger.

(ii) I have cut my finger.

The first sentence indicates that the finger is bandaged but the second indicates that it needs bandaging. Past time adverbial is not used in present perfect tense.

(e) Suggestion:

Better we stopped discussion.

You'd better go.

2. Past Progressive: The form is 'be' in (past) + verb + ing.

He was sleeping. She was singing.

Uses of Past Progressive

(a) An action that was in progress in past:

He was ploughing his field.

They were going to the market.

She was singing a song.

(b) Increasing or decreasing activity in the past:

It was getting darker.

The waves were rising.

She was getting weaker and weaker.

The temperature was falling down sharply.

(c) Descriptions:

It was raining heavily.

A man was going with an umbrella.

3. Past Perfect: The form: had + verb in the - en form.

He had reached before me.

She had left when I reached there.

Past perfect means (remote) past in the past.

When there are two actions in the past, the first (the earlier) one is placed in the past perfect and the second in simple past.

(i) He had been in army for ten years when I met him.

(ii) The old beggar, who had lived on the pavement box for six months, was a spy.

(iii) I saw her yesterday. We hadn't met for a longtime.

4. Past Perfect Continuous: It is past equivalent of present perfect continuous. The form is had + been + verb + ing.

I had been working in a shoe factory.

(a) A single action in the past that began before the time of speaking in the past or stopped just before it:

It was 8'o clock and we were tired because we had been working since morning.

She had been fanning me for quite a long time and so I asked her to stop.

(b) A repeated action in the past:

We had been trying to contact the minister on phone.

Auxiliary Modals

A modal determines the mood of a verb. There are thirteen modals: will, would, shall, should, can, could, may, might, ought to, used to, need, and dare. Ought to, used to, need and dare are marginal modals and the rest are the core modals. This is because the core modals are more frequent than the marginal modals.

1. Will: Normally used with second person and third person.

(i) Futurity:

He will come tomorrow.

You will do my work.

(ii) Habit:

She will come to the garden and sit there for hours together.

He will make mistakes while negotiating with the strangers.

Boys will be boys.

(iii) Permission

Will you do me a favour?

2. Shall: Normally used with first person.

(i) Futurity:

I shall do it for you. We shall start tomorrow.

(ii) Volition:

Shall I help you?

In normal speech, *shall* and *will* are not distinguished as the contracted form, he'll for he will and you'll for you will are used. The distinction is made in formal writing where "will" with first person means intention and "shall" with second and third person compulsion. For example:

The pronouncement in a judgement: "He shall be hanged to death."

3. May:

(i) Permission:

He may go.

May I come in?

(ii) Possibility:

They may visit us in the evening.

She may pass the examination.

It may rain.

(iii) Ability:

She may top the list if properly coached. He may lift a quintal.

4. Might: Might is the past form of *may*, but in some cases *might* can be used in place of *may*.

(i) Possibility:

He might come.

(ii) Ability:

He might lift the weight.

5. Can:

(i) Permission:

He can go.

You can assist him.

Here may and can are interchangeable.

(ii) Ability:

She can read and write French.

I can draw the map of India.

(iii) Possibility:

He can be seen in the restaurant.

The Siberian cranes can be seen in winter.

(iv) Capability:

I can run a mile.

He can lift a bag weighing seventy kilograms.

6. Could: It is the past form of *can* but *it* can be used with different meanings.

(i) Past ability/capability:

While I was in Assam, I could speak Assamese.

I could run a mile in my youth.

He could sing well a few years ago.

(ii) Possibility:

She could be with her friends in the drawing room.

(iii) Permission (polite use):

Could you lend me your pen?

7. Would: In general, it is the past form of will.

(i) Futurity:

I would do it.

(ii) Polite request:

Would you do me a favour?

(iii) Empty use:

I would like to acquaint you with the present situation.

8. Should: In general, it is the past form of shall.

(i) Advice:

You should follow her example.

She should listen to her mother.

(ii) Volition:

Should I help you in this matter?

9. Must:

(i) Obligation:

You must do it.

He must obey the order.

10. Ought to: *Ought to* is used in the sense of moral duty.

(i) I ought to love my country.

(ii) She ought to obey her parents' advice.

The difference among *ought to*, *should* and *must* is of degree. "Ought to" is used when there is moral duty; "should" is used in the context of advice, and must in the sense of obligation or compulsion.

11. Dare: *Dare* is used for assertion or boldness and mostly in negative sentences or with negative intention.

He dare not face me.

Dare she face her boss?

12. Need: *Need* is used when we politely ask someone not to do something or assure him/her not to worry.

(i) You need not stay any more.

(ii) He need not worry about the problem. I will help him.

13. Used to: This modal is used to refer to a habitual activity in the past, but now stopped.

(i) When I was in Delhi, I used to go to Connaught Place in the evening.

(ii) She used to come to me for guidance.

EXERCISES

A. Write the tense and time reference of the following sentences: The first and last ones are done for you.

(a) I am going to the market.

(b) They have come.

(c) I was in Delhi last year.

(d) Ice is cold.

(e) I wanted to go to London by ship.

(f) He would not come tomorrow.

(g) Sita is going to Hyderabad next week.
(h) Shatabdi Express leaves Kanpur for Delhi at 4.50 p.m.
(i) He goes to office at 9 a.m.
(j) Oil will float on water.

Answer:

(a) I am going to the market. Tense: present progressive, Time: present.

(j) Oil will float on water. Tense: simple present, Time: all time.

B. Write the tense and time reference of the following pairs of sentences and comment on their meaning. The first one is done for guidance.

(a) (i) I cut my finger.
    (ii) I have cut my finger.
(b) (i) We saw them cross the river.
    (ii) We saw them crossing the river.
(c) (i) He has gone to England.
    (ii) He has been to England.
(d) (i) She goes to office by bus.
    (ii) She is going to office by bus.
(e) (i) Mahima is writing a letter.
    (ii) Mahima is writing a novel.
(f) (i) Some one has removed my books.
    (ii) Some one is removing my books.
(g) (i) It may rain tomorrow.
    (ii) It must rain tomorrow.
(h) (i) I want to talk to you.
    (ii) I wanted to talk to you.

Answer:

(a) (i) I cut my finger. Tense: simple past, Time: past, Meaning: The cut has healed or bandaged.
    (ii) I have cut my finger. Tense: present perfect, Time: past, Meaning: The blood is still coming out.

C. Fill in the blanks with the appropriate form of the verb. Three verb forms are given in brackets against each blank:

(a) I want to ______ why you did not reply to my letter. (know, knew, known)

(b) I did not ______ your letter. (receive, received, receives)

(c) And then ______ the danger which my friend I had not anticipated before. (came, come coming)

(d) "She ______ not worry for her future", her father said. (need, needed, needs)

(e) We ______ to read for twelve hours every day during examination period. (did use, using, used)

D. Explain the difference between:

(a) Present perfect and simple past tenses:

(b) "should" and "ought to".

(c) "I was writing a letter" and "I have written a letter".

(d) "She is cooking food" and "She is knitting a sweater".

(e) "It may rain tomorrow" and " It will rain tomorrow".

E. (a) Explain the difference between tense and time.

(b) Which verbs carry tense?

(c) What is the difference between "Hari can lift the weight of 45 kgs", and "Hari may lift the weight of 45 kgs".

(d) Explain the difference between "I can eat ten rotis" and "I could eat ten rotis."

(e) Explain the difference between "She is going to see her sister", and "She was going to see her sister".

Chapter Seven

Sentence and Transformation

Outcome of the Chapter

A. Classification of sentences

B. Transformation

(a) Narration/Reporting

(b) Voice

(c) Change of degree

(d) Removal of "too"

(e) Synthesis

The Sentence

A sentence is a unit of words systematically arranged of which the verb is the nucleus. It is already said that the verb is the most important word in all languages for it indicates time of an action or event. The great Sanskrit Grammarian showed how the root verb (*dhatu*) is the nucleus of all words in Sanskrit. Following him, Noam Chomsky showed how the verb is the nucleus of the sentence in English.

A. Classification of Sentences

A sentence can be classified according to its (a) structure and (b) communicative purpose. According to structure, a sentence can be (a) simple and (b) multiple.

(a) **Simple Sentence:** A simple sentence consists of one main verb only. A clause also consists of one main verb. So we can say a simple sentence is made of one clause. John Seely defines sentence, "[It is] a unit of language consisting of one or more *finite clauses*. If a sentence contains just one clause, it is described as *simple*" (*English Grammar and Punctuation*, 147).

The term "finite clause" means a clause which contains a finite or free verb. A finite verb stands by itself in a clause.

A finite clause is the basic sentence in English Language and there are five basic patterns of its structure:

I. Subject + Verbal: We went. She laughed.
II. Subject + Verbal + Object: We ate mangoes.
III. Subject + Verbal + Object + Object: He bought me a car.
IV. Subject + Verbal + Complement: She is intelligent.
V. Subject + Verbal + Object + Complement: She made him a fool.

(b) Multiple Sentence: A multiple sentence consists of two or more clauses. If it consists of one free clause and one or more bound or dependent clauses, it is called a *complex* sentence and if there are two or more free. Independent clauses and one or more dependent clauses, it is a compound sentence. This tree diagram will explain the division.

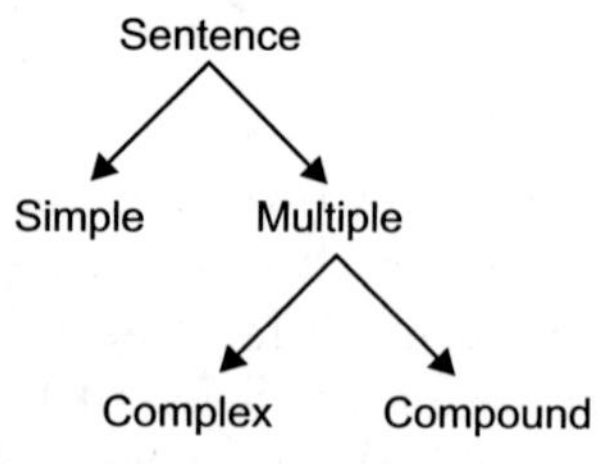

A few examples of complex and compound sentences are given here. You will read more about them in the Analysis and Synthesis sections.

Complex Sentences

1. I know that he will come.
2. She admitted that she had broken the glass.
3. You can see the tower if you go to the other side of this lane.

Compound Sentences

1. We walked about a mile and then saw a huge tree, which was 150 feet tall with ten thick branches all covered with lush green leaves.

2. They walked in the dense forest but failed to find a path, which could lead them and, so, they decided to spend the night on a tree.

As already explained, a sentence can consist of one clause or more than one clause. In analysis, only the complex and compound sentences are studied in terms of their independent and subordinate clauses. The aim of analysis is to show the relation between clauses.

A simple sentence consists of only one main verb.

There ***are*** a number of stars as big as the sun.

Those boys ***did*** not attend my class.

John and Michael ***are*** friends.

A complex sentence contains a main clause and one or more than one dependent clauses.

There are a number of stars which are as big as the sun.

Those are the boys, who did not attend my class.

The first sentence consists of the main or principal clause, "There are a number of stars" and the dependent or subordinate clause, "which are as big as the sun". The subordinate clause is structurally dependent on the principal clause. Similarly, the second sentence can be divided as:

Those are the boys: Principal clause

Who did not attend my class: subordinate clause.

A compound sentence consists of two or more main clauses (called co-ordinate clauses). It may contain one or more subordinate clause in addition to the co-ordinate clauses.

Mohan jumped four meters and so did I.

Both the clauses are independent and, so, are co-ordinate clauses. Similarly,

It is difficult to agree with all the recommendations of the Kelker committee, for it hits the middle class most and also it does not help the economic growth by any means.

This sentence has three co-ordinate clauses:

(i) It is difficult to agree with all the recommendations of the Kelkar committee.

(ii) (for) It hits the middle class most.

(iii) (and) It does not help the economic growth by any means.

Subordinate clauses are of three kinds:

(i) Complement clause

(ii) Relative clause

(iii) Adverbial clause

(a) A complement clause complements the verb in the principal clause.

I know that he will come.

That, she is intelligent, is known to us.

If we look at the complement clause from the point of view of formal classification or categorial labelling it is ingeniously a noun phrase. A complement clause can be the subject, object or complement to the main verb in the main clause. According to Chomsky, infinitives are also complement clauses. Let us take a few examples:

It is difficult *to solve this problem.*

To err is human.

I want you *to do this.*

I intend *to help you.*

The italicised words in the sentences form complement clauses.

(b) A relative clause is linked to the subject or object of the principal clause.

I saw a few boys, *who were carrying a log.*

Mr. Sanyal, *who is an officer in Canara Bank*, is my neighbour.

The italicised clauses are relative clauses:

(c) An adverbial clause modifies the main verb in the principal clause.

(a) She knows how to tease children.

(b) I do not know if he will come.

EXERCISES

1. Divide the following sentences into clauses and name each clause:
   (a) He jumped into the river but I stayed behind.
   (b) That, India is one of the oldest civilizations in the world, is a well-known fact.
   (c) The teacher said that the earth is a planet in the solar system.
   (d) I will seek your help when time comes.
   (e) Mr. Radhakrishnan is a man who, I know, is trust worthy.
   (f) Though we have made some progress, there is a lot to be done.
   (g) This is one of the best books, that are available in the market.
   (h) If you face the rising sun, your right hand will be on the south side.

We have already read that the sentence is the highest unit of language. Now we shall read the kinds of the sentence and their transformation.

1. According to meaning or communicative purposes, sentences are of four kinds.

(a) Declarative
(b) Interrogative
(c) Imperative
(d) Exclamatory/Exclamative

(a) Declarative sentences make a statement:

(a) We have eaten five apples.
(b) She did not eat anything.

(b) Interrogative sentences ask a question: They may begin with an auxiliary or a wh-word. The wh-words are who, where, what, when, why, whose, whom, which and how. Although "how" does not begin with wh-, it is close in pronunciation to the wh-words.

(i) Is he ill?

(ii) Where is he going?

(iii) What's your name?

(c) Imperative sentences begin with a verb but do not ask a question: they, ask, advise, suggest or order.

(i) Please help me.

(ii) Let us go there.

(iii) Don't make a noise.

(d) Exclamatory sentences express strong emotion:

(i) He has won the game!

(ii) You have acted wonderfully!

(iii) What a beautiful scene it is!

(iv) Alas, I am ruined!

2. From the point of view of **meaning** sentences are classified into: (a) affirmative or positive and (b) negative.

(i) I am happy: Affirmative.

(ii) I am not happy: Negative.

3. **Structurally,** sentences are divided into: (a) simple, (b) complex and (c) compound, sentences.

Rule for changing one kind of sentence into another:

1. From Affirmative to Negative

(a) If there is an auxiliary verb already present in the sentence, the negative marker "not" is attached to it. If we want to contract the negative marker to "n't", it is made part of the auxiliary.

Affirmative: It is clear.

Negative: It is not clear.

Contracted negative: It isn't clear.

The following are the contracted negative forms of the Auxiliaries:

is	isn't	should	shouldn't
are	aren't	would	wouldn't
was	wasn't	could	couldn't

were	weren't	might	mightn't
will	won't	do	don't
shall	shan't	does	doesn't

If a sentence contains the main verb only, the do-support rule is applied. The auxiliary 'do' is inserted and brought forward and placed before the subject.

(b) The sentences where there are no auxiliaries, the do support rule is applied. The contracted form of the negative marker is attached to the auxiliary "do".

Affirmative: They play.

Negative: They do not play.

Contracted negative: They don't play.

Affirmative: She sings perfectly well.

Negative: She does not sing perfectly well.

Contracted negative: She doesn't sing perfectly well.

Affirmative: He does his work methodically.

Negative: He does not do his work methodically.

Contracted negative: He doesn't do his work methodically.

2. Declarative to Interrogative

(a) If there is an auxiliary in the sentence, it is brought forward and placed before the subject. If the auxiliary "be" is functioning as the main verb, it is brought forward. In negative sentences, the contracted negative form of the auxiliary is brought forward.

Declarative: They are playing in the field.

Interrogative: Are they playing in the field?

Declarative: He plays football.

Interrogative: Does he play football?

Declarative: He allowed me to go home.

Interrogative: Did he allow me to go home?

(b) In the case of wh-words, the wh-words precede the auxiliary in interrogative sentences.

Declarative: He left the bag.
Interrogative: Did he leave the bag?

Declarative: She is not doing her work.
Interrogative: Is she not doing her work?

Declarative: We aren't responsible for it.
Interrogative: Aren't we responsible for it?

Conditional Sentences: A conditional sentence consists of a main clause and a subordinate clause. Sometimes a conditional sentence has more than two clauses. The subordinate clause may begin with subordinators like if, whether, when, unless, until, even if and provided (that).

The conditional sentences have the same tense in both the clauses, that is, if one is in present, the other will be in present, if one is in simple past, the other will be in simple past and if one is in past perfect the other will be in past perfect.

(a) **Present tense:**

(i) If it rains, the prospects of the Rabi crops will be better.

(ii) I can't say anything until he comes.

(b) **Past tense:**

(i) If he came earlier, he would meet me.

(ii) You could catch the train, if you ran fast.

(c) **Past perfect:**

(i) He would have gained more provided he had worked honestly.

(ii) She would not have succeeded even if I had helped her.

Meanings associated with conditional clauses

(a) **Present tense conditional clauses:**

(i) Possibility:

If it rains heavily, we may stay here at night.

He may pass if he studies regularly.

(ii) Permission:

You can go if you have serialized the papers.

She may leave if she is in a hurry.

(iii) Advice:

Don't take fried things, if you want to live *healthily*.

You should stop eating sugar, if you want to lose weight.

(iv) Order:

You must be regular in class, if you want to be a good student.

(v) Result:

You can see the rising sun, if you awake early.

Water will boil, if you heat it at 100 degree centigrade.

(b) **Simple past conditional sentence:** Here the supposition is contrary to the known facts or when things did not happen or would not happen. Besides it can be used for impossible situations.

(i) If I lived nearer, I would help you. (Meaning I didn't live nearly)

(ii) She would scream if a thief entered her room. (The thief did not enter her room).

(iii) She behaved if she were a queen. (she was not a queen) We use "were" with all subjects when it is an impossible situation.

(iv) I would not resign if I were you.

(c) **Past Perfect:** Conditional sentences in past perfect mean that things did not happen or the work was not done.

(i) He would have passed the examination if he had studied sincerely.

(ii) I wouldn't have signed those documents even if I had been pressurized.

(iii) The train would have arrived in time if the fog hadn't thickened densely.

(The subordinate clause may precede the principal clause, i.e. 'if he had studied....')

Question Tags: Question tags are frequently used in conversational English. The main purpose of the speaker is to get confirmation from the listener.

He'll come today, won't he?

She is intelligent, isn't she?

The tags are formed by reversing the position of the subject and the auxiliary in the main sentence. If there is no auxiliary, the auxiliary "do" is supplied. The question tag is negative, if the main sentence is affirmative and question tag is affirmative, if the main sentence is negative.

They are all right, aren't they?

It is a difficult task, isn't it?

He won't come, will he?

He can't lift 70 kgs, can he?

He writes well, doesn't he?

She sings melodiously, doesn't she?

He doesn't know English, does he?

EXERCISES

1. Change the following sentences into simple past:
   (a) If you read sincerely you will pass.
   (b) I will help her if she requests.
   (c) The patient will improve, if he regulates his diet.
   (d) John will not catch us if we move faster.
   (e) Your clothes will dry soon if you hang them in the sun.
2. Change the following sentences in past perfect:
   (a) He would reach the station in time if he started earlier.
   (b) She could avert the accident, if she applied brakes in time.
   (c) I might see the rising sun if I awoke earlier.

(d) If you took care of your health, you would not suffer from common diseases.

(e) If my friend were cautious, he would not fall on the slippery ground.

3. Write the question tags of the following sentences:

(a) They are coming home tomorrow.

(b) He assured us of his help.

(c) Our college will open next week.

(d) The train is late by an hour.

(e) They can go to any extent.

(f) There will be a cloudy day tomorrow.

(g) We shall play our final match on 19 of July.

(h) They have cheated us.

(i) She isn't going with us.

(j) He isn't that stupid.

(k) Falstaff is the greatest comic character.

Transformations

(a) **Reporting Speech:** A person's speech can be reported in two ways: first by quoting the actual words of the speaker and second in the words of the reporter or narrator. The first way of reporting is called direct speech and the second indirect speech.

1. Prakash said, "I am not well". The words within inverted commas are the actual words spoken by the speaker.
2. Prakash said that he was not well. The entire sentence is an indirect speech.

A sentence or passage in direct speech has two parts, reporting verb and reported speech. The words within the inverted commas are reported speech and the words outside them are reporting verb. In the first sentence, "Prakash said" is the reporting verb and "I am not well" is the reported speech.

A direct speech can be transformed into indirect speech. We use our words because we cannot always quote the speaker's words verbatim. There are three rules to change a direct speech into an indirect speech.

1. The rule of tense
2. The rule of pronoun
3. The specific rules of different kinds of sentences

1. Rule of Tense:

(a) If the reporting verb is in present tense, the tense of the reported speech is not changed.

He says, "I am going to London by plane."

He says that he is going to London by plane.

(b) If the reporting verb is in past tense and the reported speech is in present tense, the present is changed into its corresponding past.

He said, "I am going to London by plane."

He said that he was going to London by plane.

(c) If the reporting verb is in past and the reported speech also in past, the simple past (of reported speech) is changed into past perfect and the past progressive into past perfect continuous.

He said, "I bought the complete works of Shakespeare."

He said that he had bought the complete works of Shakespeare.

She said, "It was raining continuously."

She said that it had been raining continuously.

Note: If the reported speech states a timeless truth, the tense does not change.

The teacher said, "Tea is grown in Assam."

The teacher said that tea is grown in Assam.

2. The Rule of Pronoun:

(a) The first person of the reported speech changes according to the number and person of the subject of the reporting verb.

They said, "We are going home."

They told that they were going home.

(b) The second person of the reported speech changes according to the number and person of the object of the reporting verb.

He said to me, "You are my friend."

He told me that I was his friend.

The third person remains unchanged.

3. Specific Rules:

(a) Declarative sentences: The inverted commas are omitted and the connective "that" is inserted between the reporting verb and the reported speech. All the examples given earlier were declarative sentences.

(b) Interrogative sentences: Interrogative sentences are of two kinds:

(a) beginning with auxiliaries and

(b) beginning with wh-words.

(a) Interrogative sentences beginning with auxiliaries: The verb "say" is changed into "ask", "inquire of", "question" or "wanted to know" according to the context. The connective "if" or "whether" is inserted between the reporting verb and the reported speech and the sentence is made declarative.

(i) She said to the weatherman, "Will it rain tomorrow?"

She asked the weatherman if it would rain next day.

(ii) The manager said to the peon, "Have you locked the door?

The manager inquired of the peon if he had locked the door.

(b) Interrogative sentences beginning "with wh-words": The verb "say" is changed into "ask", "inquire of", "question" or "want to know" according to the context as it is done in the case of the sentences beginning with auxiliaries but no connective is added as wh-words are themselves connectives.

(i) He said to her, "How will you reach there?"

He asked her how she would reach there.

(ii) The stranger said to the boy, "What's the name of his village?"

The stranger asked the boy the name of his village.

(c) Imperative sentence: Imperative sentences mean order, command, request, advice and suggestion. The object is you (understood). For changing an imperative sentence into indirect speech, the first rule is to change the verb "say" into order, command, request, advise or suggest according to the meaning of the reported speech. The second rule is that the verb of the reported speech is made infinitive, generally.

(i) Order:

"Bring me a cup of coffee and some snacks" he said to the waiter.

He ordered the waiter to bring him a cup of coffee and some snacks.

(ii) Command:

The captain said to soldiers, "March on!"

The captain commanded the soldiers to march on.

(iii) Request:

He said to the officer, "Please transfer me to a hill station."

He requested the officer to transfer him to a hill station.

(iv) Advice:

My friend said to me, "Give up the bad habit of smoking."

My friend advised me to give up the bad habit of smoking.

(v) Suggestion:

He said to us, "Let us not quarrel."

He advised us not to quarrel.

(d) Exclamatory Sentence: The exclamatory sentence is made declarative and the connective "that" is inserted between the reporting verb and the reported speech. Finally, the verb "say" is changed into "wonder", "shout in joy", "exclaim in sorrow", etc., according to the meaning of the reported speech.

(i) Sita said, "Alas! I am ruined!"
Sita cried in sorrow that she was ruined.

(ii) He said, "Oh, the flood has destroyed my house!"
He exclaimed with sorrow that the flood had destroyed his house.

(iii) They said, "Hurrah! We have won the match!"
They shouted in joy that they had won the match.

EXERCISES

1. Change the following into indirect speech. The first two are done for you:
   (i) "Will you have a cup of tea?", she said to me.
   (ii) He said, "I must wash my hands first."
   Example:
      (i) She asked me if I would have/would like to have a cup of tea. (Use of 'like' makes it polite)
      (ii) He said/asserted that he must wash his hands first.
   (iii) "Where do you come from?", I asked the stranger.
   (iv) The stranger replied, "I come from a small village in Tripura."
   (v) The mistress said to the maid servant, "What have you done with my kitchen ware?"
   (vi) My friend said to me, "Come and have a glass of lassi."
   (vii) The doctor said to me, "Take two tablets thrice a day."
   (viii) Her mother said to her, "Don't delay in the market and come home by six."
   (ix) The sister said to her brother, "Will you teach me how to drive a scooter?"
   (x) He said to us, "Let us go for a walk."

(b) Voice: There are two voices in English:

(a) Active and (b) Passive

In Active Voice, the verb is used in agreement with the agent/doer; in Passive Voice the main verb is 'be' + main verb and it is in agreement with the object/action done. Read the sentences:

(i) Siddhartha made a nice doll.

Here "Siddhartha" is both the logical and grammatical subject and "Siddhartha" is the agent/doer.

(ii) A nice doll was made by Siddhartha.

Here, "Siddhartha" is the logical subject but not the grammatical subject. "A nice doll" is the object + 'be' in past tense.

Passive voice is used when the focus is on action or event. It can be also used when the "agent" is general or unknown. The following sentences are in passive voice.

(iii) The streets are cleaned every morning.

(iv) Five villages have been washed way.

(v) A dam is going to be built.

(vi) The house was burnt to ashes.

The agent/does is not known in these sentences and emphasis is on action/event.

Rules for changing active voice into passive:

1. Only transitive verbs can be changed into passive voice. Intransitive verbs are not changed into passive.
2. The subject of the first noun phrase (NP_1) is shifted to the place of the object or the second noun phrase (NP_2) and NP_2 to the place of NP_1. In short the places of NP_1 and NP_2 are interchanged. This is called NP switch rule.
3. The verb "be" and the affix "- en" are inserted before the main verb. This is called be - en insertion rule.
4. The preposition "by" is inserted before the new object.
5. Finally, the affix - en is attached to the main verb (Affix movement rule).

Let us take the following sentence:

(vii) Newton discovered the law of gravity.

The law of gravity discovered Newton. NP switch rule.

The law of gravity be - en discovered Newton (Be-en insertion rule)

The law of gravity be - en discovered by Newton (By insertion rule)

The law of gravity be past – discover - en by Newton

was discovered

Since the sentence is in the past, the verb "be" is made past and the verb "discover" is changed into - en that is, "discoved."

6. The next important rule is the agent deletion rule. It means when the agent or the doer is not specific, it may be deleted.

(viii) They elected him president → He was elected president.

(ix) Someone has stolen my car → My car has been stolen.

Some examples are given for guidance.

Declarative sentences

(i) John is observing stars.

Stars are being observed by John.

(ii) They have built the bridge.

The bridge has been built by them.

(iii) They wash cars regularly.

Cars are washed regularly.

(iv) Someone set the house on fire.

The house was set on fire.

(v) They are constructing a multi storeyed building.

A multi storeyed building is being constructed.

Interrogative Sentences: Since all sentences stem from the simple active sentences (Chomsky says they stem from the kernel sentences at the deep level) it is always better to look at the declarative form of an interrogative sentence. The declarative form of "who tore my paper?" is "someone tore my paper". Similarly, the declarative form of "where did they find him?" is "They found him somewhere". If we are to change the interrogative sentence into passive, we have to change the declarative form into passive and then make it interrogative; thus "they found him somewhere" is changed to "he was found somewhere" and its interrogative is: Where was he found?

Thus,

(i) Where did they find him? Active

Where was he found? Passive

Let us take a few more sentences:

(ii) Did you remind him of the programme?

Was he reminded of the programme?

(iii) How did he do it?

How was it done by him?

Passive of sentences with two verbs (main verb + other form of verb):

(iv) I want to clean the room myself.

Note that this sentence consists of "I want" and "I clean the room myself". Since the object of the second sentence "I clean the room myself" is 'room', the verb 'clean' will be passivized and not 'want' because 'room' is not the object of 'want'. Moreover, the verb that affects the object directly is passivized. Therefore the passive will be:

I want the room to be cleaned by myself.

The passive of the sentence:

(v) "I want you to assist her",

will be "I want her to be assisted by you"

This is because the subject of the second verb is "you" The active sentence is divided into "I want" and "you assist her."

There are sentences which are used in passive voice only. A few of them are given.

(vi) He was injured in an accident.

(vii) Five villages were washed away in the flood.

(viii) The house was badly damaged in the fire.

(ix) Passengers are advised to tighten their belts.

(x) He is supposed to be a great scholar.

(xi) My car has been removed.

Passive voice is used in the following cases:

(a) When it is not obvious who the doer is:

He was arrested.

The files are burnt to ashes.

She was sent to jail.

(b) When the doer is unknown:

The minister was shot dead.

He was killed in a plane crash.

(c) When the doer is "people" or "they":

He is supposed to be a dishonest.

She is believed to be a witch.

(d) When the doer is the indefinite pronoun one/someone:

(i) Someone has stolen my watch.
My watch has been stolen.

(ii) One mustn't touch live electric wire bare hands.
A live electric wire mustn't be touched bare hands.

EXERCISES

Change into Passive Voice by applying 'agent deletion' rule:

(a) They found him by the bank.

(b) People must not spread rumours during riots.

(c) How did they do it?

(d) They urged the Income Tax officer to check the return again.

(e) One often sees this sort of advertisement in newspapers.

(f) People suppose that the thief escaped disguised as a sadhu.

(g) Can one count the stars?

(h) How will we win the battle?

(i) Who has bought this house?

(j) We do not know when the accident took place?

(k) They took him to task for being negligent.

(c) **Change of Degree:** There are three degrees of adjectives:

1. Positive (John Seely uses the term absolute for positive)
2. Comparative
3. Superlative

There are specific rules for the change of degree.

It is possible to transform a sentence in positive degree into comparative and superlative degrees without changing its meaning. Let us take this sentence in positive degree:

Very few countries are as large as India.

It can be transformed into comparative and superlative degrees:

Comparative: India is larger than many other countries.

Superlative: India is one of the largest countries.

There are specific rules for the change of degree.

Rules for changing positive degree into comparative degree and vice-versa

1. When two nouns are compared and are equal in degree in an affirmative sentence:

(a) The positions of the nouns are interchanged.

(b) The sentence is made negative.

(c) The positive form of the adjective is changed into comparative degree.

Sita is as intelligent as Susheela.

Susheela is not more intelligent than Sita.

Bengaluru is as large as Hyderabad.

Hyderabad is not larger than Bengaluru.

2. When two nouns are compared and they are unequal in degree and the sentence is negative:

(a) The positions of the nouns are interchanged.

(b) The sentence is made affirmative.

(c) The positive form of the adjective is changed into comparative degree.

Sadananad is not so intelligent as Mahanand.

Mahanand is more intelligent than Sadanand.

Keep it in mind that the affirmative sentence in positive degree has the form "as + adjectives + as" and the negative form "not so + adjectives + as."

3. When one noun is superior to the other noun in degree:

(a) The positions of the nouns are interchanged.

(b) The positive sentence is made negative and if negative, it is made positive.

(b) The comparative form is changed into positive form.

An express is faster than a passenger train.

A passenger train is not so fast as an express train.

Prabhat is not more intelligent than Ravi.

Ravi is as intelligent as Prabhat.

One must remember that only such positive sentences as indicate a comparative sense can be changed into comparative but a sentence like 'He is a good boy' cannot be changed into comparative because it gives singular meaning.

Rules for changing the superlative degree into comparative degree

1. When the noun is in superlative degree and is supreme in the sentence, the superlative degree is changed into comparative degree and "any other" is placed after it:

Geeta is the best student in the class.

Geeta is better than any other student in the class.

2. When the adjective in superlative degree is preceded by "one of" the comparative form is followed by "many other":

Kanpur is one of the busiest railway stations in UP.

Kanpur is busier than many other railway stations in UP.

Rules for changing superlative degree into positive degree

(i) When the adjective in superlative degree is all alone the sentence will begin with the word "no" followed by the noun in the sentence under transformation;

(ii) The positions of the two nouns are inter-changed;

(iii) The superlative degree is changed into positive degree:

Delhi is the largest city in India.
No other city is as large as Delhi in India.

Harendra is the most intelligent student in the class.
No other student is as intelligent as Harendra in the class.

Most grammarians prefer to write "no other", but according to some grammarians the problem is that "than" is used after "other". The word "other" is either adjective or preposition and is followed by "than". When we write "other", the sentence is transformed into comparative degree. But here "other" in the above sentence is *indefinite determiner*, so it can be used to make a positive sentence.

(i) When the sentence contains "one of", we begin the new sentence with "very few" or "only a few" and keep it affirmative.

India is one of the largest countries.
Very few countries are as large as India.

Shakespeare is one of the greatest dramatists in the world.
Only a few dramatists are as great as Shakespeare in the world.

EXERCISES

1. Change the following sentences from positive to comparative:
   (i) Your book is as good as mine.
   (ii) She can sing as well as her music teacher.
   (iii) Iron is not so heavy as gold.
   (iv) Water is not so thick as blood.
   (v) Platinum is as costly as gold.
2. Change the following sentences from comparative to superlative and positive:
   (i) Mumbai is busier than any other seaport in India.

(ii) Jairam is more intelligent than many other boys in the class.

(iii) Jeenat Mahal was a greater fighter than any other female fighter in the first war of independence.

3. Change the following sentences from superlative to positive and comparative:

(i) Radha is the best dancer in our class.

(ii) Vipasha is the wittiest girl in her school.

(iii) John and Ratan are one of the best debaters in our town.

(iv) Pluto is the most distant planet from the sun.

(d) **Removal of "too":** The word "too" is an adverb and means "to a higher degree" than is desirable, permissible or possible. It also means exceeding the limit.

Let us take these three sentences:

1. This tea is too sweet.
2. Your words are too strong.
3. This path is too slippery to walk.

In the first sentence, the word "too" refers to desirability, the second to permissibility and the third to possibility or capacity. Besides, "too" is used in negative sense usually.

Let us take the first sense, you offer tea to your friend and he finds that there is much more sugar in it and, so, he uses the word "too".

The second sentence is a reaction to someone's undesirable language. The listener deprecates the language by using "too". If "too" is followed by an infinitive, i.e. to + verb, it can be transformed into another kind of sentence. The meaning of the infinitive should be in contrast to the word following 'too'. If it is not followed by an infinitive, it is almost impossible to transform, however, some experiments have been made, though those are considered un-English.

Let us take two examples:

1. This block of iron is too heavy for me to lift.

   The block of iron is so heavy that I cannot lift it.

2. He is too weak to rise from bed by himself.

   He is so weak that he cannot rise from bed by himself.

   In both the transformations, the following changes have taken place.

   (a) The sentences are made negative as "too" carries negative meaning.
   (b) "Too" is replaced by "so".
   (c) The infinitive is made declarative.
   (d) The pronoun "I" is supplied for the reason of "for me" being present in the first sentence. "I" is the subject of "to lift".
   (e) The pronoun "he" is supplied in the second sentence because "he" is the subject of both verbs "is" and "to rise".

Read carefully the transformation of these five sentences:

(a) She was too ashamed to speak.

    She was so ashamed that she could not speak.

    Can/could is used to show incapacity or inability on the part of the subject.

(b) This bike is too costly to buy.

    This bike is so costly that I cannot buy it.

    Here it is assumed that the speaker is unable to buy it and, so, the pronoun "I" is supplied.

(c) He is too proud to admit his mistake.

    He is so proud that he will not admit his mistake.

    Here "will" is used as "he" is able to admit his mistake but he does not want to do because of his pride. The use of "can" will be inappropriate.

(d) This tea is too sweet.

    This cannot be transformed without changing the meaning. However, it may be changed into 'This tea is sweet beyond expectation' but this is not acceptable in modern English. The sentences like 'this tea is more sweet (or sweeter) than it should be' and others are not considered English sentences; hence they are inacceptable.

(e) She is too arrogant to listen to her sister's advice.

She is so arrogant that she will not listen to her sister's advice.

(f) She is too eager to help me.

The adverb "too" cannot be removed in a normal way. The sentence means, "She is very, very eager to help me"; or "she is excessively eager to help me" and the implication is that I am unwilling to accept the same.

EXERCISES

1. Rewrite the following sentences removing "too". Write the reason why "too" cannot be removed in a particular sentence:
   (a) The weather is too bad to go out.
   (b) John is too weak in studies to pass the examination.
   (c) Sameer is too naughty to be persuaded.
   (d) She was too arrogant to admit her mistake.
   (e) They were too selfish to help us.
   (f) This ground is too slippery after rains to play football.
   (g) This car was too costly for me to buy it.
   (h) My mother was too pleased when she saw me after a long time.
   (i) The old man was too gentle to mind our misbehaviour.
   (j) This bed is too short to sleep in.

(e) **Synthesis:** Synthesis is the process to combine two or more simple sentences into one sentence. The new sentence may be a simple, complex or compound sentence. For example:

(i) I want it. You go to market.

I want you to go to market.

(ii) He saw a tiger. He ran away.

Seeing a tiger he ran away.

(iii) Mr. Chatterjee is a good man. I know it well.

I know it well that Mr. Chatterjee is a good man.

(iv) He lifted that heavy bag. I also lifted it.

He lifted that heavy bag and so did could I.

Following are the rules of combining or synthesizing sentences into a simple sentence.

(a) By changing the verb of one sentence into the - ing form:

(i) They saw a tiger. They ran away.

Seeing a tiger, they ran away. (use of Present Participle, "verb - ing")

Or

Having seen a tiger, they ran away. (use of Perfect participle, "have - ing + main verb - en)

(ii) He drew a sword. He attacked his enemy.

Drawing a sword, he attacked his enemy.

(b) By using an infinitive:

(i) I see you. I am glad.

I am glad to see you.

(ii) She is glad. She has seen her result.

She is glad to see her result.

(c) By placing the noun phrase in apposition:

Mr. Verma is a good doctor. He lives in the Civil Lines.

Mr. Verma, a good doctor, lives in the Civil Lines.

(d) By using an adjective:

This is a tower. It is revolving.

This is a revolving tower.

(e) By using preposition:

I saw a boy. He had a heavy load.

I saw a boy with a heavy load.

2. Synthesis of simple sentences into complex sentences:

Simple sentences are combined into complex sentences by using subordinators:

(i) I know it. He is intelligent.

I know that he is intelligent.

(ii) Mr. Mahendra Pratap works in the Hindustan Lever. He has met an accident.

Mr. Mahendra Pratap, who works in the Hindustan Lever, has met an accident.

3. Synthesis of simple sentences into compound sentences is done by using co-ordinators (conjunctions).

(i) He is poor. He is honest.

He is poor but honest.

(ii) Labour hard. You will fail.

Labour hard otherwise you will fail.

EXERCISE

1. Combine the following sentences into simple, complex or compound as you think fit:

(a) We saw a strange animal. It had three legs and two tails.

(b) We all know the fact. He has cheated his brother.

(c) There is a zoo in Kanpur. It is very big.

(d) At last we reached the sea-shore. Our friends were waiting there for us.

(e) I saw a few strangers. They were carrying guns.

(f) He had lost all his money. But he did not lose his honesty.

(g) The hunter saw a tiger. He raised his gun. He shot the tiger dead.

(h) India is a country. There are more than one thousand million people. India is the second largest country in population.

(i) John bought a car. The car soon started giving him trouble. So he took it to the dealer.

(j) Dinesh is the brightest boy in the college. He won the first prize in a debate competition last year. He is going to represent our university in the inter-university debate competition this year.

Chapter Eight

Punctuation

Outcome of the Chapter

(a) Understanding of punctuation marks
(b) Usage of punctuation marks

Writing is a method of recording speech for further use. Once spoken, words are lost in the air. The aim of writing is to record a speech meaningfully. When we say "meaningfully", we mean that the reader will understand all that the speaker has said verbally. While speaking, the speaker varies his/her pitch of voice, pauses in different ways, sometimes after many words, sometimes after a few words and sometimes just after a word. Punctuation marks have been developed for recording the pitch of voice and different kinds of pauses. Besides, punctuation marks are used when a reporter reproduces a speaker's exact words.

The other aspect of punctuation is that it enables the reader to move fast while reading a text. John Seely writes:

> Punctuation is part of the way in which we set out written text so that it can be read quickly, easily, and accurately. When we read, our eyes do not move steadily along the line of text reading every letter and every word. Instead, they 'dart' along, taking in small chunks of text as they go. Good punctuation makes this process much easier. It is a set of conventions: we expect it to be used in certain ways to which we have become accustomed. However, these conventions are not fixed.

Seely's last sentence needs modification. The conventions are fixed but great writers take liberty sometimes. A student must follow the conventions. Punctuation includes the following:

> Coma, semi-colon, colon, full stop/period, question mark, exclamation mark, apostrophe, inverted commas, quotation marks, hyphen, dash, brackets, braces, square brackets, capitalization and slash.

1. Comma (,): Comma indicates a short pause in speech. It is used in the following cases:

(a) counting of items in a list:

(i) I bought a pen, two copy-books, a rubber and an adhesive tape.

(b) counting of numbers:

(i) One, two, three, four, five.

(c) to mark the division of clauses in a complex sentence:

(i) I will help you, if you desire so.

(d) while using an adverbial in the beginning or at the end of a sentence:

(i) Naturally, I had to leave the job.

(ii) The little boy ran to his mother, gladly.

(e) when there is a noun or noun phrase in apposition:

(i) My friend, a well-known scholar, was given a warm welcome.

(ii) I went for my check-up to Dr. S.K. Pal, a famous cardiologist.

(f) at the end of the reporting verb in a sentence which contains a reported speech:

She said, "I am ill."

They shouted, "We have won!"

(g) In writing numbers of four digits or more:

1,000 10,000 55,374

2. Semi-colon/Semicolon (;): John Seely explains "semicolon": "Semicolons are used to mark a break between two parts of a sentence. Usually the two parts that are separated in this way could stand as sentences in their own right. You use a semicolon because you want to show that there is a close link between them."

He further says that breaking a sentence into two sentences can change its meaning.

(a) A semicolon takes a longer pause than a comma. Look at these sentences:

(i) He mistook cause for effect; the keeping of cows reflected, rather than caused, a state of war.

(ii) Not all English rulers were as forthright as went worth about motives; but they tended to adopt the same policy because it happened to satisfy economic as well as political needs.

(b) Semicolon is also used at those places where two contrasting or complementary ideas are juxtaposed:

(i) He said that he would leave the place then and there; but, at heart, he was unwilling.

(ii) Soft words soothe a sufferer; harsh words irritate him.

3. Colon (:): The pause after colon is longer than that of a semicolon. It is used to:

(a) separate a subtitle from a title:

(i) *Some Graver Subject: An Essay on Paradise Lost.*

(ii) *Ben Jonson: The Dramatist.*

(iii) *Between the Lines: Yeats's Poetry in the Making.*

(b) introduce a list:

(i) The small boys were asked to choose one of these: Knife, pistol, pen, book.

(ii) The varieties of mango are available in the market: Langra, Dasahari, Krishnabhog, Zarda.

(c) separate two parts of a sentence, which are equally important:

(i) The small boy was asked to choose between a toy and a book: he chose the book.

4. Full stop/period (.): Full stop/period is used to end declarative and imperative sentences:

(i) He left home in the morning.
(ii) He wanted to ask a question.
(iii) Stop speaking.
(iv) Do not make a noise.

5. Question mark (?): Question mark is used at the end of interrogative sentence. This is why it is called "note of interrogation".

(i) Will you do me a favour?
(ii) Are you all right?
(iii) Is he ready to help us?

6. Exclamation mark (!): Exclamation mark is used to end a sentence conveying a strong emotion, anger, wonder, fear, pleasure, etc.

(i) What have you done!
(ii) O, it's spectacular!
(iii) What a horrible scene!
(iv) Well done!

7. Apostrophe mark ('): Apostrophe is used.

(i) to show omission of one or more letters in a word in poetry;
O'er, e'er
(ii) to show omission of one or more letters in contractions;
Will not → won't
Shall not → shan't
He is → He's
They are → they're
Cannot → can't

8. Inverted commas/quotation marks (" "): The following are the uses of inverted commas:

(a) to indicate the titles of short poems and articles:

(i) Charles Lamb's "In Praise of Chimney Sweepers" is one of the most popular essays in English.

(ii) The poem "Daffodils" was written by William Wordsworth.

(b) When we reproduce or quote words of others, written or spoken, exactly:

(i) She said, "I am going to post-office".

(ii) He swore, "I did not say insulting words to her".

(iii) Wordsworth defined poetry:

"Poetry is spontaneous overflow of powerful feelings recollected in tranquillity".

9. Hyphen (–): Hyphen shows relatedness. It is used in these cases:

(a) to indicate that words joined by hyphen (–) are to be read as one word:

(i) brother-in-law, commander-in-chief, mother-in-law, up-to-date

(ii) Passer-by, multi-storey, co-opt, build-up.

(b) to indicate that the word at the end of a line is not complete and continues in the next line:

(i) un-common

(ii) extra-ordinary.

10. Dash (—): Dash is longer than hyphen and indicates distance or separation:

(i) Yeats also used the "barbed wire" or wavy line, and occasionally—if particularly dissatisfied with something—he blocked it out savagely in ink.

(ii) Of those written subsequently, there remains—thanks to Mrs. Yeats—a mass of manuscript and typescript material.

(iii) Although quite capable of writing legibly, as his fair copies show—even as late as "The Black Tower"—the preliminary workings of a poem were generally written for no eye but his own.

11. Brackets/Parentheses ( ): "Brackets" is the name of the symbol ( ) and this symbol is used in mathematics and other branches of knowledge also; but it is called parenthesis in grammar specifically. It is used mostly like the dash. John Seely is of the view that the dash is informal and the parenthesis is formal and more effective. He writes:

> when something is put "in parenthesis" it is separated off from the main part of the sentence, by a pair of brackets, commas, or dashes. This is usually because it contains information or ideas that are not essential to an understanding of the sentence. This may be because the words contain additional but non-essential information: or because they form a comment by the author on the rest of the sentence.

He is all right upto this extent that the dash and the parenthesis and the comma are used for "additional information" and the author's "comment on the rest of the sentence".

But it is difficult to agree with him when he says, that "Brackets are the most formal (and most obvious) way of showing parenthesis", "commas are less forceful" and "dashes are the least formal".

The sentences we have quoted as illustration of the use of the dash are all taken from Jon Stallworthy's "Introduction" to *Between the Lines: W.B. Yeats's Poetry in the Making* (OUP) pp. 9, 12. Stallworthy is quite formal in his "Introduction".

The fact is that we use comma, dash and bracket by observing their appropriateness. Of course, they are used for extra information and comment or explanation of the rest of the sentence.

12. Braces { }: Braces are used mostly in mathematical notation when there are more than one elements in a slot. Let us take the slot of determiner. The determiners are articles, possessives and demonstrative. We can show their occurrence in the braces to tell that only of them can be chosen:

$$\begin{Bmatrix} \text{art} \\ \text{poss} \\ \text{dem} \end{Bmatrix}$$

It follows that we can place only one of them before a noun:

a book
the book
my book
this book
that book

We cannot place an article, a possessive and demonstrative together before a noun. The slot will accommodate only one.

Brackets come within braces, that is, braces are larger than brackets.

13. Square brackets [ ]: Square brackets are the largest and braces and brackets are placed within them. There are two more uses of square brackets in writing:

(a) We place our own words within square brackets while quoting a statement or a passage of which some parts are not clear or are omitted and we want to make the entire quotation grammatically correct.

For example,

"Mrs. Yeats agrees with me, that the poem ["Sailing to Byzantium"] probably began with a tantalizingly illegible prose frequent of which Curtis Bradford makes no mention".

(b) We use square brackets with the word sic (meaning "so") when a word is misspelt in the quoted passage or year is wrongly referred, to indicate that the particular word or year is printed in the original passage. The form is [sic].

14. Slash (/): Slash is used in:

(a) either or situation, or both included:

Every candidate must produce his/her identity card before entering the examination hall.

(b) quoting two lines from a poem and showing their separation;

"A slumber did my spirit seal/ I had no human fears."

15. Ellipses (... ; ...): Ellipses is used to show that words have been omitted from the quoted passage. If a word/words are omitted from the middle of sentence, we use three dots (...) and if the sentence ends after the omission we use four dots (....) to show that the last dot is full stop.

16. Italics/Italic: It is a kind of print in the cursive style. The name takes its origin from the sixteenth century Italian handwriting. Italic is used for:

(a) emphasis:

(i) *Freedom of expression* is the first principle of democracy

(ii) Virtue is its own *reward.*

(b) indicating a book's or a long poem's title:

A Passage to India; Grapes of Wrath; Paradise Lost

In Memoriam; Queen Mab

(c) names of ships:

The Titanic, The Patna, The Atlanta

We underline a word, a group of words, a sentence or more for emphasis when we write with a pen.

17. Capitalisation. Capital letters are used in the following cases.

(a) names of days and months:

Sunday, Monday, January, February, December

(b) the first letter of each line in a poem:

"To me the nearest flower that blows can give
Thoughts that do often lie too deep for tears"

(E.E. Cummings did not follow this rule and some modern poets have deviated from the norm, occasionally).

(c) God and His pronouns begin with Capital letters

(d) Proper nouns begin with a capital letter.

(e) The personal pronoun "I" is always capital.

(The Times of India does not follow the rule)

EXERCISE 1

A. Punctuate the following sentences by rewriting them:

1. he said i am going home tomorrow.
2. they decided to go to delhi on monday.
3. the month of July is highly rainy.
4. peter asked his teacher A very Difficult Question.
5. you want to buy that mobile phone?
6. what a terrible scene it was.
7. do you go to the park daily.
8. i wandered lonely as a cloud
   that floats on high over valleys and hills
9. we went to europe and visited france, england and germany.
10. the capital of U.S.A. is Washington d.c.

EXERCISE 2

A. Rewrite the following sentences by punctuating them:

1. Kalidas a poet of the sixth century wrote the romantic meghadutam.
2. the small boy said to the teacher will you correct my answers tomorrow.
3. the stranger said to the villager how far was the railway station.
4. my friend said to me are you all right.
5. the golden treasury commends itself not only by the formal perfection of the word it presents but also by its arrangement.
6. many long poems in English contain passages of great beauty but I have included only four long poems of our period.
7. f.t. palgraves father was a historian and antiquarian of considerable reputation a friend of Southey Samuel rogers macaulay and sir walter scott.

EXERCISE 3

A. Punctuate the following passages and rewrite them:

1. his thesis is that the present despite its failures and its forebodings still draws comfort from living youth and from what has survived of lasting value from the past, he sets this out very much in his own way but his mood and even his directing idea belong to the age in which he wrote?
2. the tower which has long been a symbol in ‘yeatss poetry may stand for Ireland Or Europe or a whole system of life and is surely all three but it enshrines an unfailing loyalty to some ancient cause or tradition and presents yeatss view of the civilized life
3. it is her hour and her triumph and her little myth with its touches of Greek simplicity and sweetness is entirely apt for her need and conveys the natural purity of her feelings.
4. yet even when a poet finds himself driven to write about public affairs he has still to decide how to do so sometimes the relics of his training almost forbid him to do so directly and he resorts to a somewhat devious method which keeps his artistic conscience intact
5. chinese poetry abounds in references both to history and to myth and it is noteworthy that the communist leader Mao Tse-tung who writes in the traditional style sometimes uses them to illustrate a present occasion in 1957 he wrote a short poem for his woman friend Li Shu-yi whose husband had fallen in battle against the nationalists in 1933.

Chapter Nine

Common Errors

Outcome of the Chapter

(a) Errors of noun
(b) Errors of articles
(c) Errors of adjectives, adverbs and comparisons
(d) Errors of tense and verb forms
(e) Errors of preposition
(f) Break of the rule of agreement
(g) Defective sentence structure

Common Errors

Errors are of different kinds. They can be classified under the following heads:

(a) Errors of noun
(b) Errors of articles
(c) Errors of adjectives, adverbs and comparisons
(d) Errors of tense and verb forms
(e) Errors of preposition
(f) Break of the rule of agreement
(g) Defective sentence structure

Since we have already discussed noun, article, adjective, adverb, tense and preposition, we shall concentrate our attention on the rule of agreement and sentence structure.

1. The rule of Agreement: It states that the verb must agree with its subject in number and person.

Present	Past
I am	I was
We are	We were
You are	You were
He is	He was
She is	She was
It is	It was
They are	They were

The verb should be placed nearest to the subject as far as possible:

The main cause of obesity	**is**	**the lack of physical labour.**
Subject	**verbal**	**complement**

Sometimes people commit the error of proximity. It so happens that they assume the nearest noun to be the subject. For example:

One of my friends <u>live</u> in Dehradun.

The head word in the noun phrase "one of my friends" is "one", not friends. The error is that the noun "friends" has been thought to be the subject. In fact, the whole noun phrase is the subject. Therefore, the correct sentence is:

One of my friends lives in Dehradun.

The subsidiary rules are:

(a) When two singular nouns are joined by "and", the verb is always plural:

  (i) John and I are planning to go to Darjeeling this summer.

  (ii) Sita and Gita are best friends.

  But if two third person singular nouns refer to only one concept or object, the verb will be singular:

  (i) Bread and butter is my usual breakfast.

  (ii) The horse and carriage is waiting for you.

  (iii) The sum and substance of my arguments is that you should give up your claim over the property.

(b) The verb is singular, when the subject is a plural noun referring to a totality:

(i) Ten miles is a short distance.

(ii) Ten thousand rupees is not a large amount these days.

(c) When two nouns are joined by "as well as", "with" "together with" or "along with", the verb agrees with the number and person of the first noun:

(i) She as well as he is ready to help me.

(ii) He with his friends is going to Nainital.

(d) "Many a" is a phrase and it means "many" but it always takes a singular noun and a singular verb:

(i) Many a man was present in the meeting (nowadays "many a" is not in regular use)

(e) "Each" and "every" are distributive words. As quantifiers they take a singular noun and a singular pronoun and a singular verb:

(i) Every <u>boy</u> went to his room.

(ii) We counted each <u>tree</u>.

(iii) Each of us is ready to help Prakash.

(f) "Neither", "either", "Neither .... nor" and "either .... or" join two nouns. When either/neither is the subject of a verb, the verb is singular:

(i) Either of us is responsible for the accident.

(ii) Neither of the two is acceptable to me.

When two nouns/pronouns are joined by "either .... or", "neither .... nor", the verb agrees with the nearest subject:

(iii) Neither he nor she was willing to pay the fare of the taxi.

(iv) Either you or I am to face the music.

(v) Neither he nor his friends were responsible for the theft.

(g) The verb is the nucleus of a sentence and it must have a subject except in the case of an imperative sentence. If the same subject can govern two or more verbs in a sentence, there is no need of repeating it. But sometimes people leave a verb without a subject in a cleft sentence.

For example:

(i) Being a hot day, I took bath with cold water.

(ii) Sitting on the fence, a scorpion stung him.

The corrected form would be:

(i) It being a hot day, I took bath with cold water.

(ii) While he was sitting on the fence, a scorpion stung him.

Similarly:

(iii) Crossing the hill, the temple came in view.

It should be:

When we crossed the hill, the temple came in view.

2. Sentence Structure: Language is structure. All its components have their place in its system. The change of place of any component brings change of meaning. The meaning of a sentence is changed if a word/phrase is shifted from its place. Sometimes shifting the place of a word or phrase may make a sentence meaningless or unacceptable (i.e. incorrect). For example:

(i) I saw a blackbird this morning.

We can shift the place of the phrase "this morning".

(ii) This morning I saw a blackbird.

Here the emphasis is on "this morning" whereas the first sentence is a normal one.

But we cannot write.

* I this morning saw a blackbird.

The other examples are:

* When I was young, as a hobby I used to make paper boats.

(i) *I saw a dead horse walking on the road.

The correct form should be:

(ii) When I was young, I used to make paper boats as a hobby.

(iii) Walking on the road, I saw a dead horse.

EXERCISES

(a) Errors of Noun:

(i) The police served him a summon from the court.

(ii) He didn't play well in the first inning.

(iii) I want to buy a scissor.

(iv) This house is made of bricks and stones.

(v) She gave me a number of informations, when I returned home from London.

(vi) I requested him to give me ten thousands rupees for two months but he refused to do so.

(vii) Shyam sold all his old furnitures except the writing table.

(viii) Although many poets have praised the sceneries of the Himalayas, I find them dull and insipid.

(ix) Though Ramesh knew that I would be angry with him, he did not follow my orders.

(x) Salmon fishes are not available in market these days.

(xi) She bought two dozens eggs at a shop in the Parade market.

(xii) There are three woman doctors in this hospital.

(xiii) There was a meeting of commander-in-chiefs of America, England, France and Germany.

(xiv) We saw five rhinoes grazing in the park.

(xv) Mouses are at play when the cat is away.

(b) Errors of articles:

(i) Crow is black.

(ii) I saw a small boy carrying big umbrella.

(iii) The train left the station hour ago.

(iv) She is a graduate from an European university.
(v) Prakash is a M.Sc. from Delhi University.
(vi) Leo Tolstoy, the author of war and peace, was Russian.
(vii) Himalayas are in the north of India.
(viii) I visited Andaman and Nicobar islands last year.
(ix) He was given benefit of doubt.
(x) This is one of best book I have read so far.
(xi) Vedas are oldest books in the world.
(xii) Jupiter is biggest planet in solar system.
(xiii) More he was given more he wanted.
(xiv) I have never suffered such insult.
(xv) I retire to the bed late at night.
(xvi) Have you got one ball pen?
(xvii) Soup I was served in the restaurant was very hot.
(xviii) He was taken to the hospital after the accident.
(xix) Sorry; the father is not at home.
(xx) Times of India is one of the leading newspapers.

(c) **Errors of adjective and adverb:**
(i) They worked very hardly.
(ii) The rose smells very sweetly.
(iii) He is a hard worker but more important a good planner.
(iv) The actors came to the stage colourful dressed.
(v) I am sickly of his frequent interruption in my work.
(vi) My mother was pleasant surprised at my sudden arrival.
(vii) He ran very fastly in the race.
(viii) You have done good but you should do better.
(ix) Old enough, he didn't tell me about his future plan.
(x) I wake up generally at six but sometimes at five.
(xi) The population of Kanpur is larger than Lucknow.
(xii) Your watch is costlier than me.
(xiii) Curious enough, he spoke very politely.

(xiv) He spoke very good in the meeting.
(xv) She turned sudden towards me.

(d) Errors of tense and verb forms:

(i) He is working on the project for two years.
(ii) He had left this place two years ago.
(iii) Does she has anything more to say?
(iv) Being very much tired he lied on my bed.
(v) I have received your message in the morning.
(vi) The apple fell from the tree and hitted my head.
(vii) The whole burden of the family was born by my eldest brother.
(viii) The minister lay the foundation stone of the auditorium.
(ix) John promised that he will give me his notes on political science.
(x) This library was found by Dr. S.N. Sinha.
(xi) I will help him if he will request me to do so.
(xii) Your brother tells me that you were still working in that firm.
(xiii) I am always carrying a water bottle when I go out.

(e) Errors of tense:

(i) I am living in Kanpur.
(ii) The earth is moving round the sun.
(iii) I am hearing some strange sound.
(iv) I had met him in the morning.
(v) It is raining since morning.
(vi) I have received your letter two days ago.
(vii) He will be successful if he will be sincere in his work.
(viii) He dares not defy me.
(ix) The fence was collapsed during the storm.
(x) Do you know who did write this letter?
(xi) He will pass the examination if he read well.
(xii) He behave, as if he was a king.

(xiii) I would be happy if I was at home.

(xiv) I would not have pardoned them if I was you.

(xv) She needs not repeat the course.

(xvi) I have done the job well, isn't it?

(xvii) They lost the match; aren't they?

(xviii) I will succeed if I will labour hard.

(xix) John would get the job if he appears in the test.

(xx) Sita would have gained her father's sympathy, if she obeyed him.

(f) **Errors of Preposition:**

(i) Your performance was wonderful, you deserved for the award.

(ii) She was trying for admission in PPN college.

(iii) We must complete the work with the end of the year.

(iv) It is dangerous to see the sun by naked eyes during an eclipse.

(v) The small child ran in its mother's arms.

(vi) Rama is worrying on her examination result.

(vii) The scientist gave a talk about global warming at the conference.

(viii) I conveyed the message by phone.

(ix) He has a good command over English.

(x) Prakash thinks a lot for his career.

(xi) The government has set up a special committee to inquire about the causes of the riots in the city.

(xii) They agreed with the scheme we had proposed.

(xiii) The small child threw the ball on me.

(xiv) The recent increase in petrol prices is a blow on the middle class.

(xv) I am surprised by your way ward behavior.

(xvi) When Rakesh met me he told that he will go to Mumbai next week.

(xvii) The bird flow very high on the sky.

(g) **Errors of Preposition:**

(i) He was denied from his rights.

(ii) Naveen deserves for the reward he received yesterday.

(iii) My boss became very angry upon me when I reached office late.

(iv) It has been raining incessantly from a week.

(v) My village was cut out from other villages in the last flood.

(vi) If a stain does not come out your shirt, use our sunshine stain remover.

(vii) The chairman asked me to move on the next item of the agenda.

(viii) Our aeroplane landed in Mumbai airport at 4. p.m.

(ix) We apologise any inconvenience caused.

(x) They stayed in Hotel Ashoka in Delhi for two days after their return from London.

(xi) Sanjeev is available is his office between 10 to 5.

(xii) Tilak suggested me that I should walk two kilometers every day in the morning.

(xiii) Every body agreed but Vikas objected my proposal.

(xiv) Rakesh cut the rope by a knife.

(xv) Finding no other way out I had to break from them.

(h) **Break of the Rule of Agreement:**

(i) The main aim of his arguments are to prove us guilty.

(ii) He as well as his friends are ready to help us.

(iii) Each boy went to their respective rooms.

(iv) The number of students have declined this year.

(v) One thousand rupees are a small amount these days.

(vi) Bread and butter are favourite items of my morning breakfast.

(vii) Neither Jatin nor his sister have broken this toy.

(viii) I think every one of these men are incompetent and lazy.

(ix) The manager of the bank besides his colleagues are responsible for the forged bank drafts.

(x) The reviewers agree that this is one of most interesting novels that has been published this year.

(xi) The principal advised every one of the boys to buy a standard dictionary for their use.

(xii) The Alekhine Chess Club which has more than 100 members organize a national meet every year.

(xiii) The police is looking for two young men aged about 24.

(xiv) The biggest of these multi-coloured insects are only two centimetres long.

(xv) Neither of Mr. Shaym's sons are computer engineers.

(i) **Faulty or disordered sentence structure:**

(i) I saw a dead pig walking on the road.

(ii) Sitting on the fence, a scorpion stung him.

(iii) Being a hot day, I remained indoors.

(iv) The boy said firmly that he would rather starve than stealing to get what he needed.

(v) The orphanages in the large cities of India, they are funded by generous donors.

(vi) The guide told us that where the island was is went on narrating its history.

(vii) He arrived at Monday on 3o' clock.

(viii) Since the day the strike was declared illegal, fifty persons have been appointed and sixty resigned.

(ix) He complained to the police his neighbour was noisy.

(x) We are not in an enough strong financial position to expand our business.

(xi) She said me good-bye.

(xii) He studied briefly the problem.

(xiii) In the accident I was thrown against the door violently.

(xiv) We together walked to the end of the garden.

(xv) After climbing the hill, the lake came in view.

EXERCISES

(a) Correct errors in the following sentences.

(i) He was the most wisest man I ever knew.

(ii) My sister gets privileges because she is more older.

(iii) He lain the sick child for a nap and then sat watching over her.

(iv) Defeated at Waterloo, they sent Napoleon into exile.

(v) Bread and batter are good for breakfast.

(vi) I am looking forward to see him.

(vii) English as well as Hindi are medium of higher education in this state.

(viii) Being a wet day, I had to stay indoors.

(ix) He never has and never will say such things in public.

(x) Sixty miles are a long distance.

(xi) I have never nor will ever use strong words.

(xii) Dafla is living here since 1998.

(xiii) The soup will taste better if it had more salt in it.

(xiv) We must be true to our words.

(xv) Your daughter is twelve years old, isn't it?

(xvi) It is an unique privilege to welcome our guests.'

(xvii) A herd of cattels were grazing in the farm.

(xviii) One of my friend is a good poet.

(xix) When you are going to London to meet with your friends there?

(xx) You are the teacher here, isn't it?

(xxi) Shakespeare, the playwright and poet, was born in Stratford-upon-Avon.

(xxii) For heaven's sake, please don't ask me that why am I not coming.

(xxiii) Either his parents or brother is going today.

(xxiv) If you would have studied hard, you should have passed.

(xxv) I cannot be able to play cricket this evening.

(b) (i) May I now take your leave?

(ii) It was because of his headache why he didn't come in time.

(iii) Is he used to come late everyday?

(iv) A twenty miles walk is really very hard.

(v) We watched the man disappear in the woods.

(vi) Let's have coffee.

(vii) Cricket has become so popular that even elderly people are discussing the game when they meet.

(viii) Hardly did she finish the typing when the Manager entered the room with some more work.

(ix) Suraj along with his wife and children were invited to the party in a three star hotel.

(x) Geeta asked me that what was wrong with me.

(xi) Despite of many attempts to introduce a universal language, the effort has met with very little success.

(xii) We should drink the mineral water when we have stomach trouble in summer.

(xiii) He appears to be unreasonable anxious of solving his neighbour's problems.

(xiv) No sooner he left the office, than it started raining heavily.

(xv) He is very rude and behaves as if he was a king.

(xvi) Your watch is more costly than me.

(xvii) The chief minister exhorted us to fight corruption with tooth and nail.

(xviii) He never has and never will play at a gaming table.

(xix) The reason for the train being late was because a tree had fallen on the track.

(xx) Under no circumstances passengers are permitted to open the doors.

(xxi) Her watch is superior and costlier than mine.

(xxii) Young people are studying computer science in order to that they could get better jobs.

(xxiii) Every one of these who have come here are rowdy and arrogant.

(xxiv) He would have cached the train, if he had left home earlier.

(xxv) He was given benefit of doubt.

C. (i) The only people who are interested in this book is botanists.

(ii) The latest news of the people killed in the recent floods are highly disturbing.

(iii) Measles are still a fairly serious childhood disease in India.

(iv) Seldom we do have goods returned to us because they are faulty.

(v) At no time he did actually break the rules of the game.

(vi) So successful his coaching classes were that he decided to resign from the post.

(vii) I felt confident to pass my driving test.

(viii) She goes often to see her ailing mother.

(ix) They very admired my painting.

(x) Roasted chicken is my most favourite dish.

(xi) We did as efficient job as we could.

(xii) My wife asked me to go to market with her but I didn't want.

(xiii) My sister is quite younger than me.

(xiv) She is always complaining on her music teacher.

(xv) Do you care if I smoke a cigarette?

(xvi) There never has been such heavy rain like it in Kanpur for the last ten years.

(xvii) Have a cup of tea before you will go.

(xviii) Ravi won't be able to qualify in the premedical test unless he doesn't join a coaching institute.

(xix) Who are coming to your birthday party?

(xx) When I shall go to Delhi, I shall bring you a nice gift.

(xxi) What to speak of tea and snacks, he didn't offer me even a glass of cool water.

(xxii) The house is made of bricks and mortar.

(xxiii) A ball pen is more preferable than a pencil.

(xxiv) Please sign the papers by ink.

(xxv) The roads of Delhi are wider than Kanpur.

(xxvi) It is easier talking of getting a job than of find one.

(xxvii) Rani is blind with one eye.

(xxviii) As an artist Shubham is as good if not better than Shivam.

(xxix) Bible is the main source of Paradise lost.

Chapter Ten

Idioms and Phrases

Outcome of the Chapter

(a) Idioms and its usage
(b) Phrases and its usage
(c) Common phrasal verbs
(d) Common foreign phrases and words

Common Idioms and Phrases

1. **A gala day:** *a day of festivity*
   For little Shruti her birthday is a gala day.
2. **A red letter day:** *a day to remember*
   Fifteenth August is a red letter day in Indian history.
3. **A rainy day:** *a period of economic trouble*
   We should be economical in our living otherwise a rainy day may come to us.
4. **Above board/fair and square:** *honest beyond doubt*
   We must follow his advice. He has always been above board.
5. **At random:** *disorderly, here and there*
   When I entered my room I found everything at random. Perhaps, some burglar had sneaked in.
6. **At sixes and sevens:** *disorderly*
   She is really untidy. Look, her books are lying at sixes and sevens.

7. **Abide by:** *accept or obey a rule or decision*

   We should abide by the decision of the committee.

8. **Achilles heel:** *weak or vulnerable point*

   He loves his daughter so fondly that she has become the Achille's heel.

9. **A bee in one's bonnet:** *have obsession with some idea*

   His recent success in the competitive examination has turned his mind and has become a bee in his bonnet.

10. **At a low key:** *modest or restrained*

    The Shanti Swarup Bhatnager award has not made Dr. Shrivastava proud; he talks about it at a low key.

11. **A big shot:** *an important person*

    I saw Sharma after a long time. Now he is a big shot.

12. **Live in an ivory tower:** *be away from reality*

    The world has changed and you are still living in an ivory tower.

13. **A storm in a tea cup:** fuss on a trivial matter.

    When he forgot the date of his marriage anniversary, his wife's anger was like a storm in a tea cup.

14. **As a rule:** *usually*

    We do not allow any person to park his car at this place, as a rule.

15. **At a stretch:** *without break*

    He completed the work at a stretch.

16. **A bull in a china shop:** *a rough and crude fellow*

    Please do not include Prakash in our concert; he is like a bull in a china shop.

17. **A close shave:** *a narrow escape*

    The state transport bus hit our car from behind; luckily we had a close shave and suffered minor injuries.

18. **A feather in one's cap:** *an achievement to be proud of*

    The Man Booker award added a feather in Salman Rushdie's cap.

19. **At stake:** *in danger*

    Rohan must be given immediate protection. His life is at stake.

20. **A cry in the wilderness:** *a fruitless effort*

    All my efforts to persuade him to change his ways was a cry in the wilderness.

21. **A wild card:** *a person whose character is uncertain*

    It is difficult to rely on a wild card like Shyam.

22. **Between Scylla and Charybdis:** *between two equal dangers*

    Prashant is between Scylla and Charybdis. If he pleases his wife, his mother will be angry and if he listens to his mother, his wife will go back to her home.

23. **Beat about the bush:** *discuss a matter without coming to the point*

    It is Sushant's habit to beat about the bush and never come to the point.

24. **Bury the hatchet:** *reconcile*

    The two adversaries decided to bury the hatchet and live peacefully.

25. **Bone of contention:** *cause of quarrel*

    The mango tree is the bone of contention between the neighbours.

26. **Bring something home:** *to lay emphasis on*

    In spite of all our efforts we could not bring the importance of the proposed project home to the minister.

27. **Blow hot and cold:** *be inconsistent*

    I can't rely on him; he always blows hot and cold.

28. **Bona fide:** *authentic, genuine*

    All his credentials are bona fide.

29. **A bolt from the blue:** *a sudden and unexpected event*

    When she filed a case of divorce in the court, everybody said it was a bolt from the blue for her husband.

30. **By all means:** *certainly*

    We must help him by all means.

31. **Brown study:** *day dream*

    His sudden entrance into the room broke my brown study.

32. **Beggar description:** *beyond description*

    The beauty of the Taj is beggar's description.

33. **Bear fruit:** *yield positive result*

    Her hard work is now bearing fruit.

34. **Bear in mind:** *remember*

    She always bears in mind her mother's advice.

35. **Be in touch with:** *possess up-to-date knowledge*

    We should be in touch with the developments in science and technology.

36. **By dint of:** *by means of*

    He succeeded in the endeavour only by dint of his hard labour.

37. **Carry the day:** *win after a long effort*

    We could not do anything at the start but after a long struggle we carried the day.

38. **Cut and dried:** *simplistic*

    There is no cut and dried method to get success in a competitive examination.

39. **Cut no ice:** *make no effect*

    The long high sounding lecture of the M.L.A. cut no ice.

40. **Clinch the issue:** *decide*

    Sumitra clinched the issue after arguing for about two hours.

41. **Call something in question:** *cast doubt*

    People have started calling in question the new structure of income tax.

42. **Catch someone's eye:** *arrest someone's attention*

    Her matchless beauty caught our eyes.

43. **Catch sight of:** *suddenly notice*

While I was returning home, I caught sight of a burning house.

44. **Cover one's tracks:** *conceal evidence of one's actions*

The murderer has very cleverly covered his tracks.

45. **Do or die:** *persist, even if death comes*

It was a do or die game at Karachi between India and Pakistan.

46. **Dog in the manager:** *a person who prevents others from the things they need*

His dog in the manager policy will benefit neither me nor him.

47. **Die in harness:** *die while working*

The poor man died in harness.

48. **Beg to differ:** *politely disagree*

I beg to differ from you on this point.

49. **Come back to earth:** *return to reality*

My friend Ashish has come back to earth after some harsh experience.

50. **At a low ebb:** *in a poor state*

The loss of the job has put her at a low ebb.

51. **Egg someone on:** *urge someone to do something foolish or risky*

They egged me on to buy the shares which were sure to go down in market but I knew their intention.

52. **Ever and anon:** *occasionally*

They come to me ever and anon.

53. **Fall short of:** *be deficient or inadequate*

The supply of edible oil has fallen short of demand.

54. **Fair and Square:** *honest*

We should be fair and square in our dealings.

55. **Out of favour:** *having lost favour*

Mr. Mishra is now out of favour of the boss.

56. **In favour of:** *in support of*

    The American people cast their vote in favour of Barak Obama.

57. **Far and wide:** *widespread*

    Mahatma Gandhi's name spread far and wide after the Dandi march.

58. **Build castles in the air:** *be unpractical*

    Be realistic, don't build castle in the air.

59. **Fall flat:** *fail to produce what is intended*

    All her efforts to win him fell flat.

60. **Frame of mind:** *a particular mood*

    At present, I cannot guess his frame of mind.

61. **Free and easy:** *informal and relaxed*

    This is your home, be free and easy.

62. **A free hand:** *freedom to act completely at one's own discretion*

    The party's secretary was given a free hand to handle the situation.

63. ***French leave:** *absence without permission*

    Some officials are in the habit of taking French leave.

64. **Forty winks:** *a nap, a short sleep*

    Being tired I wanted to have forty winks after meal.

65. **Fancy price:** *high price*

    You can get things at Rave-3 at fancy price.

66. **Face value:** *printed value on a coin*

    The actual value is usually less than the face value of a coin these days.

67. **Find fault with:** *make an adverse criticism, usually unjustified*

    Don't take notice of her words. She always finds fault with others.

---

* This idiom is considered offensive now.

68. **Fool's paradise:** *ignorance of troubles*

I should have been pragmatic. In fact, I was living in fool's paradise.

69. **Given to:** *inclined*

Prakash is not given to luxurious things.

70. **Gain ground:** *become more popular or accepted*

The film, after initial setbacks, is gaining ground.

71. **Break new ground:** *be innovative*

You should break new ground if you want to be a successful entrepreneur.

72. **On the ground:** *be practical*

Don't build castles in the air; be on the ground.

73. **Give ground:** *retreat*

After a battle lasting three days, the Pakistani army gave ground.

74. **Good for nothing:** *worthless*

Your servant is really a good for nothing fellow.

75. **Halfhearted:** *without enthusiasm*

Although he told me that he would help me, I feel that it was a halfhearted assurance.

76. **Half mast:** *half lowered*

The national flag was unfurling half mast to mourn the death of the chief minister.

77. **Hard and fast:** *definitive and fixed*

There must be a few hard and fast rules to run an organization.

78. **Hue and cry:** *a loud clamour or public outcry*

There was a great hue and cry when a young cyclist was run over by a speeding truck.

79. **In camera:** *in a secret room*

The prime minister held an important meeting in camera.

80. **Laugh up one's sleeve:** *be secretly or inwardly amused*

The husband laughed up his sleeve at his wife's tantrum.

81. **Latchkey child:** *a child who is alone at home after school until a parent returns from work*

    A latchkey child has every possibility to feel loneliness.

82. **In the prime of:** *while young*

    She died in the prime of life.

83. **Have the last laugh:** *be finally vindicated*

    They ridiculed my assessment of the situation in the beginning, but I had the last laugh.

84. **Latter-day:** *modern or contemporary mirroring some person or thing in the past*

    We can call him a latter-day Kautilya.

85. **Laughing stock:** *object of ridicule*

    His clumsiness has made him a laughing stock.

86. **Lay claim to:** *assert one's rights to*

    They should not lay claim to the lawful property of the poor widow.

87. **Be a law unto oneself:** *behave in an unconventional or unpredictable manner*

    The manager of this college is a law unto himself.

88. **To let:** *available on rent*

    This house is to let.

89. **To the letter:** *in all details*

    I shall follow your advice to the letter.

90. **Do one's level best:** *make all possible efforts*

    He did his level best to help, when I was in trouble.

91. **Lift a finger (or hand):** *make the slightest effort*

    She did not lift a finger even, when her friend cried for help.

92. **Light up:** *become animated with joy*

    The mother's eyes lit up when she saw her son come back home after a year.

93. **Travel light:** *travel with minimum luggage*

    I prefer to travel light.

94. **(Be) littered with:** *(things) lying untidily*

The tenant vacated the house and gave me the keys but when I entered it, I found all the rooms littered with broken things.

95. **Little by little:** *gradually*

Success comes little by little, not in a day.

96. **Little people:** *common or ordinary people*

The government should pay attention to the little people also.

97. **Lock, stock and barrel:** *completely*

They were defeated badly and they left the place lock, stock and barrel.

98. **In the long run:** *at last*

We came out successful in the long run.

99. **A lot of:** *a large amount*

He went to America and earned a lot of money there.

100. **Make up one's mind:** *decide*

I must make up my mind about my future.

101. **The man in the street:** *the common man*

The man in the street is more important for a political party than the people in palatial buildings.

102. **Man of letters:** *a male scholar or author*

Johnson is a famous man of letters.

103. **Be man enough:** *be brave enough*

You should not shirk from reality. Be man enough to face it.

104. **Meek and mild:** *gentle*

A cultured person is usually meek and mild.

105. **Man of the world:** *practical in approach*

He is not a novice. He is experienced and man of the world.

106. **Mare's nest:** *a complex and difficult situation*

We started our campaign with gusto but later on realised that we found a mare's nest.

107. **Make no bones:** *be straight forward*

He is a straightforward man and will make no bones about anything which he considers to be right.

108. **Null and void:** *invalid*

The old rule has been superseded by the new rule and now it is null and void.

109. **A hard nut to crack:** *a difficult problem*

Crossing this turbulent river is a hard nut to crack.

110. **Out and out:** *thoroughly*

Mr. Mishra is an orthodox Hindu out and out.

111. **Old maid:** *a single woman regarded as too old for marriage*

Many a girl suffers the fate of an old maid because of the dowry system.

112. **Of course:** *undoubtedly*

He is a good athlete. Of course, he is.

113. **Old wives' tale:** *a traditional belief which is incorrect*

The belief that spirits possess human beings is an old wives' tale.

114. **Olive branch:** *an offer of reconciliation*

The two enemies compromised and met together each with an olive branch in his hand.

115. **All at once:** *suddenly*

The roof of the house fell all at once.

116. **At one:** *in agreement*

There is no dispute among us; we are all at one.

117. **Open to:** *accessible to new ideas*

We all believe in innovation and are open to new ideas.

118. **Once in a blue moon:** *rarely*

She comes to me once in a blue moon.

119. **Out of order:** *not functioning*

My watch is out of order.

120. **Play truant:** *run away from school*

The children who play truant during school time will be punished.

121. **Play to the gallery:** *aim to attract popular attention*

Politicians usually play to the gallery.

122. **Pillar to post:** *one place to another*

The young man ran from pillar to post for a job but didn't get it.

123. **Play fast and loose:** *be inconsistent*

Those who play fast and loose cut a sorry figure towards the end of their life.

124. **The point of no return:** *the point in journey or enterprise at which it becomes essential to continue*

After devoting so much of time to this project, we reached the point of no return.

125. **Play possum:** *feign unconsciousness or death; feign ignorance*

He is very clever and plays possum occasionally to fool others.

126. **(keep) a low profile:** *remain inconspicuous*

Sometimes, it is better to keep a low profile.

127. **Feel or take the pulse of:** *ascertain the mood or opinion of*

Generally, political parties feel the pulse of the public before election.

128. **Born in the purple:** *born in a privileged family*

Jawaharlal Nehru was born in the purple.

129. **Cut to the quick:** *cause deep distress*

Your remark has cut me to the quick.

130. **Read between the lines:** *find out the hidden meaning*

We should read poetry between the lines.

131. **Rise from ashes:** *revive from destruction*

After the big loss he had become a destitute but now has risen from the ashes.

132. **Run with the hare and hunt with the hound:** *be an opportunist*

You should not rely on him; he runs with the hare and hunts with the hound.

133. **Rise to:** *respond to a challenging situation*

She rose to the occasion and came out triumphant.

134. **Roll up one's sleeves:** *prepare to fight or work*

He rolls up his sleeves on a slight provocation.

135. **At root:** *fundamentally*

He is a wicked man at root.

136. **Rule of thumb:** *principle based on practice*

In many cases, the rule of thumb prevails over theory.

137. **Run-of-the-mill:** *common*

We should not be very particular about the things of the run-of- the mill.

138. **Rise like a phoenix:** *revive*

Although we are defeated by adverse circumstances, we shall rise like a phoenix.

139. **Raise a dust:** *create confusion*

Let us face the problem calmly and not raise a dust.

140. **Raise the roof:** *make a loud noise or cheer*

The clapping of the audience at the arrival of the great cricketer raised the roof.

141. **Stick to one's guns:** *refuse to compromise in spite of criticism*

The young boy didn't listen to his friends and stuck to his guns.

142. **Soft spot:** *a liking or weakness for*

Everybody has a soft spot in his heart for something.

143. **Soft corner:** *weakness*

All mothers have a soft corner for their children.

144. **Sleeping partner:** *an investor who is not active*

Ravi is the sleeping partner in the firm among us.

145. **Split hairs:** *make over fine distinction*

Let us stop arguing and splitting hairs over this petty topic.

146. **Skeleton in the cupboard:** *embarrassing fact that a person wants to keep secret*

When we asked about his past life, he remained rather silent as if there was a skeleton in the cupboard.

147. **Sound a red alert:** *raise an alarm*

A red alert was sounded when it was reported that two terrorists had entered the town.

148. **Set the Thames (or the world) on fire:** *do something remarkable or sensational*

The first flight of the aeroplane by the Wright brothers set the world on fire.

149. **For goodness' sake/*For God's sake:** *expression of impatience, irritation or annoyance*

For goodness' sake, please stop criticizing my friend.

150. **Save the day or situation:** *provide a solution to a problem*

His timely help saved the situation.

151. **Save one's breath:** *not bother to say something pointless*

I must save my breath on this issue.

152. **Settle the score:** *take revenge on someone*

India settled the score with Pakistan in the hockey final of the Asian Games.

153. **Scratch one's head:** *think hard*

Scratch your head; you'll soon find the solution.

---

* "For God's sake" is out of use.

154. **Make sense:** *be intelligible*
Your words fail to make sense.

155. **Make sense of:** *find meaning or coherence in*
Can you make sense of his long loud speech?

156. **Set the wheels in motion:** *put a plan in action*
We have drafted a good plan. Now let us set the wheels in motion.

157. **Sinking ship:** *a failing organization*
Most of the government run factories are sinking ships.

158. **Shot in the arm:** *encouragement*
His help of one lakh rupees was a shot in the arm of my business.

159. **On show:** *being exhibited*
The newly released film is on show.

160. **Have a thick skin:** *be insensitive*
He has such a thick skin that my harsh words did not affect him.

161. **Slip of the pen (or the tongue):** *a minor mistake in writing or speech*
Please excuse me; it was a slip of the pen/tongue.

162. **The small screen:** *television*
Now famous heroes are coming to the small screen.

163. **End in smoke:** *be abortive*
All my plans have ended in smoke.

164. **In spirit:** *in intention or thought*
Please take my words in spirit.

165. **Stake a claim:** *assert one's right to something*
She stakes a claim on your property.

166. **Stand on one's own feet:** *be self-reliant*
It is the demand of time we stand on our own feet and be not our parent's burden.

167. **Put a stop to:** *end*
Let us put a stop to the evil custom of dowry.

168. **In store:** *about to happen*
His ruin is in store.

169. **At a stretch:** *without break*
We completed the job at a stretch.

170. **At full stretch:** *with all energy*
Make preparation for the examination at full stretch.

171. **At one stroke:** *by single action*
She cut the plant at one stroke.

172. **Sweep the board:** *win every event or prize*
Heeralal swept the board in the short distance races.

173. **In full swing:** *at the height of activity*
His study is going on in full swing.

174. **Sword of Damocles:** *impending danger*
He is hardly aware that the sword of Damocles is hanging over his head.

175. **Talk shop:** *talk business at an inappropriate time*
Some businessman talk shop even in birthday parties.

176. **The talk of:** *subject of current discussion*
Her elopement with her lover of a lower caste was the talk of the town.

177. **The salt of the earth:** *a person of goodness and character*
Man like Netaji Subhash Chandra Bose is the salt of the earth.

178. **Take something with a pinch (or grain) of salt:** *believe only a part of something*
We all listened to her ghost story with great interest but took it with a pinch of salt.

179. **Through thick and thin:** *In sorrow and happiness*
Kasturba followed Gandhiji through thick and thin.

180. **Tell tales:** *gossip about another person's secrets or faults*
It is a bad habit to tell tales of one's neighbours.

181. **Tenant at will:** *a tenant that can be evicted without notice*

In India, the law of tenant at will is not in force.

182. **Come to terms with:** *reconcile*

The two friends quarrelled yesterday but now they have come to terms with each other.

183. **Test the water:** *certain feelings or opinions before processing further*

A good leader tests the water of his followers before he advises them to go in action.

184. **In theory:** *in an ideal or hypothetical situation*

Your project is valid in theory only.

185. **Second thought:** *more than the slightest consideration*

The committee did not give second thought to his proposal.

186. **A tight corner:** *in a difficult situation*

Rajan is in a tight corner after the loss of his job.

187. **On time:** *punctual*

Rajdhani Express runs on time, usually.

188. **Time immemorial:** *ancient time*

Legends are stories of heroes of time immemorial.

189. **Time will tell:** *Truth will be known in future*

Only time will tell whether the new economic policy is good for the welfare of people or not.

190. **Time-honoured:** *a custom observed for a long time*

The sacred thread ceremony is a time-honoured custom.

191. **(with) Tongue in cheek:** *insincerely or ironically*

They admired her make up with tongue in cheek.

192. **Tongue-tied:** *shy and speechless*

The prince remained tongue-tied when the princess addressed him.

193. **Through and through:** *completely*

Anil Kumar is a criminal through and through.

194. **From top to bottom:** *completely, thoroughly*

The rain drenched us from top to bottom.

195. **From top to toe:** *all over*

The mad dog bit the young boy from top to toe.

196. **In touch:** *in communication*

Even after leaving our town, she was always in touch with us.

197. **Out of touch:** *lacking up to date knowledge or awareness*

I have been out of touch with the developments in local politics.

198. **Touch of the sun:** *a light sun stroke*

I went out for about two hours at 12 o' clock in day time and now am suffering from the touch of the sun.

199. **Tour de force:** *a performance or achievement that has been accomplished with great skill*

Rag Bhairavi is the tour de force of Shruti Sadolikar.

200. **Shrug one's shoulders:** *raise ones shoulders to show doubt or difference*

She did not trust my words and shrugged her shoulders.

201. **Blow one's trumpet:** *talk openly and boastfully about one's achievement*

He blew his trumpet and we simply smiled.

202. **Tried and tested:** *proved reliable*

The HMT watches are the best; they are tried and tested.

203. **Out of tune:** *not in harmony*

Our football team is out of tune. The engine of my car is out of tune.

204. **To the tune of:** *amounting to*

He suffered a loss to the tune of one lakh rupees.

205. **Turn coat:** *opportunist*

Most of the political leaders are turn coats.

206. **Ugly duckling:** *a person who turns out to be beautiful or talented against all expectations*

The last bencher who used to sit silently in the class has proved himself an ugly duckling, he has passed in first division.

207. **Dark horse:** *an unknown competitor who wins a game or contest*

Shanu was the dark horse in the local election.

208. **Under way:** *having started and making progress*

The preparations for the annual meeting are under way.

209. **Up and doing:** *active*

Young people should be up and doing.

210. **Give vent to:** *release a strong emotion*

Neurotic people should be allowed to give vent to their emotion.

211. **Versed in:** *experienced or skilled*

My sister is well versed in music.

212. **Vest (something) in:** *confer or bestow*

The executive power is vested in the prime minister.

213. **Be vested with:** *give someone the legal right to power*

The vice-chancellor is vested with the power to confer degree on graduates.

214. **With a view to:** *with intention*

I went to my friend with a view to consulting him on a serious matter.

215. **By virtue of:** *because of*

He obtained first class by virtue of his hard labour.

216. **Warm up:** *prepare for hard physical exercise, be animated*

The tennis players are warming up for the match.

His assurance warmed us up.

217. **Wash one's dirty linen in public:** *discuss the personal affairs in public*

It is foolish for us to wash our dirty linen in public.

218. **Be washed out:** *a game postponed because of rain*

The cricket match was washed out on the last day.

219. **Of the first water:** *of the best quality*

This pearl is of the first water.

220. **By the way:** *incidentally*

I met him by the way.

221. **In no way:** *not at all*

In no way, I am going to surrender under their pressure.

222. **The way of the world:** *the manner in which people typically behave*

Corruption in government offices has become the way of the world.

223. **White elephant:** *an uneconomical possession*

This old car has become a white elephant for me.

224. **White lie:** *harmless lie told to avoid hurting some one's feelings*

I had to tell a white lie about her brother otherwise the truth would have shocked her.

225. **White paper:** *a government report*

The government has issued white paper on the recent riots in the town.

226. **White-collar job:** *job in an office*

White-collar jobs are still preferred in India.

227. **On the whole:** *taking every thing in account*

On the whole, your proposal cannot be accepted by us.

228. **Wide open:** *not predictable*

Both the teams are equally strong and the result of the match is wide open.

229. **Wide of the mark:** *far from the target, irrelevant*
He thought that he had said something very witty but it was wide of the mark.

230. **Wide awake:** *fully awake*
I was wide awake when the burglar entered my room.

231. **At will:** *as one pleases*
You can use all these articles at will.

232. **With a will:** *energetically and resolutely*
We started the work with a will.

233. **Get wind of:** *hear rumour*
We have got wind of his future plan.

234. **Wind up:** *close in a specific way*
Now it is time that I wind up my agreement.

235. **Nine day's wonder:** *something that attracts great interest for a short time*
His tricks were a nine day's wonder.

236. **Be unable to see the wood for the trees:** *fail to grasp the main point because of over-attention to details*
He read the minister's speech so minutely that he was unable to see the wood for the trees.

237. **Out of the wood/woods:** *out of danger or difficulty*
With great effort, we saved the boat from capsizing and came out of the wood.

238. **At a word:** *as soon as requested*
This bank advances loan at a word.

239. **Be as good as one's word:** *do what one has promised*
My friend Satyendra is as good as his word.

240. **Have a word:** *say something in brief*
I want to have a word with you.

241. **Wring one's hands:** *express despair*
After hearing the news of his team's defeat he began to wring his hands.

242. **Write something off:** *dismiss something as insignificant*
He is a worthless fellow. We have written his name off our list.

243. **In the wrong:** *guilty*
After investigation the inquiry officer found that the secretary of the company was in the wrong.

244. **Yeoman's service:** *great help*
You rendered yeoman's service in her dire need.

245. **Zebra crossing:** *a street marked by white stripes for slowing or stopping vehicles for pedestrians*
There must be zebra crossings at crossroads.

246. **Zero hour:** *the hour when an operation begins*
The army general will decide the time and date of the zero hour.

247. **A fish out of water:** *very uncomfortable*
She felt like a fish out of water when she was sent to town for further studies.

248. **Small fry:** *insignificant person*
I am a small fry in my area.

249. **Catch a tartar:** *find a stronger enemy*
The two seniors wanted to rag the junior but they soon found that they had caught a tartar in him.

250. **Make both ends meet:** *earn just enough money to live in*
With an income of five thousand rupees, I manage to make both ends meet.

251. **A dog's life:** *a miserable life*
Most of the people in slum areas lead a dog's life.

252. **At heart:** *one's real nature*
Prabhu may seem a hard man but he is good at heart.

253. **High handed:** *overbearing*
His high handed policy ruined his business.

254. **On the verge of:** *on the brim of; very close*
They teased her so badly that she was on the verge of tears.

255. **Put the cart before the horse:** *begin from the wrong end*
Please make a plan of your house before constructing it. If you start construction before the plan, you will put the cart before the horse.

256. **A black sheep:** *a wicked fellow*
There are black sheep in every society.

257. **Get better of:** *overcome*
He got better of others in the 1500 kilometer race.

258. **Crocodile tears:** *pretended sorrow*
That hypocrite shed crocodile tears on the huge loss in the business of his neighbour.

259. **Double dealing:** *deceit*
We should beware of men of double dealing.

260. **Follow suit:** *do what the predecessor has done*
When Sachin Tendulkar got out, the rest followed suit.

261. **Writing on the wall:** *Warning the coming disaster*
Take care, can't you see the writing on the wall?

262. **Harp on the same string:** *repeat monotonously*
Please change the topic. There is no use harping on the same string.

A

263. **Against the grain:** *contrary to one's nature*
Lying for some gain is against the grain of my nature.

264. **A good word:** *recommendation*
My class teacher wrote a good word in my favour.

265. **At grass:** *grazing*
Look at the cows at grass.

266. **A hair's breadth:** *a very narrow margin*
We lost the game by a hair's breadth.

267. **At hand:** *close, near*
You can buy this book. The shop is at hand.

268. **After one's heart:** *sharing one's taste*

The lunch I had today at your home was after my heart.

269. **At home (in):** *comfortable and at ease*

She is at home in drawing and painting.

270. **An iron hand:** *very strict and ruthless*

Joseph Stalin was really an iron hand.

271. **A leap in the dark:** *a daring act*

Buying shares these days is a leap in the dark.

272. **At least:** *minimum*

I will help you with ₹ 10,000/- at least.

273. **At length:** *in detail*

Our teacher explained the difficult points of his lecture at length.

274. **At the mercy of:** *completely in the power of*

A slave's life was at the mercy of his master.

275. **A hard nut to crack:** *a difficult problem*

This mathematical problem is a hard nut to crack.

276. **All at once:** *suddenly; all at the same time* (221, No 115)

He appeared before us all at once and surprised us.

We were asked to clean all the ten rooms all at once.

277. **At par/on a par with:** *the usual level*

The Indian rupees is not at par/on a par with the UK pound.

278. **A square peg in a round hole:** *a person given a job for which s/he is quite misfit*

Mayank was appointed to the post of system analyst but the management found him a square peg in a round hole.

279. **At any rate:** *whatever happens*

We have to finish the job at any rate.

280. **A bed of roses:** *a comfortable or easy thing*
Life is not a bed of roses.

281. **As a rule:** *usually but not always*
I wake early in the morning as a rule.

282. **At a stretch:** *In one continuous period*
I completed the long work at a stretch.

283. **A tall order:** *an unreasonable demand*
The students' demand to postpone the date of examination in view of the cricket match in the city is a tall order.

284. **All the time:** *at all time*
This medical shop remains open all the time.

285. **At a word:** *as soon as requested*
My friend gave me the loan of five thousand rupees at a word.

B

286. **Be in two minds:** *undecided*
We should not be in two minds while helping a needy person.

287. **Be on nodding terms:** *a slight acquaintance*
I do not know my neighbour well; we are on nodding terms.

288. **By numbers:** *following simple instructions identified*
She follows her mother's instructions by numbers.

289. **Be over:** *end*
By the time we entered the hall, the key note address was over.

290. **Bring into question:** *raise an issue*
The problem of juvenile crime was bought into question by members in the Legislative Council.

291. **Be on/at the receiving end:** *be subjected to something unpleasant*
He quarrelled with his boss and is on/at the receiving end now.

292. Be rooted in: *have source in*

Subhash Chandra Bose was deeply rooted in the Indian soil.

293. Behind the scenes: *out of public view*

Mr Kailash Satyarthi, a Nobel Prize winner, avoids publicity and remains behind the scenes, usually.

294. Be born with a silver spoon in mouth: *born in a rich family*

Most of the great men were not born with a silver spoon in mouth.

295. Bear fruit: *give good results*

Our hard and sincere work will bear fruit in due to course.

296. Be at one's wit's end: *completely at loss what to do*

The small boy was at his wit's end when he broke his father's mobile phone.

297. Be as good as one's words: *do what one has promised*

My friend's timely help proved that he was as good as words.

C

298. Call someone names: *insult verbally*

An uncultured man calls his friends names without any reason.

299. Clean sweep: *complete victory*

Sania Mirza and Martina Hingis made a clean sweep in the last tennis championship match at Wimbledon.

300. Come true: *happen actually*

His prediction that he would qualify in NEET came true this morning.

301. Go to pieces: *Become nervous and undecided*

The truck owner went to pieces when he heard of his truck's accident.

302. Go to press: *Go to be printed*

My manuscript has gone to press.

303. **Give vent to:** *release a great emotion*

After hearing sympathetic words from the doctor the rape victim gave vent to her feelings.

304. **Have a thick skin:** *be insensitive*

It is useless to tell him about our misery. He has a thick skin.

305. **Hand over:** *pass to someone else*

The retiring officer will hand over the charge to the new officer tomorrow.

306. **Hand in glove:** *very close*

The two neighbours are hand in glove.

307. **Hard and fast:** *fixed*

There is no hard and fast rule for success in life.

308. **Hard of hearing:** *inability to hear well*

Generally, people above eighty are hard of hearing.

309. **Hats off:** *admiration*

Hats off to the captain for scoring the deciding goal in the dying moments of the game.

310. **Hard luck:** *bad luck*

It was a hard luck that you suffered the leg injury in the final match.

311. **Hit-and-run:** *(the case of) an accident in which the car driver has run away*

Salman Khan's hit and run case remained national news for many years.

It is unfortunate that rich men's sons are the main culprit in hit-and-run cases.

312. **Hit the right note:** *say something in right way*

She corrected her husband's remarks by hitting the right note.

313. **Have a soft spot/corner:** *be fond of*

Every mother has a soft corner for her youngest child.

314. End in smoke: *be unsuccessful*

All my efforts ended in smoke because of the turn of events.

315. In full swing: *at the height of activity*

Preparations are going on in full swing to welcome the president.

316. In time: *at the appointed or intimated time/hour*

I received your message in time.

317. In touch: *in or into communication*

I was in touch with Shyam Nandan till the year 2015 but now I have no idea of him.

318. Knight errant: *an adventurous knight in the medieval ages*

He behaves as if he were a knight errant.

319. Leave its mark: *have a lasting or significant effect*

An earthquake leaves its mark for ever.

320. Make something out: *understand with difficulty*

I could make a little out of the politician's long speech.

321. Man of letters: *a scholarly man*

Men of letters are little valued in modern India.

322. Make use of. *benefit from*

Let us make use of this opportunity.

323. Off and on. *intermittently*

He comes to me off and on, not regularly.

324. On and on: *continually*

We climbed on and on and reached the top at last.

325. Once again/once more: *one more time*

The audience demanded the song to be sung once again. The audience requested the singer to sing the same song once more.

326. Out of order: *not working properly*

The engine of my car is out of order.

327. **Once for all:** *now and for the last time*

We have decided to settle the matter today once for all.

328. **The order of the day:** *the prevailing or required custom or state of affairs*

As the situation, we have to follow the order of the day.

329. **Out of the ordinary:** *unusual*

Your performance on the stage was out of the ordinary.

330. **Over and above:** *in addition*

He is a well-behaved worker and over and above honest too.

331. **Out of print:** *not available*

The first edition of George Orwell's novels is out of print.

332. **Out of the question:** *not possible*

That your application will be entertained again is out of the question.

333. **Out of humour:** *in bad mood*

Do not go to boss; he is out of humour.

334. **On the hour:** *on time*

We drove fast and reached the airport on the hour.

335. **Out of hand:** *not under control*

The situation is so critical that it is out of hand now.

336. **On the wing:** *in flight*

The new 380 Airbus will be on the wing tomorrow.

337. **Put heads together:** *consult together*

We four friends put our heads together to prepare the plan of our new business.

338. **Put on the map:** *bring something to prominence*

Bithoor was put on the map of India when Nana Sahab launched the first war of independence in 1857.

339. **Play foot and loose:** *behave irresponsibly*

We expelled Amit from our circle as he was playing foot and loose.

340. **Point-blank:** *shot of a gun fired from a short distance*
The dacoit shot the bank cashier point-blank.

341. **Pull someone's legs:** *deceive someone playfully*
It is bad to pull your friend's legs when he is in trouble.

342. **(A) Quixotic project:** *a foolish project or idea*
Your plan to organize a football league match at district level is a Quixotic project.

343. **The Red Planet:** *Mars*
Mars is called the Red Planet as it looks red from the Earth.

344. **Root and branch:** *thoroughly*
The system has been revamped root and branch.

345. **Reduced circumstances:** *poverty after plenty*
After a heavy loss in business I am living in reduced circumstances.

346. **Red Tape:** *the bureaucracy*
Most of the government plans are delayed by the red tape.

347. **Speak the same language:** *sharing the same opinion*
We have resolved the controversy. Now, let us speak the same language.

348. **Strong language:** *rough or coarse language*
It is not proper to use strong language when we are in the company of women or small children.

349. **Someone's days are numbered:** *someone shall not survive or remain in power*
After the revolt of sizable party members, the President's days are numbered.

350. **Slap in the face:** *an unexpected rejection*
It was a slap in the face when my application for home loan was rejected.

351. **Slip of the tongue/pen:** *a minor mistake in speech/writing*

It was only a slip of the tongue/pen and should not be taken seriously.

352. **Spill the beans:** *speak a secret indiscreetly or unintentionally*

Politicians spill the beans of their party and then say that they did not say so.

353. **Scratch one's head:** *think hard to find a solution*

The chess player scratched his head to counter reply his opponent's move.

354. **Short of:** *less than*

I wanted to buy a new bike but was short of the required money.

355. **Show of hands:** *a vote by the show of hands*

She was elected Secretary of the club by show of hands.

356. **Skeleton in the cupboard:** *something unpleasant kept in secret*

Though he wanted to keep us in dark, yet we knew there was a skeleton in the cupboard.

357. **Side by side:** *close together*

The two friends walked on the sea beach side by side.

358. **Take something for granted:** *assume that everything is true*

I am not going to take all that you have said for granted.

359. **The late:** *former or deceased*

The late Shivakant Awasthi was my father's friend.

360. **The latest:** *the most recent*

Smita asked the jeweller if he had pendants of the latest design.

361. **Turn over a new leaf:** *start to work in a better way*

The result has made the students turn over a new leaf.

362. **Take note:** *pay attention*

Please take note of your father's advice.

363. **Take notice:** *pay attention*

We must take notice of what a small child says.

364. **The order of the day:** *the prevailing or required custom/state*

We have no way out but to obey the order of the day.

365. **The salt of the earth:** *A man of great worth*

People like Kailash Stayarthi are the salt of the earth.

366. **The seven seas:** *all the seas of the world*

It is easy to navigate the seven seas now.

367. **That's the stuff:** *that is good or what is needed*

Our customer was highly satisfied with the sweets we had supplied and said, "That's the stuff."

368. **True to life:** *accurately representing real events or objects*

The people and events depicted in this novel are true to life.

369. **Tried and tested:** *reliable*

We sell only those machines that are tried and tested.

370. **Turn of mind:** *bent of mind, mind set, a particular way of thinking*

It is difficult to explain a new thing to Hari. He has a peculiar turn of mind.

371. **Up and doing:** *active*

I like the people who are up and doing, not the lazy ones.

372. **Ups and downs:** *prosperity and adversity*

I have seen ups and downs many times in my short life.

373. **Write (something) down:** *reduce the nominal value of stocks*

We had to write down our stocks due to fall in the prices of commodities.

374. **Write (something) off:** *dismiss something as insignificant*

The government wrote off the loans given to poor peasants because of the famine in 15 districts.

375. **Yeoman service:** *a very helpful help*

She gave me yeoman service during my illness.

376. **Free and easy:** *informal and relaxed*

We liked the new comer for his free and easy ways.

377. **Free hand:** *freedom to act at one's own discretion*

The officer gave our team free hand to complete the project.

378. **From hand to mouth:** *satisfy bare necessities*

We lived from hand to mouth for a year.

G

379. **Grass roots:** *the basic level of activity*

Mahatma Gandhi became successful because he launched the national movement at grass-root level.

380. **Give/lose ground:** *retreat*

As the enemy could not resist our attack they gave ground.

381. **Give a hand/lend a hand:** *assist*

My neighbours are always ready to give a hand when I need their help.

382. **Greenhouse effect:** *the retention of the sun's heat in the atmosphere*

One of the greatest causes of global warming is greenhouse effect.

PHRASAL VERBS

A phrasal verb contains one particle, usually. Sometimes there may be two particles. There is a difference between particles and prepositions. Particles cannot be separated from the main verb but a preposition can be. Besides, a phrasal verb contains a specific meaning. The preposition "in" is a preposition in the following sentences:

1. He is in the room.
2. We were left in a dark cell.
3. May I come in, Sir?

But in phrasal verbs like *call in*, *give in* and *be in for* the preposition is a particle.

Basically, a particle is a preposition but it is so called for its special position and function. In spoken English, whether formal or informal, the use of particle is quite frequent.

A few more examples will make clear the difference between a preposition and a particle.

1. He came to me in the morning. Preposition
2. He has taken to drinking. Particle
3. She came after her mother. Preposition
4. She takes after her mother. Particle
5. He went out in the morning. Preposition
6. He put out the light. Particle

Secondly, a phrasal verb is split when the object is a pronoun.

1. **They searched out Amit.**
2. **They searched him out.**

Common Phrasal Verbs

1. Attend to – pay attention

   You must attend to your duties.
2. Back out – withdraw support

   They promised to help me but backed out at the last moment.
3. Bear away – win

   My friend bore away three prizes in athletics.
4. Break out – start suddenly

   Fire broke out in my village last night.
5. Break up – end

   The meeting broke up when some members began to quarrel.

   Their friendship broke up without any apparent reason.

6. Break with – quarrel or cease relations; act against a custom or tradition

   I had to break with my friends as I could not subscribe to their views.

   The romantic poets broke with the classical tradition.

7. Bring forward – transfer the total of amount from the bottom of the page to the next

   I have brought forward the total of the previous pages to the next page.

8. Bring someone up – to rear a child upto adulthood

   She brought up her sister's children after the latter's death.

9. Brush something off – dismiss contemptuously

   He brushed off my request. His action hurt me deeply.

10. Call for – require; demand

    The situation calls for a quick action.

11. Be cast down – feel depressed

    After hearing the sad news of her mother's death, she was cast down.

12. Come out – emerge or be known

    The result of our hard work will come out soon.

13. Come through – succeed in surviving or dealing with

    At last, we were able to come through the difficulties.

14. Count down – count in the reverse way

    The class II students were asked to count down from 100 to zero.

    The count down of the launching of the rocket will begin at 9:00 am.

15. Crack down on – take strict measures

    The police cracked down on the culprits late at night.

16. Crop up – appear unexpectedly

    This problem cropped up quite unexpectedly.

17. Do away with – remove or put an end to

    You must do away with your bad habit of poking your nose into my affairs.

18. Do with – would like to do or have

    I could do with a cup of coffee.

19. Draw back – go back

    He had promised to pay me five hundred rupees but, later on, drew back.

20. Drink to – drink for someone's health

    We drank to our friend's health on his birthday.

21. Drop in/by – visit informally and briefly

    While going to Kanpur we dropped in our friend's at Unnao.

22. Drop out – cease to participate

    Earlier I was selected to play for my school but, later on, I was dropped out.

    Her name was dropped out from the list of competitors.

23. Dry up – decrease and stop

    There was a small stream here but now it is dried up.

24. Fall on/upon – attack fiercely or unexpectedly

    The enemy fell on us late at night.

25. Fall back – retreat

    When we retaliated the enemy army fell back.

26. Fall out – have an argument

    It is not proper to fall out with a stranger on a petty matter.

27. Fit in/into – be in harmony

    My friend is so good natured that he can fit in any company.

28. Flare up – suddenly become angry or violent or intense

    She often flares up for no obvious reason.

29. Focus on – pay particular attention to

    In Europe, primary education focuses on Mathematics and Language.

30. Form into – make

    We were asked to form ourselves into circle.

31. Get ahead – be successful in life or career

    If we work laboriously and sincerely, we will get ahead sometime.

32. Get away – escape

    The guards wondered how the prisoners got away.

33. Get on – make progress

    The teacher told us that we could get on in our studies if we listened to his advice.

34. Get up – rise up from bed

    I get up early in the morning.

35. Go about – begin or carry on a work

    I went about working for the poor in spite of many hurdles.

36. Go into – investigate

    The police inspector was ordered to go into the murder case.

37. Go through – undergo a difficult period

    I have gone through difficult days.

38. Go on – continue

    We should not be discouraged by adversity and must go on to achieve success.

39. Give in – cease fighting or arguing

    After a short resistance our opposite group gave in.

40. Give up – abandon

    The doctor advised the patient to give up smoking.

41. Go against – oppose

    Please don't go against me.

42. Go ahead – proceed
    My boss told me that I could go ahead in my work.
43. Go down – get defeated
    We went down fighting bravely.
44. Go over – examine or check the details
    Please go over your application before submitting it.
45. Grow up – advance to maturity
    This plant will grow up in two years.
46. Hand something down – pass something on to a successor
    Damodar handed down his property to his son and daughter equally.
47. Kick off – start
    The football match was kicked off at 4:00 pm.
48. Land in – arrive
    Our plane landed in Delhi airport at 8:00 am.
49. Make up – be reconciled after a quarrel
    The two friends quarrelled with each other two days ago but they have made up now.
50. Part with – give up possession
    It is difficult for us to part with our parental house.
51. Pass something over – avoid mentioning or considering something
    There is no need to talk about his mischief and let us pass the matter over.
52. Pick up – improve or increase
    In the beginning, she was slow in studies but picked up after sometime.
53. Pull out – withdraw
    Earlier he promised me to help but he is pulling out now.
54. Put something down – suppress a rebellion
    The riot flared up but was soon put down by the police.

55. Put something off – postpone

    The meeting was adjourned and put off for a day.

56. Put something up – present something for discussion

    The agenda was put up by the Secretary before the members of the committee.

57. Put up with – tolerate

    It is difficult for me to put up with a dishonest person.

58. (Be) rooted in – have as a source or origin

    Mahatma Gandhi was deeply rooted in the Indian tradition.

59. Rule out – reject

    The Chairman ruled out a member's proposal.

60. Run away – take flight

    The miscreants ran away when they saw the police coming.

61. Run down – reduce

    My savings are running down because of the rising prices of essential commodities.

62. Run into – collide

    The two speeding vehicles ran into each other.

63. Run on – continue

    Though I faced many difficulties, yet I ran on.

64. See through – detect something secret

    I can see through my neighbour's mischievous plan.

65. Sell out – abandon one's principles

    My friend sold out his honesty for a petty gain.

66. Set aside – *annul*

    The judge set aside the government prosecutor's objection.

67. Set out – begin a journey

    We set out early in the morning.

68. Shut down – close

After suffering a huge loss, she shut down her shop in the mall.

69. Shut up – stop speaking

She was so aggrieved that she shut up her mouth.

70. Start on – begin to work

We started on our new project after a fruitful discussion.

71. Step down – withdraw or resign

The king stepped down from the throne for his eldest son.

72. Stick to – continue

You must stick to the rules of our institution.

73. Strike off – remove

Her name was struck off from the class register because she had not paid her fees for three months.

74. Take after – resemble

She takes after her mother.

75. Take in – cheat

I was taken in by the stranger's politeness.

76. Take back – retract a statement

Earlier, he had promised to help me but has taken it back now.

77. Take off – be in the air; be successful

The aeroplane left the ground and took off at 3:00 pm.

Our economy has reached the take off stage.

78. Take over – assume control or responsibility

The new colonel will take over the charge of the command area tomorrow.

79. Take to – begin or fall into a habit

Recently, he has taken to drinking.

80. Tone down – make something less harsh in sound

In the beginning, she was very harsh to us but later toned down when we explained the fact.

81. Turn against – be hostile

The witness turned hostile in the court.

82. Turn out – prove to be the case

People were sieved to see a bag lying on the railway platform for a long time but it turned out to be a railway employee's bag.

83. Turn up – to be present; arrive

We expected a large gathering in the meeting but only a few turned up.

84. Walk away – casually or irresponsibly abandon responsibility

We asked for their help but they walked away.

85. Walk out – depart suddenly or angrily

The opposition walked out protesting the introduction of a controversial bill.

86. Warm up – stretch the body or play gently before a game

We warm up generally before playing a game.

87. (Be) washed out – game postponed because of rain

The one day cricket match between India and Australia was washed out because of a heavy rain last night.

88. Write off – cancel a bad debt

The government ordered the bank to write off the debts of flood-stricken peasants.

COMMON FOREIGN PHRASES AND WORDS

Many of the Latin, Greek and French idioms, and phrases are frequently used in English Language. A few of them are given here.

1. Ab initio – from the beginning (Latin)
2. Ad hoc – formed, arranged or done for a particular purpose only (Latin)
3. Ad nauseum – excessively tiring (Latin)

4. Ad valorem – tax in proportion to the value of goods (Latin)
5. A la carte – price list of individual items in a menu (French)
6. Anno Domini (A.D.) – In the year of our Lord (Latin)
   Nowadays C.E. (Christian Era) is being used at the place of A.D. and B.C.E. at the place of B.C. (Before Christ).
7. a.m. (ante-meridiem) – before noon (Latin)
8. Ante-mortem – before death (Latin)
9. Apex – topmost, highest point (Latin)
10. Apropos – with reference/regard to (French)
11. Aqua-vitae – strong alcoholic spirit, especially brandy (Latin)
    Originally, it meant "water of life".
12. Ad hominem – associated with a particular person (Latin)
13. Ad infinitum – endlessly; forever (Latin)
14. Ad interim – for the meantime (Latin)
15. Ad libitum/Ad lib – speak or perform in public without previous preparation (Latin)
16. Ad litem – appearing in court on behalf of a child (Latin)
17. Ad rem – to the point (Latin)
18. Avant-garde – new and unusual; experimental (French)
19. Bona-fide – genuine, real (in law without intention to deceive) (Latin)
20. Bona-fides – honesty and sincerity of intention (Latin)
21. Charge d' affaires – an ambassador's deputy; a state's diplomatic representative in a minor country (French)
22. Cul-da-sac – a street or passage closed at one end (French)
23. Debut – a person's first appearance in public or formal gathering (French)
24. Debutant – a person making a debut (French)
25. Debutante – a young upper class woman making her debut (French)

26. Decoupage – decoration of a surface by paper cuttings (French)
27. Debonair – (of a man) confident, stylish and charming (French Debonaire)
28. Ejusdem generis – of or as the same kind (Latin)
29. Fin de siècle – relating to the end of a century, especially the nineteenth century (French)
30. Fons et origo – the origin of something (Latin)
31. Geist – the spirit of an individual or group (German)
32. Grand Prix – any of the world championship series of international motor-racing or motorcycling contests (French)
33. Habeas corpus – a writ requiring a person to be brought before the judge (Latin)
34. In esse – in actual existence (Latin)
35. Incognito – an assumed or false identity (Italian)
36. Ipse dixit – a dogmatic and unproven statement (Latin)
37. Ipso facto – by that very fact or act (Latin)
38. In absentia – while not present (Latin)
39. Interregnum – the period when normal government is suspended; the gap period between two reigns (Latin)
40. Laissez-faire – a policy of non-interference by government in market economy (French)
41. Modus operandi – a way of doing something; the way in which something works (Latin)
42. Modus Vivendi – an arrangement allowing conflicting parties to coexist peacefully; a way of living (Latin)
43. Magnum opus – the most important work (s) of an artist or author (Latin)
44. Nuoveau riche – a person who has become rich recently (French)
45. Oeuvre – the body of work of a painter, composer or author (French)
46. Par avion – by airmail (French, meaning by aeroplane)

47. Poete mandit – a poet neglected by her/his contemporaries in her/his lifetime
48. Pro forma – a standard document or form (Latin)
49. Pro rata – proportionally (Latin)
50. Raison d'etre – the most important reason or purpose for someone or something's existence (French)
51. Sinecure – a position which requires a little but gives the holder status or financial benefit (Latin)
52. Sine die – indefinite period (Latin)
53. Sine qua non – a thing that is absolutely essential (Latin)
54. Suo motu – action or decision taken by the court itself (Latin)
55. Sui generis – unique, the only of its kind (Latin)
56. Tant mieux – so much the better (French)
57. Ultimatum – final warning (Latin)
58. Ultra vires – beyond one's legal power or authority (Latin)
59. Vade mecum – a handbook or guide constantly kept at hand (Latin)
60. Zeitgeist – the defining spirit or mood of a particular period of history (German)

Chapter Eleven

Synonym and Antonym

Outcome of the Chapter

(a) List of words to memorize

Concise Oxford Dictionary defines synonym "a word or phrase that means the same as another word or phrase in the same language". According to *Webster New Dictionary and Thesaurus* it is "a word having the same, or very nearly the same, meaning as another or others in the same language." *Concise Oxford Dictionary* gives the example, *shut* and *close*.

Although synonyms have the same or nearly the same meaning, they cannot be always substituted by the other when they are used in sentence. For example, we can write:

Naveen Market is closed today *but not* **Naveen Market is shut today.**

The knowledge of synonyms is necessary for effective writing. It will be monotonous if the same word is used again and again in a paragraph. For example:

I asked my little daughter to shut her eyes. She closed them slowly.

The repetition of "shut" will make the second sentence dull.

Antonym is a word opposite in meaning to the other word in the same language, e.g., close and open. The great use of an antonym is that it helps the writer present quantitative and qualitative contrasts or differences.

1. They were friends but different in appearance, one tall, the other short.
2. The two rival teams marched towards the centre of the playground, the Kanpur team in white and the Lucknow team in black.

The commonly used words and their synonyms and antonyms are given:

	Word	Synonym	Antonym
1.	abandon	forgo, forsake, give up	continue, persist
2.	abase	belittle, degrade	elevate, honour
3.	abate	alleviate, reduce, decrease	increase, strengthen
4.	abject	base, miserable	exalted
5.	able	capable, competent	incapable, incompetent
6.	abolish	eradicate, terminate, abrogate	continue, retain
7.	absence	lack, unavailability	existence, presence
8.	absolute	supreme, unrestricted	conditional, partial
9	abstemious	abstinent, restrained	gluttonous, intemperate
10.	abstruse	abstract, enigmatic	concrete, obvious
11.	absurd	silly, irrational, ludicrous	logical, rational, sensible
12.	abysmal	bottomless, deep, unfathomable	shallow
13.	accelerate	expedite, speed up	decelerate, slow down
14.	accentuate	intensify, strengthen	weaken, play down
15.	access	approach, ingress	egress, outlet
16.	accidental	adventitious, chance	intentional, deliberate
17.	accurate	exact	inaccurate, wrong
18.	acme	apex, zenith	nadir
19.	acquiescence	acceptance, compliance	disagreement
20.	acquire	achieve, attain	forfeit, forgo, relinquish
21.	acquisitive	avaricious, avid	generous
22.	acquittal	absolution, deliverance	conviction
23.	acrimony	acerbity, bitterness	friendliness
24.	acute	astute, intense	mild, faint, obtuse
25.	adamant	firm, obdurate	pliant, flexible
26.	adept	able, deft	inept
27.	admit	accept, grant	exclude, gainsay
28.	adorable	attractive, charming	hateful
29.	adroitness	adeptness, skillfulness	clumsiness, ineptitude
30.	adventitious	accidental, extrinsic	inherent, intrinsic
31.	adverse	contrary, antagonistic	advantageous, propitious
32.	affability	amiability, amicability	coolness reticence
33.	affectionate	cordial	cold
34.	affinity	alliance, similarity	dissimilarity
35.	affluence	abundance, plenty	poverty
36.	aggravate	heighten, increase	alleviate, mollify
37.	aggressive	forceful, invasive	submissive
38.	agile	active, quick	clumsy, sluggish
39.	aggrandise	enhance, magnify, glorify	belittle, debase
40.	akin	affiliated, allied	alien

41.	align	join, ally, associate	break, dissociate
42.	allay	alleviate, diminish	exacerbate, intensify
43.	allegiance	fidelity, loyalty	defiance, enmity
44.	alleviation	abatement, palliation	aggravation
45.	alliance	affiliation, combination	hostility, estrangement
46.	allure	attract, charm	repel
47.	aloofness	remoteness, alienation	concern, sociability
48.	amalgamate	combine, comingle	separate
49.	amateur	layman, novice	professional
50.	ambiguous	ambivalent, equivocal	clear, univocal
51.	ameliorate	better (v), improve	worsen, exacerbate
52.	amenable	docile, tractable	intractable
53.	amiable	affable	hostile
54.	amity	accord, cordiality	discord, hostility
55.	amnesty	forgiveness, mercy	cruelty, revenge
56.	amorphous	shapeless, inchoate	shapely, distinct
57.	anarchy	apostasy, pandemonium	order, control
58.	ancient	old	modern
59.	anemic	pallid, sickly	sanguine
60.	animosity	acrimony, antagonism	goodwill, sympathy
61.	annihilate	destroy, exterminate	create
62.	annoyance	irritation	pleasure
63.	annul	abolish, nullify, repeal	enact, restore
64.	anodyne	analgesic, palliative	irritant
65.	anomaly	aberration, inconsistency	normality, consistency
66.	anonymous	unknown	named, identifiable
67.	antedate	precede, predate	follow, post date
68.	anticipate	foresee	look back
69.	antipathy	aversion, abhorrence	sympathy, rapport
70.	antiquity	ancientness, oldness	modernity, novelty
71.	anxious	worried, concerned	composed
72.	apathetic	emotionless, impassive	concerned, responsive
73.	apocryphal	concocted, phony	true
74.	apogee	acme, apex	nadir, perigee
75.	apologetic	excusatory, penitent	defiant
76.	apostasy	heresy, perfidy	loyalty
77.	appeal	daunt, dismay	encourage, reassure
78.	apparent	obvious, clear, seeming	obscure, real
79.	appear	arrive, arise, emerge, seem	vanish, disappear
80.	appearance	advent, emergence, illusion	disappearance, reality
81.	appease	soften, allay, assuage	aggravate
82.	appetite	hunger	distaste
83.	appetizing	savoury, delicious, stimulating	disgusting
84.	applaud	acclaim, praise, extolled	censure, disparage

85.	appoint	assign, engage	dismiss, reject
86.	appreciate	admire, esteem, acclaim,	despise, neglect, depreciate
87.	apprehensive	increase	confident
88.	approximate	close, estimated	exact
89.	apt	accurate, proper	inapt
90.	arbitrary	disputable, illogical	reasoned, rational
91.	arcane	abstruse	commonplace
92.	ardent	amorous	dispassionate
93.	arduous	rigorous	easy
94.	argumentative	contentious	complaisant
95.	arid	barren, dry	fertile
96.	arouse	awaken	calm, lull
97.	arrest	capture, detain	release
98.	arrogance	haughtiness, imperiousness	humility
99.	artful	skilful	naive
100.	artificial	factitious	natural, genuine
101.	ascend	climb, rise	descend
102.	ascension	ascent	descent
103.	ashamed	abashed	defiant, shameless
104.	aspersion	abuse, animadversion	commendation, compliment
105.	assert	affirm, profess	deny
106.	asset	advantage, aid, resource	liability
107.	assimilation	absorption	rejection
108.	assured	certain	uncertain
109.	astringent	harsh	bland
110.	astuteness	acumen	stupidity
111.	asymmetrical	awry, irregular	Symmetrical, regular
112.	atrocity	cruelty	kindness
113.	attenuate	dilute	intensity
114.	attraction	charm	repulsion
115.	audacious	daring	timid
116.	augment	increase	decrease, lessen
117.	august	venerable, majestic	ignoble
118.	austere	plain	extravagant
119.	authentic	genuine, accurate	spurious, counterfeit
120.	authoritarian	despotic	liberal, democratic
121.	autocrat	absolutist, dictator	democrat
122.	autonomous	self-governing	-
123.	avant-garde	innovatory, experimental	conservative, conventional
124.	average	medium	extreme
125.	averse	opposed	sympathetic
126.	aversion	abhorrence	liking, sympathy
127.	avert	avoid, parry	face
128.	avidity	acquisitiveness	indifference

129.	avoid	parry, ward off	face
130.	avoidable	avertable	inevitable
131.	awaken	arouse, activate	lull, quench
132.	awareness	sentience	insensitivity
133.	awe	admiration, wonder	contempt
134.	awkward	clumsy, cumbersome	elegant
135.	awry	asymmetrical	straight, symmetrical
136.	axiom	adage, aphorism	-
137.	back	hind, posterior	front
138.	baffle	puzzle	enlighten, clarify
139.	banal	hackneyed	original
140.	baneful	deadly, venomous	beneficent
141.	banish	ban, expel	welcome, recall
142.	bankrupt	insolvent, beggared	solvent, wealthy
143.	barbarian	savage, vandal	civilized, humane
144.	barren	arid, unproductive	fertile, productive
145.	bashful	shy, hesitant	confident
146.	bawdy	lustful	chaste
147.	beatific	angelic	devilish
148.	bedraggled	dirty	tidy
149.	befitting	appropriate, becoming	unbecoming, derogatory
150.	belated	delayed	timely
151.	belligerent	aggressive beatitude,	peaceable
152.	benediction	blessing	anathema, curse
153.	benefaction	benevolence	malevolence
154.	beneficial	benevolent, benign	mean, harmful
155.	berserk	amok, crazy	calm, sane
156.	betrayal	deception, treachery	loyalty
157.	bewildered	baffled, mystified	co[illegible]osed
158.	bewitched	charmed	disenchanted
159.	bicker	dispute	agree
160.	bigamy	diandry	monogamy
161.	bigot	dogmatist	liberal
162.	biased	prejudiced	fair, impartial
163.	bilingual	diglot	monolingual
164.	bizarre	strange, abnormal	normal
165.	blanch	bleach	blush, colour
166.	blasphemous	impious, irreligious	reverent
167.	blemish	spot, flow	spotless
168.	blithe	buoyant	morose
169.	boast	brag	deprecate
170.	bogus	fake	genuine
171.	boisterous	exuberant	quiet, restrained
172.	bombastic	verbose	laconic

173.	bookish	erudite	lowbrow
174.	boost	augment	hinder
175.	bountiful	abundant	meager
176.	brazen	flagrant, impudent	shamefaced, shy
177.	brevity	briefness	longevity
178.	bribable	buyable	incorruptible
179.	bright	luminous	dull
180.	brisk	active, agile	sluggish
181.	broad	wide	narrow
182.	brotherly	affectionate	heartless, callous
183.	brusque	impolite, gruff	courteous
184.	brutal	cruel, beastly	humane, kindly
185.	bucolic	rural	urban
186.	burnish	brighten, glaze	tarnish
187.	bygone	antiquated	recent
188.	cacophonous	discordant	harmonious
189.	cajolery	blandishment	bullying
190.	calamitous	devastating	fortunate
191.	calamity	devastation, catastrophe	blessing, godsend
192.	caliber	capacity, ability	weakness
193.	calumny	derogation	admiration
194.	camouflage	cover	reveal
195.	cantankerous	bad-tempered, peevish	good-natured, pleasant
196.	capacious	spacious	cramped
197.	capricious	inconstant	steady
198.	captious	critical, carping	amiable
199.	captivate	allure, enthrall	repel
200.	captive	prisoner	free
201.	captivity	[illegible]	freedom
202.	caricature	distortion	normal
203.	carnal	physical, earthly	spiritual
204.	cascade	cataract, falls	trickle
205.	casual	accidental, incidental	deliberate, planned
206.	catastrophe	calamity, denouement	success, triumph
207.	catchy	attractive	boring, dull
208.	categorical	clear, explicit	qualified, vague, tentative
209.	cautious	alert, vigilant	heedless, imprudent
210.	celebrated	acclaimed, eminent	obscure, unknown
211.	celebrity	dignitary, luminary	nobody, obscurity
212.	celestial	heavenly, astral	earthly, mundane
213.	censure	castigate, denounce	approve, praise
214.	censorious	captious	approving, laudatory
215.	central	focal, main	peripheral
216.	centrifugal	diffusive	centripetal

217.	ceremonial	formal	informal
218.	ceremonious	civil, courteous	informal
219.	certain	sure, confident	doubtful, hesitant
220.	certainly	assurance, certitude	doubt, hesitation
221.	cessation	end, abeyance	commencement
222.	chagrin	annoyance, discomfiture	delight, pleasure
223.	chance	accident, haphazard	certainty
224.	change	alter, vary	fix
225.	chaotic	disordered	organized
226.	charitable	benevolent, philanthropic	malignant
227.	charity	benevolence	malevolence
228.	chaste	pure, austere	lewd
229.	cheeky	insolent, saucy	respectful, polite
230.	cheer	applaud, clap	jeer
231.	cheerful	enthusiastic	sad
232.	chimeric	hallucinatory	real
233.	chivalrous	heroic, brave, gallant, valiant	cowardly
234.	chronic	deep-sated, persistent	temporary
235.	churlish	harsh, rude	polite
236.	circumspect	attentive, cautious	unwary, unguarded
237.	civilization	acculturation, advancement	barbarity
238.	clairvoyant	diviner, intuitive, soothsayer	-
239.	clamorous	noisy	silent
240.	classic	abiding, standard	second-rate
241.	classy	elegant, exquisite, stylish	dowdy, plain
242.	clean	pure, tidy	dirty, polluted
243.	clear (v)	clean, absolve,	defile, block
243B.	clear (adj)	clean, pellucid	dirty, vague
244.	cleft (n)	breach, chasm, gap, crack	-
244B.	cleft (adj)	divided, torn	solid
245.	clemency	compassion, kindness	harshness, ruthlessness
246.	close	adjacent	far
247.	clumsy	awkward, inept	graceful
248.	coarse	tough, rude	fine, polite
249.	cocksure	arrogant, overconfident	modest
250.	cognizance	acknowledgement	unawareness
251.	cohere	bind, unite	separate
252.	collapse (n)	breakdown,	revival
252B.	collapse (v)	fall, faint	revive
253.	colloquial'	conversational	formal
254.	colossal	enormous	tiny
255.	combative	aggressive	peaceful
256.	comic	amusing, humorous	serious, tragic
257.	commence	begin, start	cease, finish

258.	commend	acclaim	criticize
259.	commendable	admirable	blameworthy
260.	common	average, ordinary	noteworthy
261.	communication	loquacious, voluble	reticent
262.	compassion	clemency, kindness	indifference
263.	compatible	accordant, congenial	incompatible
264.	compendious	abbreviated, abridged	enlarged
265.	complacent	self-assured	diffident
266.	compliant	acquiescent	intractable, disobedient
267.	complicate	entangle	simplify
268.	complicity	collusion	innocence
269.	composed	calm	agitated
270.	compress	condense	expand
271.	compulsory	binding	optional
272.	conceal	hide	reveal
273.	concentrate	condense	disperse
274.	conciliatory	placatory	antagonistic
275.	concord	accord	discord
276.	condone	allow, forgive	censure, disallow
277.	conducive	beneficial	adverse
278.	confess	acknowledge, disclose	deny, conceal
279.	confidential	secret	common, public
280.	confirm	approve	reject
281.	confuse	baffle	clarify
282.	conglomerate	accumulate	separate
283.	conservatism	orthodoxy	radicalism
284.	conspicuous	apparent	inconspicuous, insignificant
285.	constant	changeless	variable
286.	construct	build	demolish
287.	consummate	perfect	imperfect
288.	continuous	unbroken	sporadic, intermittent
289.	contrast	difference	similarity
290.	converge	combine	diverge
291.	copious	plentiful, abundant	scarce
292.	corporal	bodily	spiritual
293.	corpulence	fatness	thinness
294.	correspondence	agreement	divergence
295.	counterfeit	fake	genuine
296.	crass	coarse	refined, sensitive
297.	credibility	integrity, plausibility	unreliability, implausibility
298.	crestfallen	disappointed	elated
299.	cryptic	abstruse	clear, straight, forward
300.	culpable	blameworthy	innocent
301.	cumbersome	burdensome, cumbrous	convenient, manageable

302.	curious	inquisitive	indifferent
303.	curtail	shorten	extend
304.	customary	conventional	unusual
305.	cynical	contemptuous	genial
306.	dainty	delicious	tasteless
307.	dampen	moisten	dry
308.	dappled	brindled, freckled, pied	plain
309.	darken	blacken, eclipse	lighten, illumine
310.	dastardly	cowardly, pusillanimous	heroic, noble
311.	dauntless	brave, bold	discouraged
312.	dawn	daybreak, day-peep	dusk, sunset
313.	daybreak	sunrise	sundown, sunset
314.	dazzling	brilliant	dim
315.	deaden	benumb	enliven
316.	deadly	fatal	harmless
317.	debase	degrade	elevate
318.	debatable	arguable	certain
319.	debate	argue	agree
320.	debauch (v)	corrupt	purge, purify
321.	debauched (adj)	corrupt	virtuous
322.	debilitating (adj)	enfeebling	strengthening
323.	decadent	delaine	rise
324.	delegant	debased	moral
325.	deceive	cheat, beguile	enlighten
326.	deception	guide	openness
327.	decipher	construe	encode
328.	decisive	final, absolute	insignificant, indecisive
329.	decorative	adorning, ornamental	plain
330.	decrease	abate	increase
331.	decrepit	aged, crippled	youthful
332.	decry	belittle, blame	praise
333.	dedication	devotion	apathy
334.	deep	profound	shallow
335.	deface	disfigure	repair
336.	defame	asperse	praise
337.	defeat (n)	debacle	triumph, win
338.	defeated (adj)	beaten	triumphant
339.	defective	faulty, flawed	normal
340.	defend	guard	attack
341.	defensive	apologetic	offensive
342.	defer	adjourn	continue
343.	defer	accede, yield	resist
344.	deference	regard, respect	arrogance
345.	defiance	challenge, disobedience	acquiescence

346.	defiant	aggressive, audacious	acquirement, supmissive
347.	defray	clear, meet, repay	incur
348.	defunct	dead, extinct, inoperative	alive, operative
349.	deft	able, adept	clumsy
350.	degenerate (adj)	corrupt	virtuous, upright
351.	degrade	abase	improve
352.	dejected	depressed	happy
353.	delay	temporize	expedite
354.	deliberate	calculated, intentional, planed	unintentional
355.	delicious	dainty	unpleasant, tasteless
356.	delinquent	miscreant	blameless
357.	delirious	hysterical, frenzied	sane
358.	demand	ask	supply
359.	demolish	destroy	establish
360.	demote	relegate	promote
361.	demure	modest	forward, affirmation
362.	denial	negation	approval
363.	douse	thick	sparse
364.	denude	strip, defoliate	cover
365.	deny	negate	admit
366.	dependence	reliance	independence
367.	deposit	place	withdraw
368.	depravity	baseness	uprightness
369.	depreciate	devaluate, devalue	appreciate
370.	deprived	bereft	fortunate
371.	dereliction	neglect	devotion
372.	descent	comedown	ascent
373.	design	arrangement, plan, pattern	haphazard (adj)
374.	repair	hopelessness	hope
375.	desperate	despondent	confident
376.	desperado	bandit, brigand	-
377.	despot	tyrant	democrat
378.	destination	goal	-
379.	destitute	insolvent, impoverished	prosperous
380.	desultory	aimless	methodical
381.	detach	disconnect	attach
382.	detention	custody	release
383.	deteriorate	decline	improve
384.	determination	restiveness	irresolution
385.	deterrent	restraint	incentive
386.	detraction	aspersion	praise
387.	detrimental	harmful	conducive, advantageous
388.	development	growth	retardation
389.	deviant	aberrant	normal

390.	dexterity	ability	ineptitude
391.	diatribe	abuse	encomium praise
392.	difference	unlikeness	similarity
393.	difficult	abstruse, hard	easy
394.	diffident	dispersed	concentrated
395.	dignify	exalt, honour	degrade
396.	dilute	diffuse	concentrate, increase
397.	diminish	reduce	enhance
398.	directness	straight forwardness	crookedness
399.	dismal	bleak	bright
400.	dismantle	demolish	assemble
401.	disposal	relinquishment	provision
402.	dissolve	disintegrate, diffuse	-
403.	distinguish	differentiate	-
404.	distinguished	eminent	ordinary
405.	distress	trouble, pain	comfort, ease
406.	distribute	dispense	collect
407.	disturbance	agitation, interruption	peace, calmness
408.	docile	amenable, submissive	truculent
409.	dodge	avoid, duck	face
410.	dolorous	miserable, anguished	happy
411.	domestic	house-trained	wild
412.	dominate	dictate, control	accommodate
413.	domineering	arrogant	meek
414.	doomed	catastrophe, judgment day, accursed	saved
415.	dither	hesitate	decide
416.	divergent	different, diverse	convergent, identical
417.	divine	holy, heavenly	satanic
418.	divorce	annulment, break	unify
419.	doctrinaire	dogmatic, rigid	flexible
420.	dogged	determined	irresolute
421.	dreamy	unreal	realistic
422.	dreary	bleak	bright
423.	dubious	doubtful	certain
424.	duplicity	guile	honesty
425.	durable	lasting	fragile
426.	dwindle	abate, diminish	increase
427.	dynamic	active, driving	inactive, lethargic
428.	eager	agog, desirous,	apathetic
429.	earnest	ardent, serious	flippant
430.	ebb (v)	abate, decrease	increase
430B.	ebb (n)	low tide	flow
431.	ebullient	buoyant	dull, lifeless
432.	eccentric	idiosyncratic	sane

433.	éclat	acclamation	disapproval
434.	economic	budgetary	expensive
435.	edible	eatable	inedible
436.	effective	efficacious, powerful	useless
437.	effeminate	delicate, womanly	manly
438.	efflorescent	animated, ebullient	apathetic
439.	effusive	demonstrative	quiet, restrained
440.	egregious	arrant, flagrant	slight
441.	elaborate	amplify	simplify
442.	elastic	adjustable, stretchy	rigid
443.	elation	exaltation	depression
444.	elementary	basic, fundamental	advanced
445.	eligible	qualified	ineligible
446.	eliminate	annihilate, remove	accept
447.	eloquent	articulate, liberate	tongue-tied
448.	emancipate	liberate, free	enslave
449.	emerge	appear, arise	disappear, fade
450.	emigration	departure, migration	immigration
451.	emotional	poignant	calm, odd
452.	empty	unfilled	full, replete
453.	enclosed	bound	open
454.	encourage	animate, improve	discourage
455.	encumbrance	burden	aid
456.	endure	abide	cease, end
457.	energetic	active, spirited	idle, sluggish
458.	enervate	debilitate	activate
459.	enfeeble	weaken	strengthen
460.	engage	appoint	discharge
461.	engrossed	absorbed	bored
462.	enhance	augment	minimize
463.	enigmatic	puzzling	straight
464.	enlighten	illuminate	confuse
465.	enormous	gigantic	small, tiny
466.	enterprise	venture	inertia
467.	enterprising	venturesome	lethargic
468.	entertaining	amusing	boring
469.	enthusiasm	ardour	apathy
470.	entire	whole	partial
471.	entrance	admission, admittance	exit, departure
472.	entrepreneur	industrialist	employee
473.	entwine	interlace, enlarge	unravel
474.	enumerate	calculate, count	-
475.	enunciate	declare, pronounce	-
476.	environment	atmosphere	-

477.	envisage	visualize	-
478.	epic	gluttonous	abstemious
479.	epigrammatic	aphoristic	lengthy
480.	episode	incident, adventure	-
481.	episodic	anecdotal	-
482.	epitomize	condense	elaborate, expand
483.	equanimity	aplomb, composure	alarm, anxiety
484.	equipoise	balance	imbalance
485.	equivalence	agreement	dissimilarity
486.	eradicable	erasable, removable	permanent
487.	erudite	scholarly, cultivated	vulgar, ignorant
488.	escapable	academic, recondite	unlettered
489.	esoteric	avertable	inevitable
490.	especial	abstruse, occult	familiar, popular
491.	estrange	exclusive	common
492.	eternal	alienate	ally, unite
493.	eulogize	abiding, deathless	ephemeral
494.	euphony	extol	deprecate
495.	euphoria	harmony	cacophony
496.	evade	bliss, elation	depression
497.	evanescent	avert, brief, ephemeral	face
498.	even	balanced	odd
499.	evidence	proof	-
500.	evident	clear, obvious,	uncertain
501.	evince	display	conceal
502.	evoke	call	quell
503.	exaggerate	amplify, hyperbolize	belittle, understate
504.	exactly	absolutely, accurately	inaccurately
505.	excellence	distinction, eminence	inferiority
506.	exceptional	extraordinary	mediocre
507.	excess	abundance, surplus	death
508.	excruciating	acute	mild
509.	excuse	pardon	punish
510.	exemplary	admirable, model	imperfect
511.	exemption	absolution, exoneration	liability
512.	exhale	eject, breathe	inhale
513.	exhausted	tired, expended, finished	conserved
514.	exhaustive	thorough	incomplete
515.	exhort	advise, admonish	-
516.	exhume	unearth	bury
517.	exigency	acuteness, urgency	idleness
518.	exonerate	acquit, absolve	inordinate
519.	expansion	amplification	contraction
520.	expedience	advantage	useless

521.	expedite	accelerate	delay
522.	expensive	costly	cheap
523.	expire	cease, close	begin
524.	explicate	clarify	confuse
525.	extricate	liberate, disentangle	involve
526.	extrinsic	alien, external	intrinsic
527.	extrovert, extrovert	amiable	introvert
528.	fabricate	assemble	-
529.	fabrication	concoction	truth
530.	fabulous	amazing, unreal, mythical	moderate, real
531.	fact	actuality	fiction
532.	factual	actual	fictitious
533.	faction	group	-
534.	factious	conflict	agreement, peace
535.	factious	conflicting, seditious	calm, cooperative
536.	fade	artificial, affected	genuine
537.	faded	wane, disappear	flourish
538.	failure	dim	bright
539.	fake	fiasco, unsuccessful	success
540.	false	counterfeit	genuine
541.	falter	hesitate	true
542.	famished	starved	sated
543.	fanaticism	devotion	-
544.	fantastic	absurd, wonderful	ordinary, plain
545.	farcical	comic	sensible
546.	fascinate	charm	bore, repulse
547.	fastidious	choosy, fussy	undemanding
548.	feigned	affected, simulated	genuine, sincere
549.	ferment	agitate	calm
550.	ferocious	barbaric, fierce	gentle, mild
551.	fester	chafe, decay	dissipate, heal
552.	fetid	foul	fragrant
553.	fiasco	debacle, failure	successful
554.	fidelity	accuracy, loyalty	inaccuracy, betrayal
555.	fillip	boost	damper
556.	filth	dirt, carrion	cleanliness, purity
557.	firmness	constancy	infirmity, hesitancy
558.	fixed	arranged	alterable
559.	flamboyance	brilliance	restraint, modesty
560.	flash	blaze	-
561.	flattery	adulation, sycophancy	criticism
562.	flaw	blemish	-
563.	flawless	perfect	flawed
564.	flexible	adaptable	rigid

565.	flimsy	thin	sturdy
566.	flippant	frivolous	earnest
567.	flourish	prosper	wane
568.	fluctuate	alter	stabilize
569.	fluent	articulate	tongue-tied
570.	follow	accompany	precede
571.	forbearance	abstinence, tolerance	intolerance
572.	forcible	active, aggressive	feeble
573.	foreground	forefront	background
574.	forerunner	predecessor	aftermath
575.	formidable	appalling	genial
576.	fortitude	brace, strengthen	weaken
577.	fortuitous	accidental	cowardice, weakness
578.	fragmentary	broken	intentional
579.	frank	candid	complete
580.	frivolous	childish	evasive
581.	frustrate	baffle	serious
582.	flummox	condemnation	fulfill
583.	furnish	decorate, provide	praise
584.	fusion	fruitless	fruitful
585.	futile	profit, achieve	lose
586.	gain	chivalrous	cowardly
587.	gallant	big	small
588.	gargantuan	beautify, embellish	divest
589.	garnish	lean	plump
590.	gaunt	accumulate, collect	scatter
591.	gather	awkward	graceful
592.	gawky	ancestry, lineage	-
593.	genealogy	general	specific
594.	generic	bountiful	mean, selfish
595.	generous	allied	irrelevant
596.	germane	bud, develop	-
597.	germinate	babble, balderdash	sensible, intelligible
598.	gibberish	blaze	dim
599.	glare	darkness	brightness
600.	gloom	worldwide	parochial, local
601.	global	adore	condemn
602.	glorify	fanciful	dull, plain
603.	gorgeous	airy	opaque, thick
604.	gossamer	successive, step-by-step	sudden
605.	gradual	bombastic, affected	plain, simple
606.	grandiloquent	wrestle	modest, unpretentious
607.	grandiose, grapple	catch, comprehend	evade
608.	grasp	appease	miss, frustrate

609.	gratify	affable, sociable	unsociable
610.	gregarious	allow	refuse
611.	grant	assumed, baseless	justified, reasonable
612.	gratuitous	seriousness, sobriety	lightness, gaiety
613.	gravity	adamant, doom-laden	benign, congenial
614.	grim	bad-tempered, cantankerous	contented
615.	grouchy	absurd, misshapen	elegant
616.	grotesque	development, expansion	stagnation, stoppage
617.	growth	artfulness, duplicity	artlessness, honesty
618.	guile	credulous	skeptical, astute
619.	gullible	delight	apathy
620.	gusto	courage	cowardice
621.	guts	accustomed	occasional
622.	habitual	clichéd, stereotyped	new, arresting
623.	hackneyed	careworn	hale, fresh
624.	haggard	balmy, prosperous, golden	stormy
625.	halcyon	barrier, impairment	-
626.	handicap, handsome	elegant, personable	-
627.	harass	annoy, disturb	assist
628.	hard	tough, arduous	soft, easy
629.	harmonize	accord	clash
630.	harmony	unity, accord	discord
631.	harrow	agonize, harass	assuage, hearten
632.	hassle	altercation	assist
633.	hasten	accelerate	dawdle
634.	haughty	arrogant	humble
635.	hazard	risk	safety
636.	hazy	vague, indistinct	clear, definite
637.	hearsay	gossip, rumour	fact
638.	heathen	infidel	believer
639.	hectic	intense, animated	leisurely
640.	hedonism	epicureanism	asceticism
641.	heresy	apostasy	orthodoxy
642.	heritage,	bequest, inheritance	-
643.	heterogeneous	assorted	homogeneous
644.	hiatus	aperture, breach	continuity
645.	hindrance	obstruction, bar	aid, assistance
646.	historic	momentous	insignificant
647.	histrionic	affected, theatrical	-
648.	histrionics	dramatics	-
649.	homage	tribute	-
650.	holocaust	annihilation	-
651.	homogeneity	uniformity	difference

652.	horizon	skyline	zenith
653.	horrid	abominable	agreeable
654.	hospitality	cordiality	hostility
655.	hotchpotch	jumble	order
656.	huddle	clump	disperse
657.	huffy	angry, cross	cheerful
658.	humane	benevolent	barbaric
659.	humidity	clamminess, dampness	dryness
660.	humiliate	abase	triumph
661.	humour (v)	gratify	thwart
662.	hurry	haste, accelerate	delay
663.	hybrid	cross, breed	pure
664.	hyperbole	enlargement, over statement	understatement
665.	hypocrisy	cant, deceit	humility, sincerity
666.	hypothesis	assumption, postulate	-
667.	hypothetical	postulated	actual, real
668.	hysterical	berserk, mad	calm, composed
669.	iconoclasm	criticism, demythologization	credulity, trust fullness
670.	iconoclast	image-breaker, critic	believer, devotee
671.	idealist	perfectionist, utopian	pragmatist, realistic
672.	idealize	apotheosize, deify	caricature
673.	identify	ascertain, recognize	-
674.	idiosyncrasy	eccentricity, oddity	generality
675.	idolatry	adoration	vilification
676.	idolize	adore	vilify
677.	idyllic	pastoral	prosaic
678.	ignite	burn, combust	quench
679.	ignoble	abject, base	noble, honourable
680.	ignominy	contempt, discredit	honourable
681.	ignorance	benightedness	knowledge
682.	illness	ailment	health
683.	illuminate	clarify	darken
684.	illusion	deception	reality
685.	illustrate	adorn, clarify	blur, confuse
686.	illustrious	brilliant, celebrated	shameful
687.	imaginary	assumed, fancied	real
688.	imagine	assume, visualize	realize, experience
689.	imbalance	bias, inequity	parity
690.	imbecile	fool, fatuous	intelligent, sensible
691.	imbibe	absorb	reject
692.	imbroglio	confusion	order
693.	imitate	copy	-
694.	imitation	copy	genuine
695.	immaculate	flawless, pure	contaminated, spoiled

696.	immediate	close, nearest	distant
697.	immense	great	insignificant
698.	imminent	approaching	far-off, remote
699.	immortal	abiding, deathless	mortal
700.	immune	invulnerable	susceptible
701.	impact	impression	-
702.	impair	blunt, damage	enhance
703.	impasse	deadlock	-
704.	impeach	impugn	-
705.	impeccable	blameless	flawed
706.	impediment	hindrance	aid
707.	imperative	compulsory	optional
708.	imperious	arrogant	humble
709.	impetus	stimulus	hindrance
710.	implicate	entangle	exonerate
711.	imposing	commanding	modest
712.	impostor	charlatan	-
713.	impoverish	pauperize	enrich
714.	imprison	jail	release
715.	impudence	audacity	politeness
716.	impulsive	impetuous	restrained
717.	impurity	pollution	pure
718.	inscrutable	enigmatic	comprehensible
719.	insidious	crafty, artful	-
720.	insinuation	suggestion	-
721.	inspire	activate	dull
722.	instant	immediate	distant
723.	instigate	actuate, incite	pacify
724.	insubordination	defiance	obedience
725.	intend	aim	-
726.	intoxicate	inebriate	sober
727.	intrusion	incursion	withdraw
728.	intuitive	instinctive	reasoned
729.	insular	blinkered,	cosmopolitan
730.	insularity	isolation	openness
731.	intelligible	comprehensible, decipherable	enigmatic
732.	intermediate	halfway	extreme
733.	interpret	explain	-
734.	intervene	interfere, intercede	-
735.	intimate (n)	familiar, friend	stranger
736.	intimate (adj)	friendly, close	strange
737.	intimate (v)	communicate	-
738.	intimidation	threats, menaces	persuasion
739.	intractability	stubbornness	amenability

740.	introduction	acquaintance, initiation	withdrawal
741.	intrinsic	basic, inherent	extrinsic
742.	inundate	overflow	recede
743.	invest	authorize	divert, disinvest
744.	inveterate	chronic	impermanent
745.	invidious	offensive, hateful	desirable
746.	invincible	impregnable	beatable
747.	involuntary	automatic, instinctive	voluntary
748.	irascible	petulant	placid
749.	irksome	annoying, brighten	pleasing
750.	irritate	annoy	gratify, please
751.	isolate	separate	assimilate
752.	issue	problem, topic	-
753.	itinerary	plan	-
754.	jaded	fatigued	refreshed
755.	jarring	discordant	harmonious
756.	jaundiced	biased	neutral
757.	jeopardize	endanger	protect
758.	jovial	affable	morose, sad
759.	jubilant	elated	depressed
760.	judicious	discreet, sagacious	partial, injudicious
761.	jumble	confuse	order
762.	junior	inferior, younger	superior
763.	jurisdiction	area	-
764.	juvenile	adolescent	adult
765.	juxtaposition	adjacency, contact	separation, dissociation
766.	keen	interested	apathetic
767.	kindle	lighten, activate	thwart, dampen
768.	kudos	applause	deprecation
769.	labyrinth	maze	-
770.	lackadaisical	indolent, spiritless	active
771.	lackluster	spiritless, dull	brilliant
772.	laconic	pithy, terse	verbose, garrulous
773.	laden	burdened, loaded	empty
774.	lambaste	beat, berate	praise
775.	lambent	licking, flickering, luminous	dull
776.	lament	bewail, grieve	rejoice
777.	languish	pine, wither	flourish
778.	lassitude	apathy, languor	vigour
779.	latent	concealed	active
780.	laud	acclaim	blame
781.	lavish	prodigal	economical
782.	legendary	heroic	common
783.	legible	decipherable, readable	illegible

784.	legitimate	authentic, lawful, legal	illegitimate
785.	lenient	clement, soft	severe
786.	lethargy	sluggishness	liveliness
787.	liability	accountability, burden	asset
788.	liberal	generous, bountiful	conservative
789.	linger	abide, remain	leave, rush
790.	livid	angry	calm
791.	loathe	abhor	like
792.	loose	baggy, free	compact, tight
793.	loquacious	talkative, voluble	taciturn, reticent
794.	lousy	despicable	superb
795.	lush	abundant, flourishing	sparse
796.	lustrous	bright	dull
797.	luxuriant	abundant	barren
798.	luxurious	sumptuous, deluxe	ascetic, austere
799.	Machiavellian	amoral, unscrupulous, wily	-
800.	magnanimity	bountifulness	meanness
801.	magnate	aristocrat, mogul	-
802.	magnificent	august, elegant	humble
803.	magnify	enlarge	belittle
804.	magniloquence	grandiloquence	simplicity
805.	magnum opus	masterpiece	-
806.	main stream	central	peripheral
807.	major	main, bigger	minor
808.	maladroit	awkward	comfortable
809.	malaise	anguish	happiness
810.	malapropos	inappropriate	appropriate
811.	malapropism	misapplication	-
812.	malcontent	troublemaker	-
813.	malediction	anathema	blessing
814.	malefactor	convict, criminal	-
815.	maleficent	baleful, harmful	beneficent, harmless
816.	malice	animosity	kindness
817.	malignant	cancerous, inimical	benignant
818.	malleable	adaptable, compliant	intractable
819.	malnutrition	undernourishment	nourishment
820.	make-believe	imagined	real
821.	malinger	dodge	toil
822.	malleable	adaptable	intractable
823.	mammoth	huge	small
824.	manacle	shackle	unshackle
825.	manage	accomplish	fail
826.	mandate	command	-
827.	mandatory	binding, compulsory	optional

828.	mangy	dirty	clean
829.	mania	obsession	-
830.	manifest	clear, evident	hidden
831.	manifesto	declaration	-
832.	manipulate	manoeuvre	simplify
833.	manufacture	assemble, build	-
834.	manuscript	holograph, text	-
835.	marginal	bordering, peripheral	central
836.	martial	combative,	pacific
837.	marvellous	wonderful	ordinary
838.	masculine	manlike	feminine
839.	massive	big; enormous	small
840.	match	accord	clash
841.	material	worldly	ethereal
842.	matrimony	marriage	divorce
843.	mature	adult	adolescent
844.	maximum	utmost	minimum
845.	meager	paltry, little	substantial
846.	meandering	serpentine, circuitous	straight
847.	measure (n)	amount	-
848.	measure (v)	weigh	-
849.	meddle	interfere	-
850.	mediocre	average	extraordinary, outstanding
851.	melancholy	dejected	cheerful
852.	mellow	ripe	miniature, unripe
853.	memorial	cairn, monument	-
854.	morale	confidence, spirit	-
855.	morals	ethics, ethos	-
856.	moratorium	postponement	go-ahead
857.	moribund	standstill	flourishing
858.	morose	cheerless	cheerful, gay
859.	mortgage	pawn, pledge	-
860.	mortify	abase	jubilate
861.	motivate	stimulate	deter
862.	muddle	confuse	clarify
863.	muffle	choke	amplify
864.	multifarious	diverse, manifold	-
865.	multitude	crowd	handful
866.	mysterious	arcane	comprehensible
867.	mythical	fabled	actual, historical
868.	naive	artless, simple	sophisticated
869.	narcissistic	self-loving	-
870.	nascent	budding, growing	dying
871.	nasty	dirty	clean

872.	nauseating	repulsive	agreeable
873.	nebulous	shapeless, amorphous	clear
874.	nefarious	abominable	exemplary
875.	neglect	ignore	cherish
876.	nemesis	destiny	-
877.	nervous	shaky	confident
878.	neurotic	abnormal	nominal
879.	neutral	impartial	biased
880.	niggardly	avaricious	bountiful
881.	nimble	agile	clumsy
882.	nominal	formal	actual
883.	non-chalant	impassive, detached	anxious
884.	nostalgia	homesickness	-
885.	notion	concept, idea	-
886.	nourish	cherish, nurture	-
887.	nourishing	nutritive, health giving	detrimental
888.	novelty	newness	familiarity
889.	novice	amateur, inexperience	professional, experienced
890.	noxious	baneful, foul	innocuous
891.	nuance	degree, gradation	-
892.	nucleus	core	periphery
893.	nugatory	futile	important
894.	null	abrogate, invalidate	validate
895.	numbness	insensitivity	sensitivity
896.	nuptial	bridal, espousal	-
897.	nutrition	nourishment, nutriment	-
898.	nutritious	nourishing, wholesome	bad, unwholesome
899.	oath	avowal, swearing	-
900.	obdurate	stubborn, obstinate	tender, submissive
901.	obesity	corpulence	thinness
902.	objectionable	abhorrent	acceptable
903.	obligation	accountability	discretion
904.	obligatory	binding	optional
905.	oblivion	forgetfulness	consciousness
906.	obscene	indecent	decent
907.	obsequious	sycophantic	assertive
908.	observance	adherence	-
909.	observant	alert	careless
910.	obsessed	haunted, preoccupied	detached
911.	obsolete	extinct, anachronistic	current
912.	obstacle	hindrance, bar	advantage
913.	obstinacy	doggedness, obduracy	flexibility
914.	obstruct	bar, block, hinder	allow, help
915.	obtain	achieve, attain	lose

916.	obvious	apparent	obscure
917.	occasional	casual	frequent
918.	occult	esoteric	-
919.	oddment	fragment	-
920.	odious	abhorrent	pleasant
921.	odour	aroma, fragrance	-
922.	offend	affront	please
923.	offhand	abrupt	planned, calculated
924.	official	authentic, authorized	unofficial
925.	officious	dictatorial	-
926.	offish	aloof, cool	sociable, friendly
927.	offspring	child	parents
928.	ominous	sinister, portentous	auspicious
929.	omit	drop	add
930.	omnipotent	all-powerful, almighty	powerless
931.	omnipresent	ubiquitous	-
932.	omniscient	all-knowing	-
933.	opaque	thick	transparent
934.	opinionated	biased	open-minded, disinterested
935.	opponent	adversary	ally, proponent
936.	optimum	best, highest	worst
937.	optimism	hopefulness	pessimism
938.	optimistic	hopeful	pessimistic
939.	opulence	abundance, affluence	penury
940.	opus	brainchild, composition	-
941.	oracle	prophecy	-
942.	oral	verbal, spoken	written
943.	orator	speaker, declaimer	-
944.	ordeal	suffering	-
945	orient	enlighten	-
946.	orientation	introduction	-
947.	origin	ancestry, source	end
948.	original	first, genuine, prototypical	duplicate
949.	originality (n)	singularity	-
950.	ornament (n)	adornment	-
951.	ornament (v)	adorn, decorate	
952.	oscillate	swing	fix
953.	ostensible	apparent	real
954.	ostentatious	aggressive	modest
955.	ostracize	exclude	accept
956.	oust	depose, evict	ensconce, install
957.	outcast	castaway, exile	favorite, idol
958.	outlandish	alien, strange	familiar, ordinary
959.	outstanding	eminent	ordinary

960.	oversight	carelessness, inadvertence	-
961.	overthrow	depose	install
962.	overwhelming	overpowering	resistible
963.	pacific	appeasing, peace-loving	aggressive
964.	pacify	appease	anger
965.	pagan	heathen	unbeliever
966.	pageant	display	-
967.	palatable	acceptable, tasteful	unacceptable, tasteless
968.	palatial	grand, magnificent	cramped
969.	palliate	abate, soothe	irritate
970.	palmy	flourishing	difficult, stormy
971.	pandemonium	bedlam, disorder	calm
972.	palpable	clear	elusive
973.	palpitate	beat	-
974.	panic	alarm	assurance
975.	panorama	scene	-
976.	panoramic	scenic, extensive	limited
977.	paradigm	pattern	-
978	paragon	epitome	-
979.	paramount	cardinal, first	inferior, last
980.	parasite	bloodsucker	independent
981.	pardon	excuse, forgive	punish
982.	parochial	provincial, narrow-minded	cosmopolitan
983.	paroxysm	attack, outbreak, convulsion	-
984.	parsimony	frugally	liberality
985.	partiality	bias	justice, neutrality
986.	partisan (n)	adherent, supporter	opponent
987.	partisan (adj)	biased	neutral
988.	passion	emotion	coolness
989.	passionate	amorous, emotional	frigid
990.	pastoral	agrarian, idyllic	urban
991.	pasty	pale	healthy
992.	pathetic	deplorable, pitiable	admirable, cheerful
993.	patronage	aegis, foster	-
994.	pauper	bankrupt	solvent
995.	peculiar	abnormal, unusual	normal
996.	peculiar	mercenary, commercial	-
997.	pedestrian (n)	walker	-
998.	pedestrian (adj)	commonplace, mediocre	brilliant
999.	pedigree	ancestry, breed	-
1000.	peevish	acrimonious	good-tempered
1001.	pejorative	belittling	complimentary
1002.	penalize	punish	reward
1003.	penchant	inclination	dislike

1004.	penetrate	enter, pierce	-
1005.	penetrating	acute	gentle, soft
1006.	perceive	apprehend	-
1007.	perceptible	noticeable	imperceptible
1008.	percolate	drain, drip	-
1009.	perennial	eternal	ephemeral
1010.	perilous	dangerous	safe
1011.	persecute	afflict, harass	accommodate
1012.	persevere	adhere	give up
1013.	persist	abide, continue	-
1014.	perspective	angle, view	-
1015.	perspicacity	clarity	obscurity
1016.	persuade	actuate	dissuade
1017.	pertinent	apt, relevant	irrelevant
1018.	perverse	stubborn	normal
1019.	phenomenon	event	-
1020.	phenomenal	amazing	common
1021.	phobia	anxiety, dread	
1022.	phosphorescent	bright, luminous	liking
1023.	physiognomy	countenance	-
1024.	physique	build	-
1025.	picturesque	colorful, scenic	-
1026.	pilfer	steal	-
1027.	pillage	plunder	-
1028.	plagiarism	appropriation	-
1029.	plausible	believable	implausible
1030.	plebeian	common	aristocratic
1031.	plenary	complete, full	-
1032.	plenitude	abundance	scarcity
1033.	plenty	abundance	lack
1034.	pliable	adaptable	rigid
1035.	pluck	boldness, bravery	feebleness
1036.	plump	buxom, fat	thin
1037.	podium	dais, platform	-
1038.	polemic (s)	argument	-
1039.	pomp	ceremony, grandeur	austerity
1040.	populace	people, crowd	elite
1041.	popular	accepted, widespread	exclusive, unpopular
1042.	porous	absorbent, permeable	improbable
1043.	portray	depict, delineate	-
1044.	posterity	descendants	ancestors
1045.	postmortem	autopsy	-
1046.	postpone	defer	advance
1047.	potentate	chief despot	-

1048.	potpourri	collection, jumble	-
1049.	pragmatism	practical	idealistic
1050.	preamble	exordium	epilogue, postscript
1051.	precede	antecede	follow
1052.	predecessor	ancestor, forerunner	successor descendant
1053.	preclude	avoid, debar	incur, involve
1054.	precocious	ahead	backward
1055.	predicament	impasse, quandary	-
1056.	prediction	prognostication	-
1057.	predilection	affection, bias	antipathy
1058.	preliminary	earliest, introductory	closing final
1059.	preponderance	ascendancy, dominance	decline wane
1060.	preposterous	absurd, crazy	reasonable
1061.	prerogative	advantage, authority	-
1062.	prescient	clairvoyant	-
1063.	preserve	protect, maintain	destroy
1064.	prestige	honour	dishonor
1065.	presumptuous	overweening, arrogant	modest
1066.	pretension	ostentation	simplicity
1067.	prevail	predominate	lose
1068.	pretty	attractive, beautiful	ugly
1069.	previous	earlier	later
1070.	pride	arrogance	humility
1071.	primitive	aboriginal	advanced, developed
1072.	primordial	earliest, archetypal	developed
1073.	principal	main, head	subsidiary
1074.	principle	rule, assumption, morality	perversion, corruption
1075.	prior	former, before	later
1076.	pristine	earliest, first, virgin	later, spoiled
1077.	privilege	advantage	disadvantage
1078.	proclaim	declare	-
1079.	procrastinate	defer, delay	proceed
1080.	prodigal	extravagant	thrifty
1081.	profane	blasphemous	sacred
1082.	proficient	accomplished, adept	incompetent
1083.	profuse	abundant	scarce
1084.	progress	advancement	regress, decline
1085.	prohibit	hamper, restrict	permit
1086.	proliferate	breed, multiply	dwindle
1087.	promiscuity	licentiousness, wantonness	chastity
1088.	promiscuous	disordered, haphazard	-
1089.	prompt	instant, ready	controlled
1090.	promulgate	proclaim, declare Conspicuous,	slow, lazy
1091.	pronounced	distinct	-

1092.	propaganda	publicity	vague
1093.	propagate	disorientate, spread	restrict
1094.	propinquity	adjunct	remoteness
1095.	propose	advance, advocate	oppose, withdraw
1096.	proponent	profounder	opponent
1097.	prescribe	ban, bar	admit, allow
1098.	prospect	future, perspective	-
1099.	prosperity	affluence	poverty
1100.	prostrate	abject, fallen	elate
1101.	protean	inconstant	stable
1102.	protest	compliant	acceptance
1103.	protract	extend	shorten
1104.	protrude	bulge	-
1105.	protruding	bulging	flat
1106.	providential	heaven-sent	untimely
1107.	provoke	anger, incite	pacify
1108.	prudence	care, discretion	imprudence
1109.	prurient	lascivious	decent
1110.	publicity	advertising	secrecy
1111.	puckish	frolicsome	solemn
1112.	puerile	childish	mature
1113.	pulsate	beat	stop
1114.	pulpy	soft	hard
1115.	punctilious	careful, formal	informal, easy-going
1116.	puny	diminutive	large
1117.	purify	chasten	defile
1118.	pursue	follow	eschew
1119.	pusillanimous	timid	courageous
1120.	puzzle	baffle	clarify
1121.	pygmy	dwarf, Lilliputian	giant
1122.	quackery	charlatanism	sincerity
1123.	quaint	strange	common
1124.	quarantine	isolation	-
1125.	queer	aberrant, bizarre	common, ordinary
1126.	querulous	cantankerous	placid, contented
1127.	quest	search, pursuit	-
1128.	questionable	disputable	certain
1129.	quicken	accelerate	retard
1130.	quiescent	silent, calm, dormant	active
1131.	quite	calm, abate	aggravate
1132.	quixotic	impracticable	practical, realistic
1133.	quotidian	day-to-day, common	-
1134.	rabies	hydrophobia	-
1136.	radiance	brightness	-

1137.	raise	lift	suppress
1138.	ramble	wander, saunter	-
1139.	ramification	branch	-
1140.	rancour	acrimony	goodwill
1141.	rancid	foul	sweet
1142.	random	haphazard	systematic
1143.	range	area	-
1144.	ransack	rummage	-
1145.	ransom	redemption	captivity
1146.	rapacious	avaricious	contented
1147.	rapid	brisk, quick	slow
1148.	rapprochement	agreement	discord
1149.	rapture	beatitude, exaltation	-
1150.	rare	scarce	abundant
1151.	rash	hasty	careful
1152.	rational	logical	crazy
1153.	raucous	harsh	melodious
1154.	ravage	demolish	construct
1155.	realm	area	-
1156.	rebellion	uprising, revolt	obedience
1157.	rebut	confute	accept
1158.	recede	ebb, abate	proceed, advance
1159.	receive	accept, get	give, donate
1160.	recipient	assignee, receiver	giver, donor
1161.	reciprocate	exchange	isolate
1162.	reckon	consider	-
1163.	reconcile	reunite, accord	estrange
1164.	recondite	difficult	simple
1165.	recalcitrant	refractory, defiant	amenable
1166.	recapitulate	recap, restate	-
1167.	recent	fresh, contemporary	dated, old
1168.	recession	decline, slump	boom
1169.	reclaim	recapture, recover	surrender
1170.	recollect	remember	forget
1171.	rectify	amend	-
1172.	recumbent	flat, prostrate	erect
1173.	recurrent	repetitive	-
1174.	redeem	acquit, free	enslave, bond
1175.	reduce	lessen, shorten	boost, increase
1176.	redundant	extra, superfluous	essential
1177.	reference	allusion	-
1178.	reflect	reveal	-
1179.	regenerate	renew	-
1180.	regime	reign, administration	-

1181.	region	area	-
1182.	rehabilitate	reestablish	-
1183.	reinforce	strengthen	weaken
1184.	reject	spurn, disallow	accept, select
1185.	relax	ease, slacken	intensify, weaken
1186.	relegate	downgrade, demote	promote
1187.	relent	slacken	yield
1188.	relit	trace	-
1189.	reluctance	unwillingness	eagerness, willingness
1190.	rely	depend, trust	mistrust
1191.	remit	mail, send	-
1192.	remnant	remainder, vestige	-
1193.	remorse	sorrow	impenitence
1194.	remote	distant	close
1195.	rendezvous	converge, assemble	-
1196.	renegade	apostate	adherent
1197.	renounce	abandon, forgo	adhere
1198.	renovate	refurbish	-
1199.	renowned	famous	anonymous, obscure
1200.	reparable	corrigible, curable	irreparable
1201.	repeal	abolish, annul	enact
1202.	repeat	duplicate, redo	-
1203.	repent	atone	-
1204.	repercussion	aftermath, backlash	-
1205.	repertory	collection, list	-
1206.	replenish	furnish	-
1207.	replete	abounding	scarce
1208.	repress	suppress	encourage
1209.	reproach	chide	praise
1210.	reprobate	degenerate	upright
1211.	repute	fame	defame
1212.	requisite (n)	condition, requirement	-
1213.	requital	amends	-
1214.	requite(v)	respond, satisfy	unsatisfy
1215.	rescind	abrogate, cancel	enforce
1216.	resent	grumble	like
1217.	resentment	discontentment	contentment
1218.	residue	balance, rest, extra	core
1219.	resilience	buoyancy	rigidity
1220.	resolute	firm	Irresolute, flexible.
1221.	resolve	agree, decide	waver
1222.	resonant	resounding	faint
1223.	respect	regard	scorn
1224.	respite	relief, recess	continuation

1225.	respond	answer	-
1226.	resplendent	lustrous	dull
1227.	restive	agitated	calm, relaxed
1228.	restraint	control	freedom
1229.	resume	summary	-
1230.	resurrect	revive	bury
1231.	resurgence	rebirth	-
1232.	resuscitate	quicken, revive	-
1233.	retain	hold	spend
1234.	retard	clog	advance
1235.	reticence	reserve	communicativeness
1236.	retrench	economize	increase
1237.	retribution	vengeance	-
1238.	retrieve	redeem	lose
1239.	retrograde	regressive, renegade	progressive
1240.	revamp	overhaul	-
1241.	reveal	expose	hide
1242.	revelry	festivity	sobriety
1243.	reverberate	echo	-
1244.	reverie	daydream	-
1245.	reverse (n)	back	-
1246.	revoke	retract	maintain
1247.	reward	prize	punishment
1248.	ridicule	banter, mock	praise
1249.	right	just	wrong
1250.	rigmarole	nonsense	-
1251.	repost	answer	-
1252.	risk	hazard	safety
1253.	rival	adversary	associate
1254.	robust	stout	weak
1255.	rogue	blackguard	saint
1256.	romantic	fanciful	realistic
1257.	roomy	spacious	cramped
1258.	rosy	blushing, optimistic	depressed
1259.	rotation	alternation	-
1260.	rouse	agitate	calm
1261.	royal	kingly, majestic	-
1262.	rude	blunt	polished
1263.	rueful	penitent	glad
1264.	ruffle	agitate	calm
1265.	ruin	destruction	reconstruction
1266.	rumpus	commotion	calm
1267.	rupture	breach	continuity
1268.	rush	hasten	-

1269.	rust	blight, oxidation	-
1270.	ruthless	brutal, merciless	compassionate, merciful
1271.	sabotage	damage	-
1272.	sack (v)	dismiss	appoint
1273.	sacred	holy, consecrated	profane
1274.	sacrifice	renunciation, oblation	-
1275.	sacrilege	blasphemy	piety
1276.	sacrosanct	hallowed	profane
1277.	sadism	brutality	-
1278.	sagacious	judicious, discerning	short-sighted, foolish
1279.	salacious	bawdy	decent
1280.	salient	prominent, striking	minor
1281.	sallow	pale	rosy
1282.	salubrious	health-giving wholesome	insalubrious
1283.	salvage	conserve, reclaim	abandon
1284.	salvation	redemption	damnation
1285.	sanctify	anoint	defile, desecrate
1286.	sanction	approve, grant	disapprove
1287.	sanctity	holiness	impurity
1288.	sanctuary	asylum, shelter	-
1289.	sanguine	animated, hopeful	cynical, gloomy
1290.	sanitary	aseptic, hygienic	insanitary
1291.	sanity	normality, rationality	insanity
1292.	sarcasm	satire, irony, vitriol	-
1293.	sardonic	cynical	-
1294.	satanic	devilish, diabolic	divine
1295.	satisfy	appease	disappoint
1296.	savory	agreeable, dainty	tasteless
1297.	scan	check, scrutinize	-
1298.	scarcity	dearth	abundance
1299.	scavenger	forager	-
1300.	scheme	plan, program	-
1301.	scintillate	shine, sparkle	dim
1302.	scourge	affliction	blessing
1303.	scrap	fragment	-
1304.	scrupulous	careful	careless
1305.	scramble	chamber, crawl	-
1306.	scribble	jot	-
1307.	scrivener	scribe	-
1308.	scurry	hurry	stroll
1309.	seasoned	acclimatized, experienced	novice
1310.	secondary	-	primary
1311.	secret	confidential, clandestine	public
1312.	sedate	calm, dignified	flippant

1313.	sedentary	seated, desk-bound	active
1314.	sedition	treason	loyalty
1315.	seduce	entice, mislead	-
1316.	seductive	bewitching	repulsive
1317.	sedulous	industrious, persistent	halfhearted
1318.	segment	part	whole
1319.	segregate	separate	unite
1320.	sensational	ling	dull
1321.	semblance	likeness	dissimilarity
1322.	sentient	sensitive, conscious	insentient, unaware
1323.	serene	tranquil	troubled
1324.	serious	grave	light, trivial
1325.	servility	submissiveness, slavishness	boldness, aggressiveness
1326.	severe	acute	mild
1327.	shabby	shoddy	smart
1328.	shackle	trammel	-
1329.	shallow	frivolous	deep
1330.	shameful	humiliating	honorable
1331.	sharp	cutting, piercing	blunt
1332.	shatter	break	assemble
1333.	shock (v) & (n)	blow (v) & (n)	reassure (v) delight (n)
1334.	shoot (v)	dart, fire (v)	-
1335.	shortcoming	defect	-
1336.	shrewd	cunning	naive
1337.	shriveled	wrinkled	-
1338.	shroud (v)	cover	expose
1339.	significant	important, meaningful	meaningless
1340.	simplistic	naive	analytical
1341.	simulate	assume, counterfeit	-
1342.	simultaneous	concurrent, synchronous	separate
1343.	singular	unique, unparalleled	usual
1344.	sinister	dire	harmless
1345.	skeptic	rational	credulous
1346.	skill	ability	-
1347.	slender	slim, little	considerable
1348.	sluggish	slow	brisk
1349.	smooth	bland, frictionless	coarse, rough
1350.	sober	grave	frivolous
1351.	solace	comfort	trouble
1352.	solemn	serious, dignified	frivolous
1353.	solicit	beg, entreat	-
1354.	solitude	loneliness	companionship
1355.	sophisticated	cultivated, intricate	artless, naive
1356.	sordid	foul, dirty	clean

1357.	spacious	large commodious	small, cramped
1358.	specific	characteristic, explicit	general
1359.	speculate	guess, hypothesize	-
1360.	spell (n)	course, charm	-
1361.	spineless	irresolute, weak	resolute, strong
1362.	splendid	grand	ordinary
1363.	spontaneous	unpremeditated	planned, deliberate
1364.	spurious	fake, bogus	genuine
1365.	stable	constant	shaky
1366.	stagnate	rot	-
1367.	stagnant	motionless	flowing
1368.	staple	main, major	minor
1369.	stark	stiff	mild
1370.	start	begin	end
1371.	startle	alarm	calm
1372.	starve	furnish	provide
1373.	stately	dignified, majestic	ordinary
1374.	stationary	motionless	moving
1375.	staunch	constant, strong	wavering, weak
1376.	steady	constant	wavering
1377.	stereotype	convention, mould	-
1378.	stereotyped	hackneyed	Different, unconventional
1379.	sterility	barrenness	fertility
1380.	sterilize	disinfect	infect
1381.	stern	hard	soft, mild
1382.	stimulate	spur, encourage	discourage
1383.	sling	pierce	soothe
1384.	stoicism	imperturbability	depression, fury
1385.	stoic	dispassionate, imperturbable	depressed, furious
1386.	stoop	bend	erect
1387.	straight	direct	circuitous
1388.	strain	exert	relax
1389.	stratagem/strategy	plan, scheme	-
1390.	stratum	category	-
1391.	streamlined	rationalized, modernized	clumsy, old-fashioned
1392.	strenuous	arduous	easy
1393.	stringent	rigorous	mild
1394.	stubborn	obdurate	compliant
1395.	stupendous	enormous	unimpressive, small
1396.	sturdy	stout	decrepit
1397.	suave	affable, polite	coarse
1398.	subjection	bondage, slavery	freedom
1399.	sublime	lofty, grand	lowly
1400.	subordinate	inferior	superior

1401.	subscribe	contribute	-
1402.	subsequent	consequent, following	previous
1403.	subservient	ancillary,	domineering
1404.	substantial	considerable	insignificant, small
1405.	substantiate	prove	disprove
1406.	subterfuge	deception	honesty
1407.	subtle	artful, impalpable	open
1408.	subversive	seditious, disruptive	loyal
1409.	succinct	concise	wordy
1410.	succor	aid	undermine
1411.	succulent	juicy, luscious	dry
1412.	sultry	humid	cool
1413.	superannuated	retired, aged	young
1414.	superb	excellent	poor
1415.	supercilious	arrogant	humble
1416.	superficial	cursory, apparent	detailed
1417.	supersede	overrule	-
1418.	supine	prostrate, indolent	alert
1419.	supple	soft, flexible	rigid
1420.	suppliant	importunate	-
1421.	suppress	repress	encourage
1422.	supreme	ultimate, highest	lowly
1423.	surfeit	superabundance	lack
1424.	surpass	surmount, out do	-
1425.	surplus	excess	lack
1426.	surrender	concede, resign	fight (on)
1427.	surreptitious	secret, veiled	open
1428.	surveillance	watch, observation	-
1429.	surly	growling	contented
1430.	surrogate	substitute	-
1431.	sustain	bear, continue	break
1432.	sustenance	ailment, maintenance	-
1433.	swell	expand, enlarge	contract, shrink
1434.	swelling	bulge, inflammation	-
1435.	sweltering	airless, suffocating	airy, fresh
1436.	sycophancy	feattery	-
1437.	symbiosis	cooperatively	-
1438.	symmetry	regularity, harmony	asymmetry
1439.	symptom	indication, syndrome	-
1440.	synthesis	integration	analysis
1441.	systematic	rationalized	disorderly
1442.	tableau	picture, representation	-
1443.	taboo	prohibition	acceptance
1444.	tacit	silent, implicit	explicit

1445.	taciturn	reticent	talkative, communicative
1446.	tackle	handle	avoid
1447.	tact	adroitness, skill	tactlessness
1448.	tag	tack, adjoin	-
1449.	talent	ability	inability
1450.	tangle	complication	disentangle
1451.	tantalize	tempt, telltale	satisfy
1452.	tape	band	-
1453.	taper (v)	narrow, reduce	swell, widen
1454.	tardy	sluggish, slow	prompt, punctual
1455.	target	aim, goal	-
1456.	tariff	levy, tax	-
1457.	tarnish	stain, spoil	brighten, enhance
1458.	task	assignment, work	-
1459.	taunt	deride	praise, admire
1460.	tautology	repetition	economy, succinctness
1461.	tedious	lonesome, tiring, boring	exciting interesting
1462.	teenager	adolescent	mature
1463.	teetotaler	abstainer, nihilist	-
1464.	temperate	balanced, sober	excessive, extreme
1465.	tempestuous	furious	composed, calm
1466.	temporal	mundane, earthly	spiritual
1467.	temptation	allurement	-
1468.	tenable	justifiable	untenable, unjustifiable
1469.	tenacity	doggedness, steadfastness	slackness
1470.	tenacious	persistent	slack
1471.	tenet	maxim, principle	-
1472.	tenor	purpose, trend	-
1473.	tense (adj)	anxious, strained	relaxed
1474.	tension	strain, tightness	laxness
1475.	tentative	provisional, speculative	conclusive, final
1476.	tenuous	insignificant, delicate, slight	significant, strong
1477.	tenure	incumbency, term	substantial
1478.	tepid	indifferent, apathetic	-
1479.	terminal	final, ultimate	animated
1480.	terminate	discontinue, stop	initial
1481.	terrestrial	earthly	initiate, begin
1482.	terrain	land, ground	heavenly, cosmic
1483.	terrify/terrorize	affright, frighten	-
1484.	terse	pithy	encourage
1485.	testament	will, covenant	verbose
1486.	testify	attest	-
1487.	testimonial	certificate, recommendation	-
1488.	tether	cord, rope	-

1489.	theme	leitmotif, idea	-
1490.	theoretical	abstract, academic	-
1491.	thick	dense	applied, practical
1492.	thesis	treatise, dissertation	-
1493.	thorough	exhaustive, comprehensive	-
1494.	thought	idea	partial
1495.	thrash	beat	-
1496.	thrifty	economical	-
1497.	thrill	excitement	prodigal
1498.	thrive	prosper	-
1499.	throughout	everywhere, widely	anguish
1500.	thrust	pressure	-
1501.	tidy	neat, clean	-
1502.	tidings	news, intelligence	untidy
1503.	timorous	timid, lily-livered	-
1504.	tinge	colour	bold
1505.	tinsel	trash, superficial, gaudy	-
1506.	tint	colour	-
1507.	tiny	small	-
1508.	tireless	diligent, energetic	big
1509.	tiresome	tedious	tired
1510.	titanic	colossal	easy
1511.	tolerance	endurance	small
1512.	toothsome	agreeable	intolerance
1513.	tongue	language	-
1514.	topple	oust, outset	-
1515.	torpor	dullness, inactivity	-
1516.	tortuous	arduous	straight
1517.	totalitarian	authoritarian, dictatorial	democratic
1518.	touching	pitiable, pathetic	-
1519.	towering	outstanding, lofty	small, timid
1520.	trace (n)	mark	
1521.	trace (v)	sketch	-
1522.	traditional	conventional	modern, avant-garde
1523.	trafficker	trader	-
1524.	tragic	catastrophic	comic
1525.	Tranquility	calmness	agitation
1526.	transact	negotiate	-
1527.	transcend	exceed	-
1528.	transient	evanescent, transitory	permanent
1529.	transit	conversion	-
1530.	transition	alteration, change	beginning, end
1531.	transitional	changing	initial, final
1532.	transparent	lucid	opaque

1533.	trauma	agony	relaxation
1534.	traverse (v)	cross	-
1535.	treacherous	deceitful, unreliable	loyal, reliable dependable
1536.	treason	treachery	loyalty
1537.	treaty	alliance, agreement	-
1538.	tremendous	amazing & stupendous	tiny, little
1539.	tremulous	trembling	steady
1540.	trespass	intrude	-
1541.	tribute	homage	blame
1542.	triple	insignificant, unimportant	important, significant
1543.	triumph	victory	defeat
1544.	trivial	unimportant	important, significant
1545.	truant	absentee	-
1546.	truism	axiom	-
1547.	truly	really, actually	falsely
1548.	true	real	false
1549.	truncate	curtail, cut	lengthen
1550.	trust	faith	mistrust
1551.	tumult	turmoil, uproar	calm
1552.	turpitude	baseness	honour
1553.	tutelage	patronage, aegis, guardianship	-
1554.	twilight	dusk	-
1555.	twinkle	blink	-
1556.	tycoon	baron, magnate	-
1557.	typical	representative	atypical
1558.	tyranny	despotism	democracy
1559.	ubiquitous	all pervasive, omnipresent	rare
1560.	ugly	deformed	beautiful
1561.	ulterior	hidden	declared, overt
1562.	ultimate	final, terminal	-
1563.	umpteen	numerous	few
1564.	unanimous	concordant, agreed	split
1565.	unanimity	accord, agreement, unity	disagreement, disunity
1566.	underline	emphasize	-
1567.	underhand	secret, clandestine	overt
1568.	undertake (v)	pledge, guarantee	-
1569.	undervalue	underestimate	overrate
1570.	underworld	gangland	-
1571.	underwrite	endorse	-
1572.	unite	join	separate, sever
1573.	universal	global, worldwide	-
1574.	universe	cosmos	-
1575.	unkempt	shabby	tidy
1576.	uplift (v)	advance, elevate, advancement	downgrade

1577.	uplift (n)	improvement	-
1578.	upheaval	cataclysm, turmoil	calm
1579.	upkeep	care, support	neglect
1580.	uprising	insurgence, rebellion rising	-
1581.	uproar	clamour, rumpus	calm
1582.	upset (v)	agitate	-
1583.	upset (n)	defeat	win
1584.	upshot	outcome, result	-
1585.	upstart	parvenu, nouveau-riche	-
1586.	urchin	brat	
1587.	urge	exhort	-
1588.	urgent	extent, compelling	deter
1589.	usher (v)	conduct, lead	-
1590.	usher (n)	attendant	-
1591.	usual	common, normal	unusual, exceptional
1592.	usurp	annex, appropriate	-
1593.	usury	money-lending	banking
1594.	utensil	gadget, apparatus	-
1595.	utopian	idealistic	realistic
1596.	utter (v)	articulate	-
1597.	utterly	completely	-
1598.	vacant	empty, void	occupied, engaged
1599.	vacate	abandon, quit	occupy
1600.	vacillate	fluctuate, waver	-
1601.	vacuous	stupid, empty	-
1602.	vacuum	emptiness	-
1603.	vagary	prank	-
1604.	vague	unclear, unspecified	clear, specified
1605.	valediction	adieu, farewell, manservant	greeting
1606.	valetudinarian	feeble	
1607.	valid	approved	stoical
1608.	valour	bravery	invalid
1609.	value	price, utility	cowardice
1610.	vanish	disappear	-
1611.	vanity	affectation	appear, materialize modesty
1612.	vaporous	flimsy	substantial
1613.	variable	changeable	constant
1614.	variance	difference	agreement
1615.	variety	assortment, range	-
1616.	vegetate	stagnate	-
1617.	vehemence	force, fervour	indifference
1618.	venal	corrupt	incorruptible
1619.	vendetta	enmity, feud	-
1620.	venerable	reverend, respected	-

1621.	veracity	accuracy	-
1622.	verbatim	literally, exactly	-
1623.	verdict	opinion, judgment	-
1624.	verge	border	centre
1625.	verify	attest	falsify
1626.	versatile	all-round	-
1627.	versed	accomplished, skilled	-
1628.	vertex	acme, zenith	nadir
1629.	verve	zeal, vigour	apathy
1630.	veto	negate	approve
1631.	viable	feasible, workable	impossible
1632.	vibrate	tremble, throb	-
1633.	vicarious	surrogate	-
1634.	vice	sin	virtue
1635.	vigil	lookout, watch	-
1636.	view	outlook, opinion	-
1637.	vigilance	watchfulness	-
1638.	vigilant	watchful	careless
1639.	vigour	potency, energy, vitality	impotence, weakness
1640.	vile	debased, sinful	-
1641.	vilify	debase, defame	adore, glorify
1642.	villain	miscreant	hero, heroine
1643.	vindicate	justify	accuse
1644.	vindictive	ivengeful	merciful
1645.	vintage	ripe, mature	-
1646.	violate	transgress, disobey	obey, uphold
1647.	virgin (adj)	chaste, pure	-
1648.	virile	forceful, vigorous	feeble, effeminate
1649.	virtue	goodness	vice
1650.	virtuosity	mastery, skill malignant, poisonous	-
1651.	virulent		-
1652.	visible	noticeable	invisible
1653.	vision	sight, view	-
1654.	visionary	dreamer, idealist	realist, practical
1655.	visualize	envisage	-
1656.	vital	fundamental, essential	inessential
1657.	vivacious	cheerful, spirited	languid
1658.	vivid	clear, lively	dull
1659.	vocation	profession	hobby, avocation
1660.	vociferous	vocal, vehement	quiet, silent
1661.	vogue	use, fashion	-
1662.	void	vacant	full
1663.	voluble	loquacious, articulate	quiet, reticent
1664.	volume	size, capacity	-

1665.	voluntary	deliberate, willful	forced, involuntary
1666.	voracious	insatiable, devouring	-
1667.	vortex	whirlpool, eddy	-
1668.	votary	follower, devotee	-
1669.	vouchsafe	condescend, grant	-
1670.	vow (v)	swear,	-
1671.	vow (n)	oath	-
1672.	vulnerable	defenseless, pregnable	protected
1673.	wage	emolument, pay	-
1674.	waif	foundling, orphan	-
1675.	waive	abandon, relinquish	-
1676.	wakeful	alert, attentive	sleepy
1677.	wallow	bask, roll	-
1678.	wander	roam, saunter	-
1679.	wane	diminish	wax
1680.	wanton	sportive, willful	sober
1681.	warily	cautiously	heedlessly
1682.	warmth	fallibility, enthusiasm	coldness
1683.	water	aqua, Adam's ale, Adam's wine	-
1684.	weaken	enfeeble	strengthen
1685.	wearisome	tedious	refreshing
1686.	weary	tired	fresh
1687.	weird	bizarre, unearthly	normal
1688.	weld	join, fuse	separate
1689.	whimsical	capricious, eccentric	sensible
1690.	whisk	beat, whip	-
1691.	wile	artfulness, guile	guilelessness
1692.	winding	circuitous, curving	straight
1693.	wistful	longing, wishful	-
1694.	withdraw	retract, disinherit	Persist, deposit
1695.	wither	dry	flourish
1696.	wobble	waver, oscillate	-
1697.	woebegone	crestfallen, grief-striken	joyful
1698.	wonderful	marvellous	ordinary
1699.	wont	accustomed, habituated	unwanted
1700.	woolly (adj)	fleecy, shaggy	clear
1701.	woolly (n)	cardigan, jersey	-
1702.	woozy	befuddled, dizzy	alert, sober
1703.	workmanlike	professional, proficient	amateurish
1704.	worldly	mundane, earthly	heavenly, unwordly
1705.	worth	value	worthlessness
1706.	wrath	anger, rage	calm
1707.	wreath	garland	-
1708.	wreathe	adorn	-

1709.	wreck	break, demolish	repair, save
1710.	wrench	twist	-
1711.	wretched	poor, abject	happy
1712.	wrinkle	crease, crumple	smoothness
1713.	writhe	squint, twist	-
1714.	wrong	erroneous, incorrect	right
1715.	wrought	fashioned, made	-
1716.	wry	ironic, sardonic	straight
1717.	yawn	gape, open	-
1718.	yawning	wide-open	narrow
1719.	yell	shout	whisper
1720.	yield	surrender, succumb	withstand
1721.	yoke	burden	-
1722.	zeal	enthusiasm	apathy
1723.	zealot	enthusiast	apathetic
1724.	zenith	acme, culmination	nadir
1725.	zest	élan, taste	indifference, apathy
1726.	zigzag	meandering, serpentine	straight
1727.	zing	dash, élan, energy	apathy, indifference
1728.	zip	gusto, zest, dash, whiz	apathy, indifference

Chapter Twelve

Improve Your Vocabulary

Outcome of the Chapter

(a) Homograph
(b) Homonym
(c) Difference
(d) Polysemy
(e) One word for many words
(f) Acronym
(g) Blend words

You have already read some frequently used words, their synonyms and antonyms. We are, now, giving homographs, homonyms, confused words (difference), polysemy and one word substitution for increasing your vocabulary and competence in reading and writing.

1. *Homograph:* It means words with the same spelling but different in pronunciation and meaning. For example:

Bow? minute and wind.

But such words are very few in English.

2. *Homonym:* Homonym words have different meanings, different spellings but the same pronunciation. For example:

hair and hare, right, rite and write, heir and air.

3. *Difference:* Words which have the same origin but differ in meaning when different suffixes are added. Imperial and imperious, judicial and judicious, economic and economical.

Such words are a few in English.

4. *Polysemy:* Words of this category do not change their class but change their meaning in different contexts. For example:

space: space in a room, space in writing, space for admission, voyage in the space

eye: man's eye, eye of a needle, eye on the tail of a peacock, eye of a potato, the eye of the storm, the eye of the wind

A: Common Homographs

1. a. 'Abstract adj., stress on the first syllable) = theoretical
   b. abs'tract (verb, stress on the second syllable) = extract or remove
2. a. affect (verb, stress on the second syllable) = have an effect on
   b. 'Affect (noun, stress on the first syllable) = emotion or desire an influencing behavior
3. a. A'gape = wide open
   b. agape = Christian love; communal meal in Christian fellowship
4. a. bow = instrument to shoot arrows
   b. bow = bend the head respectfully
5. a. minute = a period of sixty seconds
   b. minute = precise and meticulous. For example, a minute observation
6. a. 'second (adjective stress on the first syllable) = after first
   b. sećond (verb stress on the second syllable) = support, temporarily, transfer
   c. second = (noun) stress on the first syllable, short time, a moment, 60th part of a minute of time
7. a. wind = air
   b. wind = move a thread or wire roundly over an object

B. Common Homonyms

1. altar = the holy place of consecration

   alter = change in character, appearance and direction
2. bare = uncovered, minimum

   bear = carry, tolerate, give birth to

3. bale = a large bundle of papers, hay or cotton
   bail = temporary release of an accused; a piece of wood covering the wickets in the game of cricket
4. bald = head, partly or fully hairless
   bold = courageous
5. be = verb (is, am, are)
   bee = an insect (honey bee)
6. bite = to cut with teeth
   byte = a group of binary digits (in computing)
7. bloc = a group of countries/parties united by a common interest
   block = a group of buildings
8. blue = a colour
   blew = past tense of blow
9. but = on the contrary
   butt = object of laughter; the end of a weapon
10. by = near, past, beside, through - action, means, power
    bye = the transfer to next round in the absence of the opponent
11. cast = throw, choose actors to play
    caste = a group in the social hierarchy or varnashram system of India
12. check = control, inspect
    cheque = a bank paper for withdrawal of money
13. chilli = a hot spice used in cooking vegetables
    chilly = very cold
14. choir = an organized group of singers
    coir = fibre made from the outer husk of coconut
15. coma = a state of deep unconsciousness
    comma = a punctuation mark
16. complement = the number or quantity to complete something
    compliment = a polite expression of praise or admiration

17. cense = ritually perfume with burning incense
    sense = the ability to understand or feel
18. censer = the container in which incense is burnt
    censor = an officer who examines materials if they are dangerous or against law
19. cent = a monetary unit in America
    sent = Past tense of send
20. cite = quote
    site = place
    sight = vision, the faculty or power of see
21. core = central part
    corps = a branch of army consisting of two or more divisions
22. dam = a barrier to control the flow of water
    damn = condemn; be doomed to misfortune
23. deem = regard or consider in specified way
    deme = a political division in ancient and modern Greek
24. demean = cause to suffer a severe loss of dignity or respect; humiliate
    demesne : land attached to a manor, possession and use of land as one's own property
25. dose = a quantity of medicine to be taken by a patient
    doze = sleep lightly
26. draft = a preliminary version of a piece of writing
    draught = a current of cool air in a room or confined place
27. dye = natural or synthetic substance used for colouring
    die = stop living
    die = singular form of dice; a device for cutting and moulding
28. dun = a dull grayish brown colour
    done = the third form of the verb "do"

29. earn = receive money for doing work

    urn = a decorated vessel, a tall vase for holding ashes of the cremated

30. fair = treating people equally; a gathering of people and stalls for a short period

    fare = the money people on public transport have to pay.

31. flea = a small winged insect

    flee = run away

32. fore = the front part of something

    four = a cardinal number

33. fort = castle

    forte = a thing at which someone excels

34. foul = offensive to sense; unfair

    fowl = a domesticated bird

35. fret = be constantly or visibly anxious

    freight = transport of goods in bulk

36. gait = a person's manner of walking

    gate = a hinged barrier used to close opening in a wall or fence

37. Gild = cover thinly with gold

    guild = an association of people for mutual benefit

38. glair = adhesive

    glare = shine with a dazzling light

39. hair = fine thread-like strands on human and animal bodies

    hare = a rabbit or mouse like small animal

40. hangar = a large and tall house to accommodate for housing aircraft

    hanger = a plastic or iron frame for hanging clothes, especially shirt and coat

41. happi = a loose Japanese coat

    happy = showing signs of contentment

42. heard = past tense of 'hear"
    herd = a large group of animals
43. Heroin = a drug derived from morphine
    heroine = a woman of extraordinary qualities, especially her bravery and capacity of leadership; main female character in a play or film
44. hole = an empty space in a solid body or surface
    whole = entire
45. horde = a group of people, usually very large
    hoard = a store of money and valuable things a mass large quantity of essential commodities, illegally
46. hue = colour
    hew = chop wood or coal with an axe, pick or other tool
47. humorous = causing laughter
    humerus = the bone of the upper arm
48. idle = lazy, doing nothing
    idol = an image, a statue
49. isle = a small island
    aisle = a passage between rows of seats, pews
50. in = a prefix as in + sufficient = Insufficient
    inn = a public place where journeymen take rest
51. know = have information
    no = negation
52. Knight = a respectable warrior in the medieval age
    night = the period between sunset and sunrise
53. lac = a resinous substance
    lack = absence or deficiency of something
54. main = chief in size or importance
    mane = A growth of long hair on a hover's neck
55. meat = the flesh of an animal used as food
    meet = arrange or happen to come into the presence

56. metal = a solid material which is typically hard
    mettle = a person's ability to cope with challenges or difficulties
57. modal = an auxiliary verb
    model = a three-dimensional representation of an object
58. need = want
    knead = work (dough or clay) with hands
59. new = novel, not old
    knew = past tense of know
60. not = negative
    knot = tie two ends of a string together
61. pail = bucket
    pale = containing little colour (or near yellow colour)
62. palate = the roof of the mouth
    palette = a thin board on which a painter mixes colours
63. peace = noiseless
    piece = bit, a part of something
64. peak = top, highest point
    peek = look quickly or furtively
65. peal = a ringing or thundering sound
    peel = the outer covering of a fruit; remove peel (n + v)
66. pendant = a piece of jewellery that hangs from a necklace chain
    pendent = hanging down
67. plait = a single length of hair or rope made up of three or more interlaced strands
    plate = a flat dish
68. plane = a flat surface; aeroplane
    plain = simple; ordinary looking; not decorated
69. quay = a platform lying alongside or projecting inside into water for loading and unloading of ships
    key = a piece of iron with teeth to open a lock

70. raise = lift or move to a higher position

raze = tear down and destroy a building

71. rain = falling of water in drops from clouds

reign = rule

rein = a horse's controlling strap

72. rap = strike (a hard surface) with a series of rapid audible blows; the smallest amount

wrap = cover or enclose in a paper

73. read = peruse

reed = a tall, slender leaved plant of grass family

74. right = correct; opposite of left

write = encode spoken words on a piece of paper

75. ring = circle

wring = squeeze and twist

76. sea = the great collection of water where rivers end

see = look at

77. sail = travel by boat; the movement of a boat or ship

sale = the exchange of commodity for money

78. scene = view

seen = third form of the verb "see"

79. Seam = a line where two pieces of fabric are sewn

seem = appear

80. sew = stitch with a needle

sow = plant seeds by scattering on or in the earth, a grown up female pig

81. seize = catch, hold

cease = stop

82. sell = exchange commodity for money

cell = a tiny part of living organisms

cell = a very small room, electric desice (battery)

83. sole = one and only

soul = the essence of the body; spirit

84. soot = a black thick powder

suit = a set of outer clothes; e.g., coat and trousers of the same piece of cloth

85. stair = each of a set of fixed steps

stare = look fixedly at someone with the eyes wide open

86. stationary = not moving

stationery = paper and other materials needed for writing

87. steal = take without permission

steel = hardened iron

88. step = an act of moving

steppe = a large area of flat unforested grassland in South East Europe and Siberia

89. straight = extending uniformly in one direction; not curved

strait = a narrow passage of water connecting two seas

90. suite = a set of rooms for one person's or family's use, especially in a guest house or hotel

sweet = having pleasant taste of sugar or honey

91. symmetry = correct or pleasing proportion of parts; nice arrangement

cemetery = a large burial ground; a large graveyard

92. tail = the hanging rope-like hindmost part of an animal

tale = a story

93. team = a group of players

teem = be full of or swarming with; (especially of rain) pour down, fall heavily

94. their = possessive (pronoun)

there = adverb (introductory)

95. tray = a flat rectangular plate to carry glasses and cups

trey = a playing card or dice with three spots

96. troop/s = soldiers or armed forces

troupe = a group of musicians or dancers

97. tuff = a light porous rock formed by volcanic ash
    tough = strong; unyielding
98. tyre = tough rubber covering on the rim of a car or bike
    tire = exhaust
99. vain = having an exaggerated opinion of one's appearances or abilities; useless
    vein = the tube that carries blood from all parts of the body to heart
100. waive = refrain from insisting on or applying (a right or claim)
    wave = move hands to and fro in greeting or as a signal; large ripples on the surface of a watery place
101. weak = feeble; not strong
    week = a period of seven days
102. weigh = find out the weight of an object
    way = path
    whey = the watery part of milk that remains after the formation of curds
103. wry = using or expressing dry, especially mocking, humour
    rye = a wheat-like cereal plant

C. Difference

Mark that the derivatives belong to the same word class but their meaning is different:

1. accelerate (verb) = increase speed
   acceleration (noun) = increase in speed
   accelerant (noun) = that which accelerates
2. access (noun) = the means or opportunity to approach or enter a place
   accession (noun) = the attainment of position of rank
   accessory (noun) = an addition to a thing to make it more useful

3. accompany (verb) = go somewhere with (someone)

   accompaniment (noun)= something that supplements or complements something else

   accompanist (noun) = a person who provides musical accompaniment

   accomplice (noun) = a person who helps another person in a criminal act

4. act = do something

   actant (n) = a person, creature, or object playing an active role in a play or novel

   action (n) = the process of doing something

5. address (verb) = speak formally to

   addresser (n) = the speaker, the writer

   addressee (n) = the listener, the receiver

6. challenge (n) = demanding task or situation; a call to fight

   challenging (adj) = One that challenges

   challenged (adj) = one that is suffering from impairment or disability in a specified respect

7. communalism = allegiance to one's own community rather than to the larger society

   communalist (adj and noun) = One who owes allegiance to one's community more than to the larger society

   communalistic (adj) = related to communalism

8. economy (n) = the state of a country in terms of its production, distribution and consumption

   economic (adj) = relating to economics or the economy

   economical (adj) = sparing in the use of resources or money

9. element (noun) = a basic constituent part

   elemental (adj) = fundamental; basic and primitive

   elementary (adj) = relating to the most rudimentary aspects of a subject

10. family (n) = [From Latin familia meaning "household servants, family]

    familiar (adj) = well known; usual; common

    familial (adj) = of or relating to family

11. empire (n) = a large area controlled by a monarch or an emperor; an extensive business controlled by a tycoon

    [From Latin imperium]

    (a) imperial (adj) = of or relating to an empire or emperor

    (b) imperious (adj) = arrogant and domineering

    Empiricism and empirical are not related to empire or the Latin word imperium; they have their source in Greek word emperikos meaning experience.

12. judiciary (n) = the judicial authorities of a country

    judicial (adj) = of or relating to judiciary

    judicious (adj) = having or done good judgement

13. Lyric (n) = a short poem

    lyricism (n) = of the qualities of a lyric such as melody, expression of emotion and flight of imagination

    lyricist = a person who writes lyrics

    [Lyrist is a different word and means a person who plays the lyre. Of course, a lyric was sung with a lyre and hence the name lyric arose]

14. match = correspond or resemble

    matchable (adj) = able to match

    This curtain is matchable in colour to that of our drawing room

    matching (adj) = matches actually. This curtain is wonderfully matching with the colour of your drawing room

15. milit (n) (French) = soldier

    the military (n) (English) = armed force

militia (n) (English) = a military force that is raised from the civil population to supplement the military or regular army

16. move (verb) = go or cause to go in a specified direction or manner; change position

mover (noun) = a person or thing that is moving; a person who instigates or organizes something

movement (noun) = an act of moving

movie = a cinema film

moving (adj) = in motion

moveable (adj) = capable of being moved

17. native (n) = a person born in a specified place

nativism (n) = the theory or doctrine that concepts and ways of thinking are innate rather than acquired or learned

nativity (n) = the occasion of a person's birth

18. nature (n) = the force that governs the natural phenomena of the world/universe

naturalism (n) = (in art and literature) a style and theory of representation based on the accurate description in detail

naturalist (n) = an expert in or student of natural history; an exponent or practitioner of naturalism

natural (adj) = existing in or derived from nature, not made by mankind

naturalistic (adj) = derived from or imitating real life or nature; based on the theory of naturalism

19. necessity (n) = the state or fact of being indispensable

necessary (adj) = required to be done, achieved or presented; needed

necessitous (adj) = (of a person) poor, needy

necessitate (v) = make necessary

20. pacify (v) = bring peace between two parties

pacifier (n) = a person or thing that pacifies

pacifism (n) = the belief that disputes should be settled by peaceful means and that war and violence are unjustifiable

21. precede (v) = occur before

    precedence (n) = the condition of preceding others in importance, order or rank

    precedent (n) = an earlier event or action serving as an example

22. preside (v) = be in a position of authority in a meeting, court or government

    presidency (n) = the office or status of president

    president (n) = the head of a meeting, office or government

23. project (n) = an enterprise, a plan undertaken

    projectile (n) = a missile fired or thrown at target

    projection (n) = an estimate or forecast based on present trends; a protruding thing; the projecting of an image, sound, etc.

24. protest (n, verb) = a statement or action expressing disapproval or objection to something; express objection to what is said to be done

    Protestant (n) = a member or follower of the Protestant sect of Christianity

    protestation (n) = an emphatic declaration against what is said or done

25. religion (n) = the belief in and worship of a superhuman controlling power, especially a personal good/goodness or gods and goddesses

    religiose (n) = excessively religious in practice

    religious (n) = of, concerned with, or believing in a religion

26. respect (n) = regard; deep admiration

    respectable (adj) = regarded by society as being proper, good and correct respectful (adj) = of, or relating to, respect. The small boy is respectful to his teacher

27. settle (v) = reach an agreement; pay a debt or account

    settlement (n) = the action or process of settling; a place where people establish a community

    settler (n) = a person who settles in an area

28. vary (v) = differ in size, weight, quantity and quality

    variance (n) = the fact or quality of being different or inconsistent (generally with the phrase at variance with)

    variation (n) = a change or slight difference in condition, amount, or level

D. One Word Substitution

There are many words which carry a meaning that will need many words otherwise. For example, look at these words and their meaning:

annual = that happens once a year

precocious = (mentally) more advanced than her/his age

philanthropist = one who does good to others without taking anything (except thanks) in return

A knowledge of such words helps a learner write paragraphs, letters, essays and précis effectively and precisely.

1. abate = (of something bad) become less intense (wind, noise, pain)
2. abduct = take (someone) away illegally by force or deception
3. aberration = an unwelcome or unacceptable deviation from what is normal
4. abet = encourage or assist (someone) to do something wrong, in particular to commit a crime
5. abolish = formally put an end to (a practice or institution)
6. abolitionist = A person who favours the abolition of something, especially capital punishment, bond labour, child labour, untouchability and caste system

7. abortion = the deliberate termination of pregnancy
8. abrogate = repeal or do away with (a law or agreement)
9. absolute = complete, total, unqualified or not dimished in any way
10. abstraction = the quality or process of dealing with ideas rather than events
11. academia = the academic environment or community
12. academy = a place of study or training in special field
13. accelerate = begin to move more quickly
14. accident = an unfortunate incident that happens unexpectedly or unintentionally
15. acclaim = praise enthusiastically and publicly
16. accolade = something granted as a special honour or in recognition of merit
17. accomplice = a person who helps another commit a crime
18. account = a record of financial expenditure and receipts
19. acoustic = relating to sound or hearing
20. active = moving or tending to move about vigorously or frequently
21. adage = a short statement expressing a general truth

    aphorism = a pithy observation expressing a general truth

    proverb = a short statement expressing a general truth
22. Addendum (singular) = an extra item added at the end of a book or text

    addenda (plural)

    appendix (singular)

    appendices/appendixes (plural)
23. adopt = legally take (another's child) and bring it up as one's own

24. advocate =
    1. a person who publicly supports or recommends a particular cause or policy
    2. a person who pleads on someone else's behalf in the court
25. affectation = behaviour, speech or writing that is artificial and designed to impress
26. affidavit = a written statement confirmed by oath or affirmation, for use as evidence in court
27. aggression = the action of attacking without provocation
28. agnostic = a person who believes that nothing is known or can be known of the existence or nature of God
29. ajar = (of a door or window) slightly open
30. alienation = the state or experience of being isolated
31. alignment = placement or arrangement in a straight line or into correct relative positions
32. alleviate = make (pain or difficulty) less severe
33. ally = a person or organization that co-operates with another
34. alumnus = a former pupil or student of a school/college alumni (plural)
35. ambivalent = having mixed feelings or contradictory ideas about something or a person
36. ambrosia = the food of gods (in Greek and Roman mythology)
37. ameliorate = make better; reduce the undesirable effect of
38. amnesty = an official pardon for people convicted of political offences
39. amnesia = a partial or total loss of memory
    dementia = total loss of memory
40. amphibian = a creature that lives in water and on land
41. Anachronism = a thing appropriate to a period other than that in which it exists; the attribution of something

to a period to which it does not exist. For example, reference to antibiotic medicines in the nineteenth century

42. anemia = the condition of deficiency of red cells in the human body
43. analogy = a comparison between one thing and another for the purpose of explanation or clarification; for example, comparison between a cat and a tiger
44. anarchy = a state of disorder due to lack of government or control
45. anathema = something a person strongly dislikes
46. ancillary = providing support to the primary activities of an organization or industry
47. androgynous = partly male and partly female in appearance
48. annals = a record of events year by year
49. annual = occurring once every year
50. annuity = a fixed sum of money paid to someone each year, typically for the rest of her/his life
51. annul = declare a lower contract (especially that of marriage) invalid
52. anomaly = something that deviates from what is standard or normal
53. anonym = an anonymous person or publication
54. anorexia = lack of appetite for food
55. antagonist = a person who actively opposes or is hostile
56. antenatal = before birth
57. anthem = a solemn patriotic song
58. anthology = a collection of poems or prose writings
59. anticipate = be ware of (a future event) and take action
60. antics = foolish, outrageous or amusing behavior
61. antidote = a medicine taken to counteract a particular poison

62. antique = a decorative object or piece of furniture that is valuable because of its age
63. aphrodisiac = a food, drink or drug that stimulates sexual desire
64. apiary = a place where bees are kept for honey
65. apocalypse = an event involving destruction or damage on catastrophic scale
66. apocryphal = (of a report) of doubtful authenticity, although widely circulated as being true
67. apologize = express regret for something that one has done wrong
68. apostate = a person who renounces her/his belief or principle
69. apparent = readily perceived or understood
70. arbitrary = based on random choice or personal whim
71. arcane = understood by a few
72. articulate = fluent and clear in speech
73. assiduous = showing great care and perseverance
74. astray = away from the correct path or direction
75. atheism = the theory or belief that God does not exist
76. autobiography (n) = biography written by the author himself
77. autocrat = a ruler who has absolute power
78. autograph = a celebrity's signature for her/his admirer
79. auxiliary = providing additional help and support
80. awry = away from appropriate or expected course or position
81. babble = talk rapidly and continuously in a foolish, excited or incomprehensible way
82. bachelor = a man who is not and has never been married
83. backdrop = a painted cloth hung at the back of theatre stage as part of the scenery

84. barometer = an instrument measuring atmospheric pressure
85. barren = a piece of land too poor to produce vegetation
86. bask = lie exposed in the sun for health
87. benevolent = well-meaning and kindly
88. betray = act treacherously towards (one's country) by aiding the enemy
89. bibliography = a list of sources listed at the end of a book for references
90. bibliophile = a person who collects books or has a great love of them
91. bifurcate = divide into branches
92. bilingual = speaking two languages fluently
93. bimonthly = occurring once in two months; or taking place twice in a month
94. binoculars = an optical instrument with a lens in each, used for viewing distant objects
95. bleed = lose blood due to injury, external or internal
96. blink = shut and open the eyes quickly
97. blitz = an intensive and sudden attack
98. boycott = withdraw from commercial and social relations with, as a punishment or protest
99. breakthrough = a sudden important development or success
100. bypass = a road passing round a town to avoid congestion or traffic jam; a surgical operation to make an alternative passage to aid the circulation of blood
101. cabinet = a cupboard with drawers or shelves for storing or displaying articles; the cabinet—a group of senior ministers responsible for government's policy and administration
102. cacophony = loud unpleasant mixture of discordant sounds

103. Caesarian section = an operation for the delivery of a child from its mother's womb
104. cafe = a small restaurant selling light meals and drink
105. cajole = persuade (someone) to do something by sustained coaxing and flattery
106. cakewalk = a very easy task
107. calamity = an event causing great and often sudden damage or distress
108. calibre = quality of character or level of ability
109. calibrate = correlate the readings of (an instrument) with those of a standard
110. callback = an invitation to return for a second audition or interview; a telephone call made to return one that someone has received
111. camouflage = the disguising of military personnel and equipment by painting or covering them to make them blend with the surroundings
112. campaign = a series of military operations; series of planned activities with a particular social, political or commercial aim
113. canard = an unfounded rumour or story
114. cannibal = a person who eats the flesh of other human beings
115. canon = a general rule or principle by which something is judged.

     cannon = a large heavy automatic gun
116. capable = having the ability or quality to do something
117. capacity = having the strength to do something
118. capture = take into one's possession or control by force
119. caretaker = a person employed to look after a house or guest house
120. carnivore= an animal that feeds on flesh
121. cascade = a small waterfall

122. challenged = suffering from impairment or disability in a specified respect
123. charisma = compelling attractiveness or charm that can inspire devotion
124. choke = prevent from breathing by depriving of air
125. chord = a straight line joining the ends of one or two points on the circumference of a circle; combination of notes usually sounded together in harmony
126. choreograph = compose the sequence of steps and moves for (a dance performance)
127. chronometer = a high precision watch to measure time accurately
128. cliché = an overused phrase or opinion
129. closure = an act of closing something
130. collide = hit by accident when moving
131. commemorate = honour the memory of someone as a mark of respect
132. commute = travel some distance between one's home and the place of work regularly
133. complacent = smug and uncritically satisfied with oneself or one's achievement
134. complaisant = willing to please others
135. comprehend = understand in detail
136. comprehensive = including or dealing with all or nearly all aspects of something
137. concert = a musical performance given in public, typically of several compositions
138. conference = a formal meeting of people with a shared interest, lasting between 2 and 5 days, generally
139. confess = admit to a crime or wrong doing
140. confiscate = take or seize property with authority
141. conjugal = the relationship between husband and wife
142. construe = interpret in a particular way
143. contiguous = sharing a common border

144. contingency = a future event or circumstance which is possible but cannot be predicted with certainty
145. contraband = goods that have been imported or exported illegally
146. convention = a way in which something is usually done
147. convert = change or cause to change inborn, character or function
148. corridor = a long passage from which doors lead into rooms
149. crawl = move forward on hands and knees or by dragging the body close to the ground
150. creep = move slowly and carefully to avoid being heard or seen noticed
151. crescent = the curved sickle shape of the moon
152. crude = in a natural or raw state
153. cynosure = a person or thing that is the centre of admiration or attention
154. dabble = move (one's feet or hands) around gently in water
155. daub = smear with a thick substance carelessly or liberally
156. demagogue = a political leader who seeks support by appealing to popular desires
157. demur = raise doubts
158. demurrage = a charge payable to the owner of the carrier for delay in loading or unloading the goods
159. dexterity = skill in performing tasks, especially with hands

     ambidextrous = one who is able to work with both right and left hands almost equally well
160. diagnosis = the identification of a disease by observation of its symptoms
161. dilemma = a situation in which a difficult choice has to be made

162. diminish = make or become less
163. discourse = a formal discussion of a topic in speech or writing
164. dishevelled = (of a person's hair, clothes and body) untidy
165. dispossess = deprived of land and property
166. disposition = a person's inherent qualities of mind and character
167. dissident = the person who opposes official policy
168. dissuade = advise someone against (its autonym is persuade)
169. divert = cause to change course or take a different route
170. diverge = take a different direction
171. dole = benefit paid by the government to the unemployed
172. domesticate = take a wild animal and make it a pet
173. dormant = as if in a deep sleep
174. draught = a current of cool air in a room
175. drone = make a continuous low humming sound; male honey bee
176. dummy = a model or replica of a human being
177. dynasty = a line of hereditary rulers
178. dystopia = an imaginary place or society where everything is bad. It is antonym of *utopia*
179. eager = strongly desirous to do
180. eclectic = deriving ideas or style from a broad and diverse range of sources
181. ego = a person's sense of self-esteem or self-importance
182. egoism = an ethical theory that treats self-interest as the foundation of morality
183. egotism = the quality of being excessively conceited or self-centered
184. elocution = the skill of clear and expressive speech, especially of distinct pronunciation and articulation

185. enclosure = an area that is sealed off by a barrier
186. endorse = declare one's public approval
187. environment = the surroundings in which living creatures and vegetation exist
188. equivocal = unclear in meaning or intention
189. ethereal = extremely delicate and light in a way that seems to be unearthly
190. euphemism = use of a mild word (in place of more accurate) for unpleasant experience or physical defect
191. extract = take out a part from something large
192. exuberant = lively and cheerful
193. extrinsic = not essential; not belonging to a part of the real nature of a person or thing; its antonym is "intrinsic"
194. façade = the face of a building, especially its front
195. facsimile = an exact copy, especially of a written or printed material
196. fade = gradually grow faint and disappear
197. figment = a thing believed to be real but existing only in the imagination
198. fixate = cause to be excessively interested in something or someone
199. float = rest or cause to rest on the surface of a liquid without sinking
200. freight = transport of goods in bulk, especially by truck, train or ship
201. frontier = a border separating two countries
202. funeral = a ceremony in which the dead is buried/ cremated
203. genetic = of or relating to heredity or gene
204. gentry = people of good education and position
205. glean = collect gradually from different sources
206. gouge = make a rough hole

207. granary = a storehouse for threshed grain
208. grey area = an ill-defined area of activity, not conforming to any act of rules
209. hackneyed = old and stale because of constant use
210. handicapped = physically or mentally challenged
211. hell-bent= determined to achieve something at all costs
212. heritage = property and other valuable things passed on to the next generation
213. heterogeneous = diverse in character or content
214. homogeneous = consisting of parts, all of the same kind or content
215. horizon = the line where the sky and the earth appear to meet
216. ibid = in the same source
217. illusion = a false or unreal perception
218. imminent = about to happen
219. immigrate = come to live permanently in a foreign country
220. emigrate = go to a foreign country to live there permanently
221. immunity = the ability to fight against disease causing bacteria and virus
222. incantation = a series of words said as a magic spell or charm
223. incapacitate = prevent from functioning in normal way
224. indelible = (of ink and work) unable to be removed
225. indemnify = compensate in respect of harm or loss
226. indomitable = that cannot be controlled
227. indistinct = not clear or sharply defined
228. inference = a conclusion reached on the basic of evidence and reasoning
229. insane = in an unsound state of kind
230. inscribe = write or carve (words or symbols) on a surface as a formal and permanent record

231. integrity = the quality of having strong moral principles
232. insurgent = rising in active revolt (insurgency)
233. intercept = obstruct and prevent from continuing to destination
234. itinerary = a planned route or journey
235. jubilee = a special anniversary celebrated twenty-five or fifty or seventy-five give years after the event
236. jurisdiction = the official power to make legal decision and judgements
237. juxtaposition = placing two things closely together
238. kleptomania = a recurrent urge to steal
239. labyrinth = a complicated irregular network of passages or paths; maze
240. landscape = all the visible features of an area of land
241. liaison = communication or co-operation between people or organizations
242. macabre = disturbing and horrifying because of depiction of death and fatal injury
243. magnanimous = very generous and forgiving, especially to the less powerful persons
244. magnate = wealthy and influential person, especially in business (tycoon)
245. manna = heavenly food given to Israelites (as described in Exodus, the Bible)
246. matriarchy = a system in which mother is the head of family (antonym is patriarchy)
247. memorandum = a written message in business or diplomacy
248. meteorology = a study of changes in atmosphere with special focus on weather
249. migrate = animals and birds move from one habitat to another according to the seasons
250. mince = cut or chop meat into very small pieces
251. miniature = of a very small size

252. misogynist = a man who hates women
253. moderate = average in amount, intensity or degree
254. molest = pester or harass in a hostile or indecent way
255. monologue = a long speech by one actor in a play (dialogue is its opposite; it is a conversation between two or more characters)
256. moratorium = a temporary prohibition of an activity
257. mortuary = a room or building where dead bodies are kept until burial or cremation
258. multiple = having or involving several parts
259. mute = refrained from speech or temporarily speechless
260. mutilate = injure or damage severely, typically so as to disfigure
261. mystify = utterly bewilder; make obscure or mysterious
262. nag = harass (someone) constantly to do something to which he/she is averse
263. nap = a short sleep, especially during day
264. narcissism = excessive or erotic interest in oneself and one's physical appearance (source: Greek myth of Narcissus)
265. native = a person born in a specified place or associated with a place by birth; a plant or an animal of indigenous birth
266. nausea = a feeling of sickness with an indication to vomit
267. nebulous = in the form of a cloud; of a concept or idea (vague or ill-defined)
268. neocolonialism = the use of economic, political or cultural pressure to control or influence other countries
269. nominal = existing in name only; far below the real value or cost (I purchased this second hand bike at a nominal price)
270. nonplus = surprise and confuse

271. nuisance = a person or thing causing inconvenience or annoyance
272. nursery = a room in a house for the special use of children; a place where young plants and trees are grown
273. obese = grossly fat or overweight
274. obituary = a notice of a person's death in a newspaper, typically including a short life-sketch and a photograph
275. obligation = an act or course of action to which a person is morally or legally bound
276. obdurate = stubbornly refusing to change one's opinion or course of action
277. obfuscate = make unclear or unintelligible
278. oblivious = not aware of what is happening around
279. obsolete = no longer produced or used
280. obvious = easily perceived or understood
281. occasional = occurring infrequently or irregularly
282. occident = the countries of the West, especially Europe and America
283. ocular = connected with the eyes
284. omen = an event regarded as a portent of good or evil
285. ominous = giving the worrying impression that something bad is going to happen
286. omni = of all things

    This is a prefix and its addition denotes mastery or supremacy. The common words formed with omni are omnipresent, omniscient, omnicompetent, omnifarious and omnipotent
287. onerous = involving an oppressively burdensome amount of effort and difficulty
288. onslaught = a fierce or destructive attack
289. opaque = not able to be seen through; difficult or impossible to understand. Its antonym is *transparent*

290. ophthalmology = the branch of medicine concerned with the diseases of the eyes
291. optimism = hopefulness and confidence about the future
292. optimum = most conducive to a favourable outcome
293. oracle = the enigmatic words of the possessed priest in Greek temple, especially of Delphi, about the future of the nation
294. ornithology = the scientific study of birds
295. ornate = highly decorated
296. orthopaedics = the branch of medicine that studies the deformities of bones and muscles
297. ostentation = the pretentious display of wealth, skill or knowledge, designed to impress
298. ostensible – apparently true, but not necessarily so
299. outcry = a strong public disapproval
300. outside = the external side or surface of something
301. pacific = peaceful in character or intent
302. pacifist = one who believes that disputes should be solved by mutual understanding, not by war
303. pageant = a procession of people in elaborate costumes
304. palatable = pleasant to taste
305. palliative = relieving pain or alleviating/easing a tense situation without dealing with its cause
306. pamper = indulge (someone) with a great deal of attention and comfort. For example, pampering parents
307. paragon = a person or thing regarded as a model of excellence or of a particular quality. For example, a paragon of beauty
308. paramount = more important than anything
309. parasite = an organism which lives in or on another organisms and benefits by deriving nutrients at the other's expense
310. parsimony = extreme unwillingness to spend money or resources

311. passim = (of references) at various places throughout the text
312. patron = a person who gives financial or other support to a person or organization
313. penitent = feeling or showing sorrow and regret for having done wrong (its synonym is repentant)
314. penultimate = last but one
315. perception = the ability to see, hear or become aware of something through the senses
316. peripatetic = travelling from place to place
317. perpetual = never ending or changing
318. personnel = people employed in an organization
319. pessimism = lack of hope or confidence in future; the view that the future of the world is dark
320. pestilence = a fatal epidemic disease
321. philanthropist = a person who seeks to promote the welfare of others, especially by donating money to good causes
322. pilgrim = a person who journeys to a sacred place for religious reasons
323. pilfer = steal things of little value
324. pioneer = a person who is the first to explore a possibility, or develop new ideas or techniques
325. pirate = a person who attacks and robs ships at sea
326. piracy = the act of robbing ships at sea; the unauthorized use of contents of a book or books
327. platter = a large flat dish
328. pledge (n) = a solemn promise or undertaking; a thing that is given as security for the fulfillment of a contract or the payment of a debt
329. plod = walk slowly with tired steps
330. portent (n) = a sign that a calamitous event may happen
    portend (v) be a sign that a calamitous event may happen
331. posterity = all future generations

332. post-mortem = the examination of a dead body to determine the cause of death; autopsy
333. precipitous = dangerously high and steep
334. predicament = a difficult situation
335. predict = state that (a specified event) will happen in the future
336. premature = occurring or done before the proper time
337. prevaricate = speak or act evasively
338. pretext = a false reason used to justify an action
339. prodigy = a person, especially a young one, with exceptional abilities
340. precocious = having developed certain abilities at an earlier age than usual
341. procrastinate = delay or postpone action
342. profile = an outline or something, especially a face, as seen from one side
343. prolific = producing much fruit and foliage; (of a writer) producing many works
344. proletariat = the working-class people
345. propound = put forward (an idea, theory, etc.) for consideration
346. proponent = a person who advocates a theory, proposal or project
347. puerile = childishly, silly and trivial
348. pungent = having a sharp or strong taste or smell
349. pursue = follow in order to catch or attack
350. quarantine = a state, period or place of isolation for people or animals that have arrived from elsewhere or been exposed to contagious disease
351. quintuplet = each of five children born at one birth

     quadruplet = each of four children born at one birth

     triplet = each of three children born at one birth

     twin = each of two children born at one birth

352. rack = a framework for holding or storing things
353. racketeer = a person engaged in fraudulent business dealings
354. radiate = emit (light, heat, or other energy) in the form of rays or waves
355. raid = a rapid surprise attack on people or premises
356. ramp = a sloping surface joining two different levels
357. rational = based on or in accordance with reason or logic
     rationale = a set of reasons for a course of action
358. ravage = cause extensive damage to
359. raze = tear down and destroy (a building)
360. recuperate = recover from illness or exertion
361. redeem = make up for one's past poor performance or behavior; save from sin, error or evil
362. redemption = the action of redeeming someone or something or of being redeemed.
363. referendum = a general vote by the electorate on a single political question
364. refute = prove an argument or statement wrong by logic
365. regicide = the killing of a king
366. regime = a government, especially an authoritarian one
367. reinstate = restore to a former position or state
368. relinquish = giving up a claim voluntarily
369. remainder = a part, number or quantity that is left over
370. remuneration = payment for a service done
371. renovate = restore (something old) to its former condition or shape
372. replicate = make an exact copy of; duplicate
373. replica = an exact copy
374. reprobate = an unprincipled person
375. resonant (adj) = (of sound) deep clear and continue to sound or ring

376. respiration = the action of breathing
377. ruffle = make or become disarranged
378. rumble = make a continuous deep, resonant sound
379. rupture = break or burst suddenly
380. ruthless = having or showing no compassion
381. salvation = deliverance from sin and its consequences
382. sane = of sound mind
383. sanguine = cheerfully optimistic; blood-red
384. scan = look at quickly in order to identify relevant features or information; traverse with detector to obtain image
385. scant = barely sufficient
386. scanty = small or insufficient in quantity
387. scapegoat = a person who is blamed for wrong-doing or mistakes of others
388. schedule (n) = a plan for carrying out a process or procedure giving lists of intended events and times
389. scour = clean or brighten with vigorous rubbing
390. secular = not religious, sacred or spiritual; not bound by religious rules
391. sensitive = quick to detect, respond to, or be affected by slight change
392. sensitize = cause to respond to certain stimuli
393. sensor = a device which detects or measures a physical property
394. sententious = given to moralizing in a pompous or affected manner
395. sentiment = view, opinion or feeling
396. sentimental = deriving from feelings of tenderness, sadness or nostalgia
397. sentinel = a soldier or guard whose job is to stand and keep watch
398. sentry = a soldier stationed to keep guard or to control access to a place

399. sequence = a particular way in which related events, movements and items follow each other
400. sericulture = the production of silk and the rearing of silk-warms for this purpose
401. shell = a thin hard outer cover of an egg, firework or explosives
402. shimmer = shine with a soft tremulous/trembling light
403. shower = a brief and usually light fall of rain or snow
drizzle = continuous light fall of rain
404. shroud = a length of cloth wrapped round a dead body at the time of funeral
405. silhouette = the dark shape and outline of someone
406. sinecure = a position requiring little or no work but giving the holder status or financial benefit
407. simultaneous = occurring or doing at the same time
408. sinister = suggestive of evil or harm
409. skeleton = an external or internal framework of bones
410. skim = remove (a substance) from the surface of a liquid For example, remove the cream from the surface of milk
411. slam = shut loudly and forcefully
412. slash = cut with a violent sweeping movement
413. slaughter = the killing of farm animals for food
414. slippery = difficult to hold firmly
415. smack = have a smell of
416. smart = clean, tidy and stylish
417. snap = break or cause to break with a cracking sound
418. sociable = engaging readily with other people
419. solemn = formal and dignified
420. solecism = a grammatical mistake; a piece of bad manners or behavior
421. soliloquy = an act of speaking loudly to oneself on the stage

422. somersault = an act in sports when the player jumps in the opposite direction by turning feet over head
423. sonic = related to sound
424. strategy = a long plan to achieve a specific end
425. temerity = excessive confidence or boldness
426. spark = a small fiery particle coming from a hearth or burning coal
427. squalid = extremely dirty and unpleasant
428. starve = suffer badly from hunger
429. subjugate = bring under control or subjugation
430. subsidy = a sum of money from public funds to help an industry or business to keep the price of commodity low
431. succinct = briefly and clearly expressed
432. succour = assistance and support in times of hardship and distress
433. sultry = (of weather) hot and humid
434. supercilious = having an air of contemptuous superiority
435. superficial = on the surface only
436. susceptible = easily influenced by something or someone's word
437. synchronize = cause to occur or operate at the same time
438. systematize = arrange things or ideas methodically or under certain rules
439. tableau = a group of models or motionless figures representing a scene
440. taboo = a social or religious custom to prohibit certain activities
441. tabular = (of data) consisting of or presented in columns or tables
442. tabula rasa = an absence of preconceived ideas or prejudices
443. tactics = an action or strategy carefully planned to achieve a specific end

444. talent = natural aptitude or skill
445. tantalize = torment or tease with a promise or visible object which is never fulfilled or gained
446. teetotaller = abstinence from drinking and smoking
447. teller = a person who deals with customers' transactions in a bank
448. temperament = a person's state of mind and behaviour
449. temperate = of mild climate, neither very cold nor very hot
450. temperance = absence from alcoholic drinks
451. temporal = of or relating to time; worldly affairs not spiritual
spatial = of or relating to space
452. tendentious = calculated to promote a particular cause or point of view
453. tenacious = not readily relinquishing something
454. tenacity = the quality to hold firmly
455. tender = gentle and sympathetic
456. terminate = bring to an end
457. terracotta = unglazed, typically brownish – red earthenware
458. territory = an area controlled by a ruler or state
459. testify = give evidence as a witness in a court of law
460. theme = the subject, topic or idea of a piece of writing
461. therapy = treatment to heal and cure a disorder in the body
462. thermal = of or relating to heat
463. thespian = of or relating to drama and the theatre
464. thorough going = involving every detail or aspect
465. thrash = beat repeatedly and violently with a whip or stick
466. thrust = push suddenly (to go ahead)
467. topnotch (informal) = of the highest quality

468. tortuous = full of twists and turns; excessively lengthy and complex
469. tout = a broker of low quality
470. trace = find by investigating; find or describe the origin and development; copy (drawing, map or design) by drawing over its lines on a super imposed transparent paper
471. track = a rough path or a minor road
472. trammel = restriction to freedom of action
473. transaction = the action of conducting business
474. transactions = published report of the meetings of a learned society
475. transcend = go beyond the limits of
476. transcendental = of or relating to a spiritual realm
477. transitory = not permanent, living for a short time
478. translucent = allowing light to pass through partially; semi-transparent
479. transparent = allowing light to pass through so that the objects are clearly seen on the other side
480. transmit = cause to pass on from one place to another or one person to another
481. transpire = come to be; prove to be
482. tremendous = very great amount
483. tremor (n) = an involuntary quivering moment
484. trendy = very fashionable
485. trepidation = a feeling of fear or agitation about something that may happen
486. trespass = enter someone's land or property without permission
487. triad = a group or set of three connected people or things
488. trinity = Father, Son and Holy Ghost
489. trident = a three pronged spear (Hindi *trishul*)

490. trilateral = shared by or involving three parties
bilateral = share by or involving two parties

491. triennial = lasting for or recurring every three years
biennial = lasting for or recurring every two years
biannual = occurring twice a year
annual = occurring once a year

492. trillion = one million million

493. trip (n) = a journey for pleasure
trip (v) = (or electricity) disconnect automatically as a safety measure

494. triumph = a great victory

495. trivial = of little value

496. truant = a pupil who absents herself/himself from class without permission

497. trudge = work very slowly and with heavy steps

498. truism = a statement that is obviously true but says nothing new
altruism = selfless concern for the well-being of others

499. tumble = fall down suddenly and clumsily or headlong

500. tyranny = cruel and oppressive government

501. tyrant = cruel and oppressive ruler

502. ubiquitous = present or appearing everywhere

503. ultimate = being or happening at the end
penultimate = just before the ultimate

504. ulterior = other than what is apparent or obvious

505. uprising = an act of resistance or rebellion

506. upstart = a person who has become rich or eminent suddenly, especially one who behaves arrogantly

507. usurp = take possession by force or illegally

508. uxorious = showing great or excessive fondness for one's wife

509. vacillate = waver between different opinions or actions; keep changing one's mind
510. vagrant = a person without a home or job
511. validate = check or prove the validity of
512. valetudinarian = a person who is excessively anxious about her/his health
513. vanish = disappear suddenly and completely
514. vanquish = defeat completely
515. vantage = a place or position allowing or giving a good view
516. variegated = showing different colours
517. vendetta = a bloody feud in which the family of murdered person takes or seeks revenge on the murderer or the murderer's family
518. vengeance = a punishment given for a perceived injury (eye for eye, for example)
519. veteran = a person who has a very long experience in a particular field (for example, a veteran of war)
520. vicissitude = a change of circumstances or fortune, typically for the worse
521. vindictive = showing or having a strong or unreasoning desire for revenge
522. virtual (adj) = almost as described

     virtually (adv) = nearly or almost
523. vista = a pleasing view, especially seen through a long, narrow opening
524. vivid = producing powerful feelings or strong, clear images in the mind
525. volatile = changing rapidly, for good or worse
526. voluptuous = relating to or characterized by luxury and sensual pleasure
527. voracious = wanting or devouring a large quantity of food (for example, a voracious eater)

528. vow (n) = a solemn promise
vow (v) = solemnly promise to do something
529. voyage = a long journey in the sea or space
530. vulnerable = exposed to being attacked or harmed
531. wade = walk through a liquid. (water generally)
532. wafer = a very thin light sweet biscuit
533. waft = pass easily or gently through the air
534. wag = (of an animal's tail) move to and from one side to the other quickly
535. wage = a fixed payment for a work an either daily or weekly basis
536. warble = (of birds) singing softly and with constantly changing notes in succession
537. washout = a disappointing defeat; the removal of material from the body by washing with a fluid
538. washroom = a room with washing and toilet facilities
539. wave = move hands to and fro as a mark of greeting or as a signal
540. wean = accustom an infant to food other than mother's milk
541. wild card = a playing card which can have any value
542. wince = give a slight involuntary grimace or flinch due to pain or distress
543. wobble = move unsteadily from side to side
544. wreck = the destruction of ship at sea
545. yawn = open mouth widely and take breath involuntarily when tired
546. zealot = a fanatical and uncompromising follower of a religion or policy
547. zest = a great enthusiasm and energy
548. zoom = (of a car) move very fast; (of a camera) change smoothly from a long shot to close-up or vice-versa

Abbreviation, Acronym and Blend Words

Abbreviation, acronym and blend words are products of word coinage. They are not entirely new words as they are made from the segments of existing words.

Abbreviation. Abbreviation is formed by taking the first letters of an existing compound word. For example:

Prime Minister → P.M.; Finance Minister → F.M.

Master of Arts → M.A.; District Magistrate → D.M.

An abbreviation makes it easy to pronounce a long compound words and saves times in speech and space in writing.

Acronym. An acronym is a word made from an abbreviation. Let us take the word "radar". It is basically the abbreviation of "radio detection and ranging. The underlined letters form the abbreviation RADAR. As it is possible to the abbreviate a word, it became a word in course of time; for examples:

(a) Aids = *a*cquired *i*mmunity *d*eficiency *s*yndrome

(b) Laser = *L*ight *a*mplification by *s*timulated *e*mission of *r*adiation

(c) scuba = *s*elf *c*ontained *u*nderwater breathing apparatus

Generally, long compound words used in science, medicine and technology become acronyms, if possible, as it is difficult to speak or write very long words.

Blend words or Portmanteaus. Blends are compounds of two words that at the time of blending lost some segments. After listening to the "jabberwocky", Lucy, the main character in *Through the Looking-Glass*, asks the meaning of the poem as she does not understand the meaning of many words, she never came across. She is given the explanation that words like "brillig" and "mimsy" are *portmanteau* words. "Brillig" means four *O'clock* in the afternoon, the time of broiling things for dinner and "*slithy*" means *lithe* and *slimy* and "mimsy" means *miserable* and *flimsy*. The portmanteau words convey the complex concept in minimum words possible. Even before Lewis Carroll the word *diminish* was coined by joining the Latin words "diminue" and "minish". The most common blends are given below:

brunch = breakfast and lunch
dejectent = dejected + despondent
edutainment = education + entertainment
infortainment = information + entertainment
harage = harass + ravage
smog = smoke + fog
symblem = symbol + emblem
sitcom = situation + comedy
tip = to + insure + promptness
vibgyor = violet + indigo + blue + green + yellow + orange + red

Aids, laser, radar and scuba are already explained.

Chapter Thirteen

Sequence of Sentences: Reconstruction

Outcome of the Chapter

(a) Order in sentences
(b) Unity
(c) Coherence

It is necessary that a long sentence should be a single unity and all its phrases and clauses be linked grammatically and logically. We read in the chapter on noun phrase, verb phrase, prepositional phrase and adverb phrase that every word in a phrase has a fixed slot. Similarly, clauses are closely linked.

Paragraphs, have sentences in a particular order also. The main principle is unity and coherence. By unity we mean wholeness, that is, a paragraph or an essay should have a beginning, a middle and an end. A paragraph, in other words, should be a regular sequence of sentences. This sequence can be either chronological or logical or both. Illustrations will explain the point.

Order in Sentences

Although he was born in a little village near the coast and had gone to school in the nearest seaside town, Mr. Wilmot was not a lover of the sea; even when walking along the sands he was always afraid of being cut off by the tide.

This sentence consists of two sentences joined by a semicolon. The first sentence has two subordinate clauses joined by "and". They are dependent upon the principal or main clause "Mr. Wilmot was not a lover of sea." The second sentence, traditionally considered, is a simple sentence but, in fact, it too has two subordinate clauses. All phrases and clauses are properly placed and the second part of the sentence follows the first logically.

The following sentence is disorderly and needs reconstruction.

He was a man who was loved by all those who were close to him till the end of his life if not publicly recognized. We find that the clause "if not publicly recognized" is not properly placed; it is rather hanging loosely at the end of the sentence. Its right place is after the relative pronoun. The sentence should read:

He was a man who, if not publicly recognized, was loved by all those who were close to him till the end of his life.

In examinations, candidates are required to re-order or reconstruct a sentence. The phrases or clauses are underlined and named PQRS universally accepted symbols in this category. There are four choices given. They have to put tick mark on the choice they think to be the right answer. A few examples are given.

1. When you

   P. which one is closest in meaning

   Q. read the four sentences in your text book and decide

   R. to the statement you have heard

   S. hear a statement,

   (a) SRPQ (b) SQPR (c) SPQR (d) QPSR

   Since the verb should come immediately after the subject, Q and S are the natural choices to follow the main clause. Q is eliminated because P and S do not follow S. So the proper sequence is (b) SQPR.

2. He started the book thinking

   P. he decided to

   Q. that it would be an interesting work

   R. but by the time he reached the middle

   S. throw it away

(a) (a) PSQR (b) QRPS (c) RSPQ (d) SPRQ

The main sentence ends with the word "thinking" and needs a subordinate clause. Therefore, Q follows it grammatically. Since the first sentence is complete, it can be linked only with a co-ordinator. Here the co-ordinator is "but". So the next is R. P is the next choice because it has the preposition "to" which makes the verb of s an infinitive. The choice will be (b) QRPS.

3. Almost every country in the world

   P. that they have become the best

   Q. it has some special dispensation from Providence

   R. and that others are somewhat inferior creatures

   S. believes that

   (a) PRSQ (b) RQSP (c) RSPQ (d) SQPR

   The verb should follow its subject immediately. Therefore, the first choice will be S. The next is Q because it is a full sentence to be connected by "that" to become a subordinate clause. The next choice is naturally P which begins with "that" subordinator and the final choice is R. The sequence is SQPR.

Unity and Coherence in a Passage

Candidates are required to reorder the jumble sentences to make them logically sequential. The pattern of question is the same as that of reconstructing a sentence. There are all together six sentences. The first sentence marked I is the opening sentence and the sixth sentence marked is the closing one. The sentences marked PQRS are to be reorded.

Example 1

S1: The defence expenditure next will be ₹ 2845 crore in a total budget of ₹ 18716 crore.

S6: All this is the revenue account.

P. The army naturally gets the lion's share of ₹ 1897 crore.

Q. Of the remaining amount a large proportion goes to pensions and retirement benefits.

R. This means that 16 paise out of every rupee in the central budget goes for defence.

S. The combined expenditure on the Air Force and Navy comes to another 791 crore.

The proper sequence should be

(a) PSQR (b) SQRP (c) RPSQ (d) PQSR

The sentence R follows S1 logically because it expresses the idea of S1 in different words. Sentences P and S go together but the word "another" in S makes it follow P. The last sentence is Q. Therefore, the correct sequence is RPSQ, that is (c).

Example 2

S1: This is how milk is pasteurized.

S6: Now milk becomes safer for drinking.

P. The temperature is maintained for about 15 minutes.

Q. This is done to kill bacteria.

R. The milk is first heated to a temperature of 70°C.

S. Milk is cooled rapidly to 4°C.

(a) RPSR (b) PSRQ (c) RPSQ (d) QSPR

The first sentence is R as it contains the word "first" and indicates the time sequence of the passage. The second sentence is for the word "maintain". The third sentence will be S as it has the words "cooled rapidly." Therefore, the sequence is RPSQ that is (c).

EXERCISES

(A) The first and the last parts of each sentence are given as 1 and 6 respectively. The remaining portion of the sentence is split into four parts, marked PQRS. These four parts are not given in proper order. Read the following sentences and find out the correct sequence:

(a) 1. In every country..................6. as they are.

P. they are the best and

Q. people imagine that

R. the cleverest and

S. the others are not so good

(i) RPQS (ii) PRSQ (iii) QPRS (iv) RQPS

(b) 1. In his numerous..................6. a charmed life.

P. hair-breadth escapes hitherto

Q. adventures and

R. seems to have had

S. he

(i) PSRQ (ii) QPRS (iii) SRQP (iv) QPSR

(c) 1. You are today..................6. what he wills.

P. and make him do

Q. as little man do

R. on top of

S. a great big elephant

(i) PSRQ (ii) QRSP (iii) QPSR (iv) RQSP

(d) 1. But people in ....6. written by hand.

P. which were beautifully

Q. books in libraries

R. those days wrote beautifully

S. and today we have many

(i) PRSQ (ii) SRPQ (iii) RSQP (iv) RQSP

(e) 1. To make a hut..................6. in a circle.

P. and plant them

Q. they take a number of

R. in the ground

S. long. thin wooden poles

(i) QSPR (ii) QRSP (iii) QPSR (iv) QPRS

(f) 1. Thus when the mosquito..................6. infected with malaria.

P. the black threads

Q. bites a human being

R. pass into the bloodstream

S. and a fresh patient becomes

(i) PRSQ (ii) RSPQ (iii) SRQP (iv) QPRS

(g) 1. There are ....6. its usual perfection.

P. in regard to which

Q. some matters

R. it must be admitted

S. the memory works with less than

(i) QPRS (ii) QPRS (iii) RQPS (iv) RSQP

(h) 1. There are people..............................6. they have read it.

P. not because they enjoy the book

Q. be able to say that

R. but because they want to

S. who read a book

(i) QRSP (ii) SPRQ (iii) SRPQ (iv) RSQP

(i) 1. And now they find.....................6. better off without science.

P. the distance which they enjoyed

Q. and the awe has turned to fear, and

R. turned to distrust

S. people who are by no means fools really believe that we should be

(i) PRQS (ii) PQRS (iii) PSQR (iv) PRSQ

(j) 1. But in China................................6. to left as in Urdu.

P. a kind of picture writing

Q. not from left to right as in Hindi or English or right

R. even now the writing is

S. and it is written from top to bottom

(i) RPSQ (ii) PRSQ (iii) RSQP (iv) RQPS

(B) There are altogether six sentences; the sentence marked 1 is the first sentence. The sentence marked 6 is the concluding one. The other four marked PQRS are not in order. Choose the correct sequence given at the end:

(a) S1: Many men and women used to live together and so we had the first

S6: Perhaps these were some wild nuts and fruits which men ate, but mostly they must have lived on animals they killed.

P. They had not noticed, therefore, nor did they have any wheat from which bread is made.

Q. They did not know then how to grow their food from land.

R. Before the cities were made men used to wander about from place to place, probably living in some kinds of tents.

S. There were no vegetables, and most of the things you eat today were not known then.

(i) QRSP (ii) PRSQ (iii) RSPQ (iv) RQPS

(b) S1: The Resident announced his plan to Koh and explained that it would give him prestige beyond calculation

S6: Pricked chiefly by his pride, he finally agreed to fly.

P. To give him courage, More led him to the pontoons and into the front cockpit, and tried to explain that it really wasn't dangerous at all.

Q. This seemed like invading the realm of gods and the demons.

R. It would also bring to the tribe as much glory as a successful head-hunting war.

S. But koh was dubious.

(i) SPQR (ii) PQRS (iii) RSPQ (iv) SQPR

(c) S1: Anna did not answer

S6: The husband asked if she would allow him to smoke,

evidently not because he wanted to, but to enter into conversation with her.

P. The couple sat down opposite her, attentively but stealthily examining her dress.

Q. She went back to her corner and sat down.

R. Both the husband and the wife seemed to Anna disgusting.

S. Neither the guard nor those entering noticed the horror on her face beneath the veil.

(i) RQPS (ii) QSRP (iii) PQSR (iv) PRSQ

(d) S1: The elephant was certainly tamed by the time of the Buddha

S6: In the second century B.C.E. the Chinese traveller Chang Kien found that Chinese silk was imported into Bactria by way of India.

P. Silkworms were bred and reared, chiefly in Bengal and Assam.

Q. But it is probable that silk was first introduced to India from China by way of the Burma Road, in the second half of the first millennium BCE.

R. It has been suggested that silk was known even in Vedic times.

S. The earliest certain references to silk are found in the Buddhist scriptures and the *Arthashastra* as Chinapatta.

(i) PRQS (ii) SQPR (iii) PQRS (iv) RQPS

Chapter Fourteen

Précis

Outcome of the Chapter

(a) How to write précis

The word "précis" is borrowed from French and it means precise. *The Concise Oxford English Dictionary* gives its meaning "summary of a text or speech". However, we make distinction between summary, précis and substance. Précis is highly technical and it needs a defined number of words; usually it is one-third of the text. Suppose the text is of 1000 words, then its précis would be 333 words. If the précis writer finds the text pithy he/she is given the liberty to add five to six words more and if the text is rather loose, the total may be upto 328 but never less than this. Besides the précis writer is expected to give a title to the text or speech.

Summary is like précis but much wider in scope. Summary can be a text of 5000 words, a long speech, a short story, a novel or a drama. The summary writer does not count words. Besides, he/she, while writing the summary of a novel or play is cautious enough to let the reader feel that he/she is enjoying the original. Charles Lamb's *Tales from Shakespeare* are classic summaries of the great dramatist's plays.

Substance is very short and touches the main idea and a few important points of the text or speech. The substance of a one page size poem can be written in three or four lines.

Précis is the most popular form of summarizing. Substance gives the main idea and related ideas and summary is meant for more difficult and larger texts; précis touches all the main points of the text in the simplest form. As a candidate has to write the précis of a given passage in the examination hall within a specified time, he/she must observe the following rules:

1. The précis must not exceed by two to three words of the word-limit nor should be shorter than two or three words.
2. It must cover all the important points of the given passage.
3. It should be written is candidate's own words. Quoting lines verbatim from the given passage is punishable.
4. The précis should be written in active voice as far as practicable. Passive construction is used when the writer wants to remain impersonal or the agent/doer is not known.
5. All comparisons, analogies and figures of speech in the text should not be included in the précis.
6. Examples should be avoided.
7. Supply a suitable title to the précis when asked.
8. The candidate must increase his/her vocabulary. A good knowledge of synonyms, antonyms and pithy words helps him/her write précis easily.
9. The candidate must perfect the skill of synthesizing two or three sentences into a simple sentence. Brevity is the most important aspect of précis writing.

How to Write Précis

The following steps are to be taken by a précis writer:

(a) Read the passage twice: first fast and second slow.
(b) Underline the lines that contain important points.
(c) Write the points on the answer-book.
(d) Connect all the points and write the précis. This is the rough draft.

(e) Read your rough draft and check if any points are left.

(f) Write the fair copy and revise it twice to check if any grammatical or spelling mistakes are there.

(a) Suggest a suitable title.

Example

Write a précis of the following passage and suggest a suitable title:

Students are responsible for familiarizing themselves with the University Code of Student conduct, as on enrolment with the university they place themselves under the policies and regulations of the University and all of its duly constituted bodies. Disciplinary authority is exercised through the Student Conduct Committee. The committee has procedures in place for hearing allegations of misconduct. Copies of the student conduct code are available at the Student Services Office. This includes cheating and plagiarism, which violate the Student Conduct Code and could result in expulsion or failing the course.

Cheating includes but is not limited to obtaining or giving unauthorized help during examination, getting unauthorized information about the content of an examination before it is administered, using unauthorized sources of information during an examination, altering or falsifying the record of any grades, altering of supplying answers after an examination has been handed in, falsifying any university record, and misrepresenting the facts to get exemptions from or extensions to course requirements. (Total words: 162)

First step: Points

(1) Conduct of students in the university

(2) Knowledge of and obedience to regulations of the university

(3) Disciplinary authority and Student Conduct Committee

(4) Academic dishonesty : cheating, plagiarism

(5) Cheating includes unauthorized help and receipt of the contents of examination, tempering with awarded grades, altering or supplying answers and misrepresenting facts.

(6) Plagiarism includes quoting long passages from other's works, using materials of different courses and utilizing data of others and fabrication of data to fit the expected results.

ROUGH DRAFT

After enrolment in the University students have to follow a code of conduct. The regulations are exercised by Disciplinary Authority through the Student Conduct Committee. Copies of the rules are available at the Student Services Office. Academic dishonesty is unpardonable. It includes cheating and plagiarism. Cheating means unauthorized help to others and receiving help from others in the examination. Plagiarism includes other's written material as one's own, using materials of other courses and fabrication of data to fit the expected results. 81 words.

As a rule the précis should be of 162 ÷ 3 = 54 words

Therefore, a few words are to be deleted and the language be made précis. Corrections and revisions should be made in the first fair copy.

FIRST FAIR COPY

Title: Students' Code of Conduct

Students have to follow a code of conduct exercised by Disciplinary Committee through the Student Conduct Committee of the University. The University does not condone academic dishonesty, especially cheating and plagiarism. Cheating means giving and taking help from others in the examinations, and tampering with grades. Plagiarism includes use of others' materials claiming them as one's own and fabrication of data to fit the expected results.

Total words 66

Here we have to reduce the number to 54-56.

FAIR COPY

Title: Students' Code of Conduct

Students have to follow Code of Conduct of the University, exercised by Disciplinary Committee. The University does not condone academic dishonesty. The Disciplinary Committee can punish them for violation of the code, especially for cheating and plagiarism. Cheating is use of unfair means in examinations, plagiarism and fabrication of data for the expected results.

Total 54 words

Since this passage is quite short and part of a notification, it is full of facts and it is rather strenuous to write a précis of it. But the passages which are given for practice are easier and longer.

EXERCISES FOR PRACTICE

Write précis of the following passages and suggest suitable title for each of them.

1. Pride of race is even more harmful than national pride. When I was in China I was struck by the fact that cultivated Chinese were more highly civilized than any other human beings, that it has been my good fortune to meet. Nevertheless I found a number of gross and ignorant white men who despised even the best of the Chinese solely because their skins were yellow. In general, the British were more to blame in this than Americans; but there were exceptions. I was once in the company of a Chinese scholar of vast learning, not only of the traditional Chinese kind, but also of the kind taught in Western universities, a man with a breadth of culture which I scarcely hoped to equal. He and I went together into a garage to hire a motor car. The garage proprietor was a bad type of American, who treated my Chinese friend like dirt, contemptuously accused him of being Japanese, and made my blood boil by his ignorant malevolence. The similar attitude of the English in India, exacerbated by their political power, was one of the main causes of the friction that arose in that country between the British and the educated Indians. The superiority of the race to another is hardly ever believed in for any good reason. Where the belief persists it is kept alive by military supremacy. So long as the Japanese were victorious, they entertained a contempt for the white man, which was the counterpart of the contempt that white man had felt for them while they were weak. Sometimes, however, the feeling of superiority has nothing to do with military prowess. The Greeks despised the barbarians, even at times when the barbarians

surpassed them in war like strength, the more enlightened among the Greeks held that slavery was justifiable so long as the masters were Greek and the slaves barbarians, but that otherwise it was contrary to nature. (323 words)

2. In what is sure to encourage whistleblowers, the Supreme Court has valued that the identity of the persons who tip off anticorruption agencies about corrupt deals of bureaucrats can never be revealed to the accused facing prosecution under Prevention of Corruption Act.

Anti-Corruption Bureau of Maharashtra had investigated a case of disproportionate assets against a public servant on the basic of a complaint filed by "unknown person" and chargesheeted the accused. The accused wanted a copy of the original complaint on the ground that it was essential for a fair trial. Rejecting his plea, the apex court bench said it failed to see how the accused was prejudiced by non-disclosure of the person who sent the complaint and by not being given the original copy of the complaint received by the Anti-Corruption Bureau.

"Situations are many where certain persons do not want to disclose the identity as well as the information/complaint passed on by them to the Anti-Corruption Bureau. If the names of the persons, as well as the copy of the complaint sent by them are disclosed, that may cause embarrassment to them and sometimes threat to their lives", said Justice Radhakrishnan, who authored the judgement for the bench.

The bench said what is to be borne in mind is that it was a complaint given by some person to the Anti-Corruption Bureau which triggered the investigation. "Thus complaint simply provided information to the Anti-Corruption Bureau and it is not the formation of the case or even the FIR," it said. On the case in hand the bench said, "In fact, after receiving the complaint the Anti-corruption Bureau held its independent investigation into the matter and collected the material which was forwarded to the home department. On that basis, Challan (Charge-sheet) was filed in the court pointing out that sufficient material emerged on record as a result of the said investigation to proceed against the petitioner under Prevention of Corruption Act. (330 words)

3. In the Indian Parliamentary system, the office of the President is like a "pivot" that joins the two wheels, namely the legislature and the executive, although his role is not so "pivotal". As stated earlier, the Parliamentary system belies the doctrine of strict separation of powers. Recall that, it is based on the fusion of powers wherein the executive is a part of the legislature. The office of the President is a constitutional conjunction where the legislative and the executive organs meet. At this, all executive powers are constitutionally vested in him. On the other hand, the President of India is also an integral component of the Indian Parliament. No bill without the assent of the President can become a law. The President has the power to summon either House of the Parliament, prorogue either House, and dissolve the Lower to legislate while the Houses are not in session. This will form the basic premise on which the legislature—executive relations will be discussed.

In our system, all governmental functions are carried in the name of the President. Article 74 of the Constitution puts on the President strict limitations on the exercise of executive powers. Prior to the 42nd Amendment, 1976, there was a little bit of ambiguity contained in this article. It was argued that the President is not bound to render conformity to the ministerial advice. It was no secret that President (Dr) Rajendra Prasad had disagreements on many issues with Prime Minister Nehru. The disagreement erupted into the public arena. Public statements made by the President amounted to veiled criticism of the government. Harnessing the ambiguity seemingly inherent to Article 74, Dr. Prasad ignited a public debate and called for the legal scrutiny of the President's power. The Indira Gandhi Government by the 42nd Amendment, 1976, made it obligatory upon the President to act upon the ministerial advice. The 44th Amendment, 1978, empowered the President to revert the advice for reconsideration. Most of the Presidents after Dr. Rajendra Prasad were far more restrained. (402 words)

4. The people are living beings. They have their distinct personalities. But nations are organizations of power, and therefore their inner aspects and outward expressions are

everywhere monotonously the same. Their differences are merely differences in degree of efficiency.

In the modern world the fight is going on between the living spirit of the people and the methods of nation-organizing. It is like the struggle that began in central Asia between cultivated areas of man's habitation and the continually encroaching desert sands, till the human region of life and beauty was choked out of existence. When the spread of higher ideals of humanity is not held to be important, the hardening method of national efficiency gains a certain strength; and for some limited period of time, at least, it proudly asserts itself as the fittest to survive. But it is the survival of that part of man which is the least living. And this is the reason why dead monotony is the sign of the spread of the Nation. The modern towns, which present the physiognomy due to this domination of the Nation, are everywhere the same, from San Francisco to London, from London to Tokyo. They show no faces, but merely masks.

The people, being living personalities, must have their self-expression, and this leads to their distinctive creations. These creations are literature, art, social symbols and ceremonials. They are like different dishes at one common feast. They add richness to our enjoyment and understanding of truth. They are making the world of man fertile of life and variedly beautiful.

But the nations do not create, they merely produce and destroy. Organizations for production are necessary. Even organizations for destruction may be so. But when, actuated by greed and hatred, they crowd away into a corner the living man who creates, then the harmony is lost, and the people's history runs at a break-neck speed towards same fatal catastrophe.

Humanity, where it is living, is guided by inner ideals; but where it is a dead organization it becomes impervious to them. Its building process is only an external process, and in its response to the moral guidance it has to pass through obstacles that are gross and non-plastic. (368 words)

5. Many of the developing countries will promote the growth of their economy in one way or another no matter whether they receive substantial aid in the process or not. The character of

that development, however, is likely to be strongly influenced by the types and amounts of the aid available. The outcome is much more likely to be favourable, from the standpoint of the objectives for successful development set up previously, if there is substantial international aid than if there is not.

By substantial aid I mean not only large amounts of technical assistance but also of capital. Initially, the capacity of a developing country to use capital productivity may be surprisingly small limited by lack of organization, trained personnel, and other social obstacles. At this stage technical assistance is the main need from outside, with comparatively small amounts of capital much of which may have to be in the form of grants for non-self-liquidating projects in education, health, access roads to rural areas, and the like. If at this state, substantial capital is available from outside to supplement what can be formed internally (and to stimulate internal capital formation, for it does that too) the rate of economic growth can be considerably increased, and the strains and frustrations and political risks of the development process are likely to be considerably less.

It is possible for the developing countries to modernize themselves with very little capital from outside. Japan's imports of capital were small, though some of it came at crucial times. The contribution of foreign direct investments to the advancements of technical know-how also was greater than would be indicated merely by the size of the investment. South Korea's progress has been fantastic after the implementation of FDI. India accepted the policy of FDI after liberalization in the time of Prime Minister Narsimha Rao and now that we have adopted the policy of FDI, we must work as hard as the people of Japan and South Korea and follow the new slogan Make in India.

Chapter Fifteen

Comprehension

Outcome of the Chapter

(a) Reading comprehension

(b) Ten ways to write the answers for unseen passages

What is Comprehension?

Comprehension implies an exercise of reading, thinking and understanding a group of sentences usually an article, a paragraph or a story. Most paragraphs contain a topic sentence—a sentence that states the main idea of the paragraph. Paragraphs also contain details of information that tells about the main idea. When you read an article, you may ask, "what is the point?" The point is the main idea about the article. The main idea is the central thought or meaning of a passage—what the passage is all about. Sometimes the author states the main idea of a selection in a topic sentence. The topic sentence is often the first or second sentence. The rest of the paragraph includes details that support or give information about that main idea. The details provide specific facts' examples, or reasons that support or explain the main idea. A fact is a statement that can be shown to be true. An opinion is a statement of belief, a guess, or a prediction.

The main idea of a piece of writing is its most important point. Sometimes it is not stated in the first or second, but it can be anywhere in a piece of writing. Sometimes the main idea is not stated directly, so you have to figure it out from the reading of the passage as a whole. Whether the main idea is stated or implied, the job of the supporting details is to give specific facts, examples, or reasons to support or explain the main idea. So you have to use your power of inference.

Tracking the reality behind events or statements is *inference*, you use every day. When you infer you use clues to figure out something that isn't apparently stated. For instance, you can infer people's feelings and the reasons behind their actions by watching and listening to them. Making inferences is sometimes called "reading between the lines". For example, you can use the clues in the paragraph along your experience and imagination. Your inference should be logical; it should be based on deductive reasoning, sequential analysis and critical thinking. Deductive reasoning means reaching a particular conclusion from a general principle. Deductive reasoning is sometimes referred to as top-down logic. Inductive reasoning is its opposite; it is sometimes referred to as bottom-up logic. Whereas reasoning proceeds from general premises to a specific conclusion. Inductive reasoning proceeds from specific premises to a general conclusion. Sequential analysis implies an orderly analysis based on related action/event/thought as it is developed in an order (one after another), relating to or arranged in a particular order or sequence/ happening in an order or sequence. Critical thinking employs deductive reasoning and analysis as tools. Critical thinking will enable students to understand scope as well as acquire to an awareness of the subject.

If you read a story, you know that the topic of a story is what the story is about. The theme of the story is the message or major idea the author is expressing through the story. It is a general message about life or human nature the writer wants to communicate.

However, sometimes the paragraph is about multiple ideas, so one may think that there would be more than one topic sentences but one should not forget that the central idea/theme of the paragraph would revolve round a topic. So usually there will be one topic sentence.

One should not confuse between supporting information and topic sentence. For practice students should use worksheets which will teach them how to think and read critically. Students read a passage and are then tested on their ability to understand scope, draw inferences, deduce the meaning of practical vocabulary words and find or recall details from the story/paragraph.

Ten Points to Remember

1. Read the questions first attentively.
2. Read the passage carefully but hurriedly mainly the introductory and the concluding portions.
3. Read the questions carefully and note what has been asked.
4. Read the passage again, now the whole of it. Read the bod y paragraphs more carefully as questions call for it.
5. Note the topic sentence, understand the main idea/ theme and underline the points referring to the questions.
6. Indulge in critical thinking and examine all contexts and acquire tonal awareness.
7. Try to understand the context of the questions asked. Understand the specific point being asked. Many times more than one choices will be true or partially true. Be specific and choose the best answer.
8. Do not make assumptions. You may guess or infer but your information must be based on what is actually given in the passage.
9. Avoid extreme answers—do not use words like absolutely, never, completely unless they are part of description in the passage.
10. You must not use prior knowledge in selecting or formulating your answer that can't be supported with information written in the passage.

Why should you Read the Questions First?

You should read the questions first, so that you are well aware of what to look for in the passage when you read. This helps you focus you r attention on important words and phrases.

Mark the passage lightly when you see those terms. If you first read the passage it often becomes necessary to search through the passage repeatedly.

Writing Answers

1. You should take special care to maintain subject-verb agreement depending upon tense.
2. Do not use double negatives or double comparisons.
3. Do not write run-on sentences; do not write fragments. Write small and complete sentences using connectives like when, after, because, but although, where, so, or, etc. to join independent clauses.

Comprehension Passages

1. After the historic victories at Gettysburg and Vicksburg, the situation had vastly improved for the Union, but the war was far from over. On November 22, 1863, President Lincoln delivered the Gettysburg Address at the dedication of the Soldiers National Cemetery at Gettysburg. The 272 word speech, which followed a two hour address by Harvard professor Edward Everett, would become one of the greatest speeches in American history. In March of 1864, President Lincoln appointed General Ulysses S., Grant Commander of the Army of Potomac, the main branch of the Union Army. Finally, after nearly three years of war, the President had found a general who would pursue fleeing Confederates. Grant, known as "Unconditional Surrender Grant" after his exploits at Fort Donelson, Tennessee, in 1862, was by this time a Union hero after leading the Army of the Tennessee to numerous victories in the West, including those at Shiloh and Vicksburg. Grant would spend 1864 waging his bloody Overland Campaign through much of the state of Virginia, suffering massive casualties while gradually diminishing the numbers and spirit of Lee's Army of Northern Virginia. Eventually, Grant would corner Lee's Arm y at Petersburg, Virginia, where he staged a ten-month siege. During the siege, Lincoln would visit Grant's headquarters at City Point, outside of Petersburg, where his presence excited and inspired the Union soldiers.

Meanwhile, Union General William T. Sherman struck another blow to the spirit of the Confederacy with his destructive march through the state of Georgia which would become known as Sherman's March to the Sea. Sherman's Army destroyed farm's railroad lines, and virtually anything in its path. After Sherman's capture of Atlanta, Georgia, President Lincoln easily won re-election to a second term. In contrast to his campaign platform in 1860, Lincoln made the emancipation of slaves a primary emphasis. Over 78 percent of Union soldiers would support his bid for a second term as President.

On April 9, 1865, the Confederate States of America surrendered at Appomattox Courthouse, Virginia. The Civil War was over and the Union would be preserved. At this point, President Lincoln had to consider the complicated task of reconstructing the Union and how to re-integrate the Confederate states back into the United States.

Lincoln believed in a policy of forgiveness and took a moderate approach to reconstruction, hoping to recon struct the Union as quickly as possible rather than indefinitely punish the rebel states. Unfortunately, the President did not have much of a chance to preside over Reconstruction. Just five days after the end of the war, Southern sympathizer and actor John Wilkes Booth assassinated the President while he was watching a play at Ford's Theater in Washington , D.C. Lincoln's bodyguard had abandoned his post, allowing Booth access to the Presidential box. Lincoln died at 7:22 the next morning at the Peterson House across the street from the theater. Upon his death, Secretary of War Edwin M. Stanton uttered the timeless words "Now, he belongs to the ages."

a. After the battle of Gettysburg and Vicksburg the situation had ....

(A) become impossible

(B) worsened

(C) remained the same

(D) improved

Ans. D

b. When did President Lincoln give his Gettysburg address?

(A) During the Battle of Gettysburg

(B) Before the Battle of Gettysburg

(C) After the Battle of Gettysburg

(D) After the war was over

Ans. C

c. Which of the following was not true about Ulysses S. Grant?

(A) He was the general President Lincoln was looking for since the war started.

(B) He was known "Unconditional Surrender" Grant

(C) He led the Confederacy to victories in the overland campaign

(D) He had led the *Army* of the Tennessee to many victories

Ans. A

d. How would you best describe Grant's Overland Campaign?

Ans. Grant waged a bloody Overland Campaign through much of the state of Virginia. Suffering massive casualties while gradually diminishing the numbers and spirit of Lee's Army of Northern Virginia. Eventually, Grant cornered Lee's Army at Petersburg, Virginia, where he staged a ten-month siege.

e. Which of the following was a major reason why President Lincoln was elected to a second term in 1864?

(A) People were happy that slaves were free

(B) After the capture of Atlanta it seemed as if the war was coming to an end

(C) There were no other candidates who ran against him

(D) Because the South seemed to be winning the war

Ans. B

f. How did the Union soldiers feel about President Lincoln?

Ans. Over 78 percent of Union soldiers would support his bid for a second term as President.

g. What did Lincoln think about the process of Reconstruction after the Civil War?

Ans. Lincoln believed in a policy of forgiveness and took a moderate approach to reconstruction, hoping to reconstruct the Union as quickly as possible rat her than indefinitely punish the rebel states.

h. Which of the following is not true?

(A) Lincoln died the morning after he had been shot.

(B) Lincoln's bodyguard may have been asleep or not where he was supposed to be.

(C) Lincoln died at the Petersen House.

(D) Lincoln died at Ford's Theater.

Ans. D

i. What does the word 'timeless' mean in the sentence below:

Edwin M. Stanton uttered the timeless words, "Now he belongs to the ages" (A) taking a long time, (B) irrelevant, (C) always relevant, (D) aspiring

Ans. C

2. To understand meteors, one must also understand meteoroids and meteorites. First, a meteoroid is a particle in the solar system. The meteoroid may be as small as a grain of sand, or, as large as a boulder. When the meteoroid enters the Earth's atmosphere, and becomes visible as a shooting star, it is called a meteor. If the meteor makes it to the ground, it is called a meteorite. Meteors, also called shoot in g stars, occur in the Earth's mesosphere at an altitude of about 40-60 miles. Millions of meteors enter the Earth's atmosphere every day, though the vast majority are observed at night. Their visibility in the night sky is due to air friction which causes the meteor to glow and emit a trail of gases and melted particles that lasts for about a

second. Meteor showers are relatively common events that occur when the Earth passes through a trail of debris left by a comet.

Sometimes meteoroids make it throughout the atmosphere and hit the ground, w h ere they are referred to as meteorites. There are over 31,000 documented meteorites that have been found, although only five or six new ones are found every year. The largest meteorite ever found was in the African nation of Namibia. It weighs over 100 tons and left a huge impact crater in the ground. Scientists believe the massive Berringer Crater in Arizona was formed when a 300,000 ton meteorite crashed to the ground over 49,000 years ago. On November 30, 1954, the Hodges Meteorite (actually a fragment of a meteorite) crashed through the roof of the residence of Ann Hodges in the town of Sylacauga, Alabama. It bounced off a table before striking her in the leg. Although she was badly bruised, she was not seriously injured. It was the first recorded instance of a meteorite injuring a human. The actual meteorite was donated to the Alabama Museum of Natural History after various legal battles concerning ownership. Some scientists believe the impact of a large meteorite from an asteroid or comet in Mexico's Yucatan Peninsula was responsible for the extinction of dinosaurs some 65 million years ago. Such an impact would have had catastrophic global consequences including immediate climate change, numerous earthquakes, volcano erupt ions, wildfires, and massive supertsuanims, along with the proliferation of massive amounts of dust and debris that could block solar energy and lead to a disruption in photosynthesis. Most meteorites that reach the Earth are classified as chondrites or achondrites, while a small percentage are iron meteorites and stony-iron meteorites. Most meteorites are chondrites. Chondrites contain silicate materials that were melted in space, amino acids, and other presolar grains, particles likely formed from stellar explosions. Diamond and graphite are among materials found to be present in these grains. Chondrites are thought to be over 4.5 billion years of age and to have originated in the asteroid belt, where they never formed larger bodies. Achondrites are less common. These types of meteorites seem to be similar to igneous rock. Iron meteorites make up less than five percent of meteorite finds. These types of meteorites are thought to come from the core of asteroids that were once molten. Finally, stony-iron meteorites constitute less than one percent of all meteorite falls. They are made of iron-nickel metal and different silicates.

Questions

1. Most meteorites are .... (a) achondrites, (b) chondrites, (c) iron, (d) stonyiron
2. .... meteors enter the earth's atmosphere every day. (a) Millions, (b) Hundreds, (c) Few, (d) Thousands
3. When does a meteor shower occur?
4. Which of the following actually hits the ground? (a) meteor, (b) meteoroid, (c) meteorite
5. Where are chondrites thought to have originated?
6. The largest meteorite ever discovered landed in.... (a) Alabama, (b) The United States, (c) Africa, (d) Mexico

3. Mark Rothko

Mark Rothko, one of the greatest painters of the twentieth century, was born in Daugavpils, Latvia in 1903. His father emigrated to the United States, afraid that his sons would be drafted into the Czarist army. Mark stayed in Russia with his mother and older sister; they joined the family later arriving in the winter of 1913, after a 12-day voyage.

Mark moved to New York in the autumn of 1923 and found employment in the garment trade and took up residence on the Upper West Side. It was while he was visiting someone at the Art Students League that he saw students sketching a nude model. According to him, this was the start of his life as an artist. He was twenty years old and had taken some art lessons at school, so his initial experience was far from an immediate calling.

In 1936, Mark Rothko began writing a book, which he never completed, about the similarities in the children's art and the work of modern painters. The work of modernists, which was influenced by primitive art, could, according to him, be compared to that of children in that "child art transforms itself into primitivism, which is only the child producing a mimicry of himself." In this same work, he said that "the fact that one usually begins with drawing is already academic. We start with colour."

It was not long before his multiforms developed into the style he is remembered for; in 1949 Rothko exhibited these new works at the Betty Parsons Gallery. For critic Harold Rosenberg, the paintings were a revelation. Rothko had, alter painting his first multiform, secluded himself to his home in East Hampton on Long Island, only inviting a very few people, including Rosenberg, to view the new paintings. The discovery of his definitive form came at a period of great grief; his mother Kate died in October 1948 and it was at some point during that winter that Rothko chanced upon the striking symmetrical rectangular blocks of two to three opposing or contrasting yet complementary colours. As part of this new uniformity of artistic vision, his paintings and drawings no longer had individual titles; from this point on they were simply untitled, numbered or dated. However, to assist in distinguishing one work from another, dealers would sometimes add the primary colours to the name. Additionally, for the next few years, Rothko painted in oil only on large vertical canvasses. This was done to overwhelm the viewer or, in his words, to make the viewer feel enveloped within the picture.

On February 25, 1970. Oliver Steindecker, Rothko's assistant, found him in his kitchen, lying on the floor in front of the sink, covered in blood. His arms had been cut open with a razor. The emergency doctor arrived on the scene minutes later to pronounce him dead as the result of suicide; it was discovered during the autopsy that he had also overdosed on anti-depressants. He was just 66 years old.

a. Who accompanied Mark Rothko to US?
b. How did Rothko become an artist?
c. What was Rothko's artistic vision?
d. Rothko's distinctive style ....
    (a) was inspired by Rosen berg.
    (b) resulted from moving to Long Island.

(c) resulted from his grief.

(d) evolved in 1948.

4. Students are responsible for familiarising themselves with the University Code of Student Conduct, as on enrollment with the University they place themselves under the policies and regulations of the University and all of its duly constituted bodies. Disciplinary authority is exercised through the Student Conduct Committee. The Committee has procedures in place for hearing allegations of misconduct. Copies of the student conduct code are available at the Student Services Office. Academic dishonesty is never condoned by the University. This includes cheating and plagiarism, which violate the Student Conduct Code and could result in expulsion or failing the course.

Cheating includes but is not limited to obtaining or giving unauthorized help during an examination, getting unauthorized information about the contents of an examination before it is administered. Using unauthorized sources of information during an examination, altering or falsifying the record of any grades, altering or supplying answers after an examination has been handed in, falsifying any official University record, and misrepresenting the facts to get exempt ions from or extensions to course requirements. Plagiarism includes but is not limited to submitting any paper or other document, to satisfy an academic requirement, which has been copied either in whole or in part from someone else's work without identifying that person; railing to identify as a quotation a documented idea that has not been thoroughly assimilated into the student's language and style. or paraphrasing a passage so closely that the reader could be misled as to the source: submitting the same written or oral material in different courses, without obtaining authorisation from the lecturers involved; or 'dry-tabbing', which includes obtaining and using experimental data from fellow students without the express consent of the lecturer, utilizing experimental data and laboratory write-ups from other parts of the course or from previous terms during which the course was conducted, and fabricating data to fit the expected results.

a. With what are students familiarized and who does it?
b. What is not condoned and results in expulsion?
c. Which would you consider to be a more serious offence?
d. What is not acceptable?
e. Can a student submit the same work in a different course?

5. Modern science has a good grip on most of those very few laws that drive life forward, most tellingly on how genetic material copies itself from parent to offspring. The innumerable variations however? Not so much. They are, after all, innumerable.

That does not mean that science is not trying. *Nature* publishes the latest progress reports from this colossal effort. The papers mark the completion of the 1000 Genomes Project, the largest work yet to sequence the genetic information of hundreds of individuals in an attempt to tune into Mother Nature's hum of human variation. It completes a set of genomic reference tools—resources of genetic data produced by international collaborations—that dates back 25 years to the start of such research. The bigger job, of tracking the relationships between genetic variation and human disease to help to develop effective treatments, is not finished, and may never be. But it is important from time to time to acknowledge and celebrate landmarks of achievement along the way. The data sets produced by the 1000 Genomes Project are already in use. The genetic details of the volunteers provide a publicly owned and openly available asset in the era of big data, and after a foundation for further study. Applications range from hunts for the genetic roots of human illness to analyses of population genetics and evolutionary history. As technology continues to improve, so does the ability to capture genetic variation worldwide. The research published this week demonstrates that neatly. For a start, the eponymous 1,000 genomes analysed have extended to more than 2,500. The data now come from 2,504 individuals, across 26 distinct populations. From Chinese immigrants in downtown Denver, Colorado, and the Luhya tribe in Kenya to Punjabis in the dusty streets of Lahore, Pakistan, much of human life and diversity is here. The genetic data have been analysed more thoroughly than was possible before, which throws more light on rarer forms of variation. The take home message: although most common genetic variants are shared across populations, rarer variants are often restricted to closely related groups. Many more rare variants are still to be identified. The improved precision provided in the latest data set has also enabled a more comprehensive map of structural variation across the human genome. For the first time, this includes analysis of eight structural-variation classes. What now? Sequencing projects should continue to cast the net wide, and extend it further, to seek volunteers from regional and ethnic groups that are currently under-represented in global genetic databases. Meanwhile, the astonishing increase in genetic sequencing ability—even when compared with when the 1000 Genomes Project began in 2007—has shifted the research bottleneck from generation of data to analysis and interpretation. Two challenges arc to make sense of the non-coding regions of DNA and to ease out the links between genetic variation and clinical symptoms. As links to health records are established, it is crucial that public trust is secured. The ways in which scientists collect, store and share sensitive personal information must continue to evolve to ensure adequate safeguards. The Global Alliance for Genomics and Health has offered promising alternatives and a model to follow. The final goal remains to make this flood of population-level genetic research relevant Lo personal health. Emerson would have approved. He was a proponent of individualism, a political philosophy that emphasizes the moral worth of the individual. He celebrated the non-conformist. And when it comes to the few laws that dictate the repetition of genetics, it is not just the 2,504 people whose variation is detailed this week who are the non-conformists. We all are.

a. What is the aim of genetic data research?
b. Who celebrated individualism and why?
c. What needs to be ensured?

d. What has been achieved so far by data research?

e. What is genetic data research analysis?

6. The Indian music is essentially impersonal; it reflects an emotion and an experience which are deeper and wider and older than the emotion of any single individual. Its sorrow is without tears, its joy without exultation and it is passionate without any loss of serenity. It is in the deepest sense of the words all-human. But when the Indian prophet speaks of inspiration, it is to say that the Vedas are eternal and all that the poet achieves by his devotion is to hear or see, it is then Saraswati, the goddess of speech and learning or Narada, whose mission is to disseminate occult knowledge in the sound of the strings of his vina, or Krishna, whose flute is forever calling us to leave the duties of the world and follow Him—it is these rather than any human individual, who speak through the singer's voice, and are seen in the movements of the dancer.

Or we may say that this is an imitation of the music in heaven. The master musicians of India are always represented as pupils of a god, or as visiting the heaven world to learn there the music of the spheres—that is to say, their knowledge springs from a source far within the surface of the empirical activity of the waking consciousness. In this connection it is explained why it is that human art must be studied, and may not be indentified with the imitation of our very day behavior. When Shiva expounds the technique of the drama to Bharata, the famous author of the *Natya shastra,* he declares that human art must be subject to law, because in man the inner and outer life are still in conflict. Man has not yet found Himself, but all his activity proceeds from a laborious working of the mind and all his virtue is self-conscious. What we call our life is uncoordinated and far from the harmony of art, which rises above good and evil. It is otherwise with the gods whose every gesture immediately reflects the affections of the inner life. Art is an imitation of that perfect spontaneity—the identity of intuition and expression in those who are of the kingdom of heaven, which is within us. Thus it is that art is nearer to life than any fact can be; and Mr Yeats has reason when he says that Indian music, though its theory is elaborate and its technique so difficult, is not an art, but life itself. For it is the inner reality of things, rather than any transient or partial experience that the singer voices. "Those who sing here," says Shankara charya, "sing God"; and *Vshnu Purana* adds, "All songs are a part of Him, who wears a form of sound". We could deduce from this a metaphysical interpretation of technique.

1. What does Indian music express?
2. What is the implication of Shiva's teaching to Bharata?
3. What is the status of Indian musician?
4. What is the nature of art?
5. Why does Yeats call Indian music "life itself"?

7. We are living now, not in the delicious intoxication induced by the early successes of science, but in a rather grisly morning—after, when it has become apparent that what triumphant science has done hitherto is to improve the means for achieving unimproved of actually deteriorated ends. In this condition of apprehensive sobriety we are able to see that the contents of literature, art, music—even in some measure of divinity and school metaphysics—are not sophistry and illusion, but simply those elements of experience which scientists chose to leave out of account, for the good reason that they had no intellectual methods for dealing with them. In the arts, in philosophy, in religion men are trying—doubtless, with complete success—to describe and explain the non-measurable, purely qualitative aspects of really. Since the time of Galileo, scientists have admitted, sometimes explicitly but much more often by implication, that they are incompetent to discuss such matters. The scientific picture of the world is what it is because men of science combine this incompetence and specialization is a complete picture of reality. As a matter of historical fact, however, this claim has constantly been made. The successive steps in the process of identifying an arbitrary abstraction from reality with reality itself have been described, very fully and lucidly, in Butt's excellent "Metaphysical Foundations of Modern Science": and it is therefore unnecessary for me of science have come to realize that the scientific picture of the world is a partial

one—the product of their special competence in mathematics and their special incompetence to deal systematically with aesthetic and moral values, religious experiences and intuitions of significance. Unhappily, novel ideas become acceptable to the less intelligent members of society only with a very considerable time-lag. Sixty or seventy years ago the majority of scientists believed—and the belief often caused them considerable distress—that the product of their special incompetence was identical with reality as a whole. Today this belief has begun to give way, in scientific circles, to a different and obviously truer conception of the relation between science and total experience. The masses, on the country, have just reached the point where the ancestors of today's scientists were standing two generations back. They are convinced that the scientific picture of an arbitrary abstraction from reality is a picture of reality as a whole and that therefore the world is without meaning or value. But nobody likes living in such a world. To satisfy their hunger for meaning and value, they turn to such doctrines as nationalism, fascism and revolutionary communism. Philosophically and scientifically, these doctrines are absurd; but for the masses in every community, they have this great merit: they attribute the meaning and value that have been taken away from the world as a whole to the particular part of the world in which the believers happen to be living.

Questions

1. What do the masses today crave for?
2. Which part of human experience has science ignored and why?
3. What has been described as incompetence of science?
4. Do scientists today feel comfortable with their conception of reality as a whole?
5. Describe the relation between science and total experience.

8. Answers to the riddle of the universe often have a logical form and are expressed in such a way that they raise questions of epistemology and involve the acceptance or rejection of certain scientific theories. In substance however, they are simply

rationalizations of diverse and equally valid psychological states, and are therefore neither true nor false. (Incidentally, similar states are not necessarily or invariably rationalized in the same way. Mystical experiences which, in Europe, are explained in terms of a personal god are interpreted by the Buddhists in terms of an entirely godless order of things. Which is the truer rationalization? God, or not-god, whichever the case may be, no one knows.) The life-worshipper who adopts in turn all the solutions to the cosmic riddle is committing no crime against logic or the truth. He is simply admitting the obvious fact that he is a human being—that is to say, a series of distinct psychological states, a colony of diverse personalities. Each state demands its appropriate rationalizations; or, in other words, each personality has its own philosophies of life. Philosophical consistency had some justification so long as it could be imagined that the substance of one's world-view (as opposed to the logical trappings in which it was clothed and the problems of epistemology and science connected with it) was uniquely true. But if we admit, as I think we must, that one world-view cannot be truer than another, but that each is the expression in intellectual terms of some given and undeniable fact of experience, then consistency loses all philosophical merit. It is pointless to ignore all the occasions when you feel that the world is good, for the sake of being consistently a pessimist: it is pointless, for the same of being consistently a positivist, to deny that your body is sometimes tenanted by a person who has mystical experiences. Pessimism is no truer than optimism, nor positivism than mysticism. Philosophically, there is no reason why a man should deny the thoughts of all but one of his potential selves, each self on occasion exists; each has its feelings about the universe, its cosmic tastes—or, to put it in a different way, each inhabits its own universe.

Questions

1. What is the creed of a life-worshipper?
2. What is philosophical consistency?
3. How is it relevant to attribute other's viewpoint as untrue?

4. What is author's opinion about answers to the riddle of the universe?

9. Words form the thread on which we string our experiences. Without them we should live spasmodically and intermittently. Hatred itself is not so strong that animals will not forget it, if distracted, even in the presence of the enemy. Watch a pair of cats, crouching on the brink of a fight. Balefully the eyes glare; from far down in the throat of each come bursts of a strange. strangled noise of defiance; as though animated by a life of their own, the tails twitch and tremble. With aimed intensity of loathing! Another moment and surely there must be an explosion. But no; all of a sudden one of the two creatures turns away, hosts a hind leg in a more than fascist salute and, with the same fixed and focused attention as it had given a moment before to its enemy, begins to make a lingual toilet. Animal love is a much at the mercy of distractions as animal hatred. The dumb creation lives a life made up of discreet and mutually irrelevant episodes. Such as it is, the consistency of human characters is due to the words upon which all human experiences are strung. We are purposeful because we can describe our feelings in rememberable words, can justify and rationalize our desires in terms of some kind of argument. Faced by an enemy we do not allow an itch to distract us from our emotions: the mere word "enemy" is enough to keep us reminded of our hatred, to convince us that we do well to be angry. Similarly the word "love" bridges for us those chasms of momentary indifference and boredom which gape from time to time between even the most ardent lovers. feeling and desire provide us with our motive power; words give continuity to what we do and to a considerable extent determine our direction. Inappropriate and badly chosen words vitiate though and lead to wrong or foolish conduct. Most ignorances are vincible, and in the greater number of cases stupidity is what the Buddha pronounced it to be, a sin. For, consciously, or subconsciously, it is with deliberation that we do not know or fail to understand—because incomprehension allows us, with a good conscience, to evade unpleasant obligations and responsibilities, because ignorance is the best excuse for going on doing what one likes, but ought not, to do. Our egotisms are

incessantly fighting to preserve themselves, not only from external enemies, but also from the assaults of the other and better self with which they are so uncomfortably associated. Ignorance is egotism's most effective defence against that Dr. Jekyll in us who desires perfection; stupidity, its subtlest stratagem. If, as so often happen, we choose to give continuity to our experience by means of words which falsify the facts, this is because the falsification is somehow to our advantage as egotists.

Questions

1. How do cats behave which are on the brink of a fight?
2. How are ignorance and egotism interrelated?
3. How do words affect our conduct?
4. What is deliberate incomprehension?
5. How do words impact consistency to human character?

10. In many societies at many levels of civilization attempts have been made to fuse drug intoxication with God intoxication. In ancient Greece, for example, ethyl alcohol had its place in the established religion. Dionysus, or Bacchus, as he was often called, was a true divinity. His worshipers addressed him as "Lusios", "Liberator," or as "Theoinos, "God-wine." The latter name telescopes fermented grape juice and the supernatural into a single Pentecostal experience. "Born a god" writes Euripides. "Bacchus is poured out as a liberation to the gods, and through him men receive good." Unfortunately, they also receive harm. The blissful experience of self-transcendence, which alcohol makes, possible, has to be paid for, and the price is exorbitantly high.

Complete prohibition of all chemical mind changers can be decreed, but cannot be enforced, and tends to create more evils than it cures. Even more unsatisfactory has been the policy of complete toleration and unrestricted availability. In England, during the first years of the eighteenth century, cheap untaxed gin—"drunk for a penny, dead drunk for two-pence"—threatened society with complete demoralization. A century later, opium, in the form of laudanum, was reconciling the victims of the Industrial Revolution to their lot—but at an appalling cost in terms of addiction illness and early death.

Today most civilized societies follow a course between the two extremes of total prohibition and total toleration. Certain mind-changing drugs, such as alcohol, are permitted and made available to the public on payment of a very high tax, which tends to restrict their consumption. Other mind changers are unobtainable except under doctors' orders—or illegally form a dope pusher. In this way the problem is kept within manageable bounds. It is most certainly not solved. In their ceaseless search for self-transcendence, millions of would-be mystics become addicts, commit scores of thousands of crimes and are involved in hundreds of thousands of avoidable accidents.

Do we have to go on in this dismal way indefinitely? Up until a few years ago, the answer to such a question would have been a rueful "Yes, we do." Today, thanks to recent developments in biochemistry and pharmacology, we are offered a workable alternative. We see that it may soon be possible for us to do something better in the way of chemical self-transcendence than what we have been doing so ineptly for the last seventy or eighty centuries.

Questions

1. Who is known as Greek god of wine?
2. What does a chemical mind-changer so?
3. What policy does the author suggest to restrict the use of alcohol?

11. The last three generations have witnessed a vast increase in the size and number of large cities. Life is more exciting and more money can be earned in the cities than in villages and small towns. Hence, the migration from village to city. In the van of this migrating host have marched the ambitious the talented, the adventurous. For more than a century there has been a tendency for the most gifted members of small rural communities to leave home and seek their fortune in the towns. Consequently, what remains in the villages and country towns of the industrialized countries is in the nature of a residual population, dysgenically selected for its lack of spirit and intellectual gifts. Why is it so hard to induce peasants and small

farmers to adopt new scientific methods? Among other reasons, because almost every exceptionally intelligent child born into a rural family for a century past has taken the earliest opportunity of deserting the land for the city. Community life in the country is thus impoverished; but (and this is the important point) the community life of the great urban centers is not correspondingly enriched. It is not enriched for the good reason that, in growing enormous cities have also grown chaotic. A metropolitan "wen," as Cobbett was already calling the relatively tiny London of his day, is no longer an organic whole, no longer exists as a community, in whose life individual can fruitfully participate. Men and women rub shoulders with other men and women; but the contact is external and mechanical. Each one of them can say, in the words of the Jolly Miller of the song, "I care for nobody, no, not I, and nobody cares for me." Metropolitan life is atomistic. The city, as a city, does nothing to correlate its human particles into a pattern of responsible, communal living. What the country loses on the swings. The city loses all over again on the roundabouts.

In the light of this statement of the principal reasons for the recent decline of the community and of the community sense in individuals, we can suggest certain remedies. Schools and colleges can be transformed into organic communities and used to offset, during a short period of the individual's career, the decay in family and village life. (A very interesting experiment in this direction is being made at Black Mountain College in North Carolina.) To some extent, no doubt, the old "natural" life of villages and small towns, the life that the economic, technological and religious circumstances of the past conspired to impose upon them, can be replaced by a consciously designed synthetic produce—a life of associations organized for local government, for sport, for cultural activities and the like. Such associations already exist, and there should be no great difficulty in opening them to larger numbers and, at the same time, in making their activities so interesting that people will wish to join them instead of taking the line of least resistance, as they do now, and living unconnected, atomistic lives, passively obeying during their working hours and passively allowing themselves to be entertained by machinery during their hours of leisure.

Questions

1. What is the reason of migration from countryside to city?
2. Why is it difficult for farmers to adopt scientific methods?
3. Why is community life in the countryside impoverished?
4. Explain the author's meaning when he says "...life is atomistic".
5. What does the author suggest to enrich community life of cities?

12. Now, if there is one thing that the study of history and psychology makes abundantly clear, it is that there are no such things as either "divine" or "natural" forms of love Innumerable gods have sanctioned and forbidden innumerable kinds of sexual behavior and innumerable philosophers and poets have advocated the return to the most diverse kinds of "nature." Every form of amorous behavior, form chastity and monogamy to promiscuity and the most fantastic "perversion" is found both among animals and men. In any given human society, at any given moment, love, as we have seen, is the result of the interaction of the unchanging instinctive and physiological material of sex with the local conversion of morality and religion, the local laws, prejudices, and ideals. The degree of permanence of these conventions, religious myths, and ideals is proportional to their social unity in the given circumstances of time and place.

The new twentieth-century conception of love is realistic. It recognizes the diversity of love, not merely in the social mass from age to age, but from individual to contemporary individual, accordingly to the dosage of the different instincts with which each is born, and the upbringing he has received. the new generation knows that there is no such thing as Love with a large L, and that what the Christian romantics of the last century regarded as the uniquely natural form of love is, in fact only one of the indefinite number of possible amorous fashions, produced by specific circumstances at that particular time. Psychoanalysis has taught it that all the forms of sexual behavior previously regarded as wicked, perverse, unnatural are statistically normal (and normality is solely a question of statistics), and that what is commonly called amorous normality is far from being a spontaneous, instinctive form of behavior, but must be acquired by a process of education. Having contracted the habit of talking freely and more or less scientifically about sexual matters, the young no longer regard love with that feeling of rather guilty excitement and thrilling shame which was for an earlier generation the normal reaction to the subject. Moreover, the practice of birth-control has robbed amorous indulgence of most of the sinfulness traditionally supposed to be inherent in it by robbing it of its socially disastrous effects. The tree shall be known by its fruits: where there are no fruits, there is obviously no tree. Love has ceased to be the rather fearful, mysterious thing it was, and become a perfectly normal, almost commonplace, activity—an activity, for many young people, a perfectly normal, almost commonplace, activity—an activity, for many young people especially in America, of the same nature as dancing or tennis, a sport, a recreation, a pastime. For those who hold this conception of love, liberty and toleration are prime necessities. A strenuous offensive against the old taboos and repressions is everywhere in progress.

Questions

1. Is there any universal definition of love?
2. How did the older generation react to the feeling of love?
3. What is modern conception of love?
4. How do psychologists explain love?
5. If according to the author love has neither 'divine' nor 'natural' forms, then what is it?

13. Man's progress has been contingent on his capacity to organize societies. It is only when protected by surrounding society from aggression, when freed by the organized labor of society from the necessity of hunting or digging for his food, it

is only, that is to say, when society has tempered and to a great extent abolished the struggle for personal existence, that the man of talent can exercise his capacities to the full. And is only by a well-organized society that the results of his labors can be preserved for the enrichment of succeeding generations. Any force that tends to the strengthening of society is, therefore, of the highest biological importance Religion is obviously such a force. All religious have been unanimous in encouraging within limits that have tended to grow wider and ever wider, the social altruistic, humanitarian proclivities of man and in condemning his anti-social, self-assertive tendencies. Those who like to speak anthropomorphically would be justified in saying that religion is a device employed by the Life Force for the promotion of its evolutionary designs. But they would be justified in adding that religion is also a device employed by Devil for the dissemination of idiocy, intolerance, and servile abjection. My fellow passenger from Camphell did something, no doubt to encourage brotherly love, forbearance, and mutual helpfulness among his flock. But he also did his best to deepen their congenital stupidity and prevent it from being tempered by the acquirement of correct and useful knowledge, he did his best to terrify them with imaginary fears into servility and to flatter them with groundless hopes into passive contentment with a life unworthy of human beings. What he did in the name of the evolutionary Life Force, he undid in the name of the Devil. I cherish a pious hope that he did just a trifle more than he undid, and that the devil remained, as the result of h is ministry, by ever so little the loser.

Questions

1. Why did man try to organize societies?
2. What are the benefits of organized society?
3. How can religion become a force to strengthen society?
4. How does the devil infiltrate through religion?
5. Explain "Life force".

14. Literature is also philosophy, is also science. In terms of beauty it enunciates truth. The beauty-truths of the best classical words possess, as we have seen, a certain algebraic universality

of significance. Naturalistic works contain the more detailed beauty-truths of particular observation. These beauty-truths of art are truly scientific all that modern psychologists, for example, have done is to systematize and de-beautify the vast treasure of knowledge about the human soul contained in novel, play, poem and easy. Writers like Blake and Shakespeare, like Stendhal and Dostoevsky, still have plenty to teach the modern scientific professional. There is a rich scientific harvest to be reaped in the works even of minor writers. By nature a natural historian. I am ambitious to add my quota to the sum of particularized beauty-truths about man and his relations with the world about him. (Incidentally, this world of relationships, this borderland between "subjective" and "objective" is one which literature is peculiarly, perhaps uniquely, well fitted to explore.) I do not want to do a Classical, or even a Neo-Classical, eliminator and generalize. This means, among other things that I cannot accept the Classicist's excommunication of the body. I think it not only permissible, but necessary, that literature should take cognizance of physiology and should investigate the still obscure relations between the mind and its body. True, many people find the reports of such investigations, when not concealed in scientific textbooks are couched in the decent obscurity of a Graeco-Latin jargon, extremely and inexcusably vulgar and many more find them downright wicked. I myself have frequently been accused, by reviewers in public and by unprofessional readers in primate correspondence, both of vulgarity and of wickedness—on the grounds, so far as I have ever been able to discover, that I reported my investigations into certain phenomenon in plain English and in a novel. The fact that many people should be shocked by what he writes practically imposes it as a duty upon the writer to go on shocking them. For those who are shocked by truth are not only stupid, but morally reprehensible as well; the stupid should be educated, the wicked punished and reformed.

All these praiseworthy ends can be attained by a course of shocking retributive pain will be inflicted on the truth-haters by the first shocking truths, whose repetition will gradually build up in those who read them an immunity to pain and will end by reforming and educating the stupid criminals out of their truth-hating. For a familiar truth ceases to shock. To render it familiar is therefore a duty. It is also a pleasure.

Questions

1. What is literature?
2. What does literature explore?
3. Explain the difference between "subjective" and "objective".
4. Who is formally shocked by truth?
5. How can truth-haters be removed?

Professor M.P. Sinha's Books

Critical Theories
Indian and Western

9788126918270

HB 288 2013 ₹ 795.00

Fundamentals of Effective Communication

9788126918812

HB 384 2014 ₹ 995.00

9788126918829

PB 384 2014 ₹ 395.00

Research Methods in English

9788126903580

HB 144 2018 ₹ 495.00

Send your Orders to :

ATLANTIC PUBLISHERS & DISTRIBUTORS (P) LTD.

7/22, Ansari Road, Darya Ganj, New Delhi-110 002

Tel: 40775252, 40775214, 23273880; Fax: 91-11-23285873 • Follow us at f

E-mail: orders@atlanticbooks.com

For purchase of books, please visit our website

www.atlanticbooks.com